Warner Bros. Television

Warner Bros. Television

Every Show of the Fifties and Sixties Episode-by-Episode

Lynn Woolley
Robert W. Malsbary
Robert G. Strange, Jr.

McFarland & Company, Inc., Publishers
Jefferson, North Carolina, and London

Library of Congress Cataloging in Publication Data

Woolley, Lynn, 1949–
  Warner Bros. television.

  Includes index.
  1. Warner Brothers. 2. Television programs — United
States — Plots, themes, etc. I. Malsbary, Robert W.,
1949– . II. Strange, Robert G., Jr. 1952–
III. Title.
PN1992.92.W37W66 1985   791.45′75   84-43217

ISBN 0-89950-144-3 (alk. paper)

Printed in the United States of America

McFarland & Company, Inc., Publishers
Box 611, Jefferson, North Carolina 28640

To William T. Orr
Thanks for those halcyon days

Acknowledgments

The authors wish to thank the following for valuable assistance in the preparation of this book:

Hugh Benson; The Dallas Public Library, Fine Arts Staff; Jim Duffy; Joyce Goodman, KTVT-TV, Fort Worth; The Grace Lee Whitney Fan Club, Van Nuys, California; George Henderson, Dallas Public Library; Richard V. Huisking, Jr.; Al Kohn, Warner Bros. Music, Burbank, California; The Los Angeles Public Library; Louis B. Marino, Warner Bros., New York; David Miller; Fairfax Nisbet, former TV-Radio Editor, *The Dallas Morning News*; Robert W. O'Connor, Jr., *TV Guide*, Dallas; William T. Orr; William A. Payne, former Amusements Editor, *The Dallas Morning News*; Vernon Scott, United Press International; Carl Stucke; John Thomas, KXTX-TV, Dallas; Grace Lee Whitney; Jodie Woolley.

Contents

Introduction

The 50's. Sputnik circled the earth; Eisenhower was President of the United States; the New York Yankees were the kings of baseball; and the nation had a *new* national pastime—television.

Television had been in the midst of a slow development process ever since 1817 when a Swedish scientist isolated the element selenium. From those early experiments, people like Vladimir Zworykin, Philo Farnsworth, and Allen DuMont continued the research until the first home receivers were marketed in 1939—not that there were many programs to watch in those days. NBC's New York station W2XBS was the only station with a regular programming schedule that year, so if you happened to live in Walla Walla, Washington, for example, you qualified as a bona fide fringe area.

After the second World War, five U.S. cities could boast of television outlets; in addition to the Big Apple, there were stations in Philadelphia, Chicago, Los Angeles, and Schenectady. Six outlets in the five cities beamed scattered programming to seven-thousand receivers. By the end of 1948, twenty-five more stations were in operation.

At this point, the Federal Communications Commission, which oversees broadcasting, decided to call a halt to the whole thing while it took a long, hard look at the infant industry. During the four year "freeze" on new frequency allocations, the Commission decided to designate two thousand new channel assignments. This was done by adding seventy new channels in the Ultra High Frequency (UHF) range to go with the twelve Very High Frequency (VHF) channels already in operation.

This brings us back to where we started—the 1950's. By the time the freeze thawed out, television had been accepted by the general public. Advertising rates had more than doubled, and signals were being received by more than ten million sets. (That number would increase seven fold by the mid-60's.) Also in the early 50's, four national networks had been established.

NBC took the early lead, followed solidly by CBS. ABC, the number three network, had earlier splintered off from NBC and just managed to keep in front of the DuMont network. NBC and CBS grew and prospered, but the two latter webs became victims of circumstance.

ABC, by virtue of being a late entry, entered many markets to find the choice affiliates already committed to NBC or CBS, and in those days many markets still didn't have as many as three stations. When that third station *was* there, ABC grabbed it, thereby muscling its way into some of the larger markets. By picking up the scraps from NBC and CBS's table, ABC found itself a perennial number three when the nets began to play the ratings game.

Not only did ABC find itself stuck with less desirable affiliates in the VHF band, it *also* ended up with UHF outlets in many areas. That made it hard on the network because most TV sets in those days were built to receive *only* VHF signals, and that left ABC entirely out in the cold in many homes. The problem could have been avoided if the FCC had designated each market with either VHF or UHF allocations *only* rather than mixing them up, but by the time the FCC realized that it was too late. The Commission finally saw the light, and in July of 1962 it took action to rectify the mistake. After that date, any TV set sold across state lines had to be equipped for both UHF and VHF reception. The Commission figured the new rule wouldn't harm any existing VHF station, but would give UHF the opportunity to grow.

As far as ABC and DuMont were concerned, the damage was already done. As the two webs struggled for survival, it became apparent that ABC just might make it, but DuMont's chances were slim. Toward the middle to late fifties, ABC had garnered enough affiliates to compete with the big boys, even though the number three net *still* was far behind in the station count. The network managed to pull some impressive ratings numbers on the strength of several high quality Westerns and private-eye shows that were being produced by one of the Hollywood movie houses. Each successful show begat another, and each success was a shot in the arm.

ABC lived; the net was *still* in third place, but it lived. Meanwhile, in 1955, the DuMont network died.

More than 350 commercial stations were broadcasting by that

time with hundreds more on the drawing board. CBS was still going strong with Uncle Miltie and Lucy, and NBC had introduced Wally Cox to the nation as *Mr. Peepers*. Situation comedies and quiz shows were drawing vast audiences. But over at ABC, the bread and butter came from gunslingers and private eyes.

The studio that made it happen was Warner Bros., an organization that took time out from feature movies to try its hand at the newcomer, the small screen. Shows like *Warner Bros. Presents, Maverick, Cheyenne, 77 Sunset Strip, Hawaiian Eye*, and *The Gallant Men* were added to the ABC lineup, and lo and behold, the ratings held their own — even with fewer stations and less audience potential.

The WB series all worked from the same recipe. Take a handsome hero (or two or three) and put him (or them) in a glamorous setting like Los Angeles or the old West. Add a dash of colorful supporting characters and stir well. Serve with a generous helping of adventure and romance, and don't forget one key element of most Warner Bros. shows — mystery. And that held true even for the Westerns.

The series began each episode the same way. First, a teaser, usually an intense scene cut from within the show, then a stock introduction. Then, the inevitable shield on the horizon that would grow and grow and gradually turn into a Warner Bros. emblem which would cover the entire screen as an announcer proclaimed in a rich baritone: "A Warner Bros. Television Production."

Without those WB productions, ABC might very well have gone the way of DuMont. Shows like *77 Sunset Strip* had one of the authors of this book stringing tinfoil across a rabbit-ears antenna in a near futile attempt to receive an ABC affiliate that was too far away. It wasn't until *The Fugitive* series in the 60's that ABC had a consistent winner on a dramatic series that didn't come from Warners. By that time, the web was on much stronger footing and on its way to its first number one season which would finally come along in 1976.

Left to right: Robert W. Malsbary, Lynn Woolley, Robert G. Strange, Jr.

1
A Warner Bros.
Television Production

It was 1955 — and ABC-TV had a problem. The network was in desperate need of new shows, and for a solution it was looking to the major film studios. Not to worry — help was on the way.

Jack L. Warner, the head of Warner Bros., made the decision for his company to take the plunge into TV, but apparently his was not a wholehearted effort. So he appointed a press agent as head of his new television production division.

From this appointment came the first of what was to be a long line of "Warner Bros. Television Productions."

The first series was aptly titled *Warner Bros. Presents*. However, even before the first of these shows was aired, Warners had a new man at the helm of the television division. His name: William T. Orr. Under Orr's capable guidance, Warners brought hit after hit to the small screens of America.

Bill Orr was born in New York City on September 27, 1917, and it was only twenty-one years later that he began his career in films by appearing in an Andy Hardy movie. In 1942, he was in the Air Force's first Motion Picture Unit. He was out of the Air Force in 1945 — the same year he married Jack L. Warner's stepdaughter, Joy Page.

Orr's new father-in-law talked him into moving to the other side of the camera, and there Bill developed his skills as a producer. So Bill was named Executive Producer for TV. He explains more about how the studio got involved with the "vast wasteland":

"We got into television because — if you can't lick 'em, join 'em. And the grosses on pictures had gone way down because of TV. ABC came to Warners, Fox, and Metro. Leonard Goldenson, who was president (now the chairman of the board) of ABC, was a theatre man. Before ABC, he was with Paramount Theatres, so he had been involved in films all his life. When he became president of ABC, since he had been a theatre man, he thought, 'What about our suppliers?' He said, 'Let's go get the majors to supply.' And that's how we got into television. They dragged us in. By that time, our Eastern office, not being the creative head of a studio like Jack Warner was, (they weren't as parochial about television, you see) said, 'Look. There's money there. I mean, come on already.' When they were approached, they came to us and then we had meetings. I was working with the Old Man, J.L., so we'd be at these meetings not as television people, but as studio people seeing how you did this. So they put somebody in charge of television who knew nothing. About five weeks before we went on the air, they let him go. Then they looked around and said, 'Who knows anything about television?' Nobody did—except I had been making their deals for them. I had been suggesting personnel they might use, but I hadn't been involved in their creative effort at all except for a couple of directors."

So Orr was in, and the studio never regretted the decision. Hit after hit flashed his name in the closing credits—*Cheyenne, Maverick, 77 Sunset Strip*.

And, as Orr went on to other things after his TV stint (he produced *Sex and the Single Girl* in 1962, and in 1966 formed the Wm. T. Orr Company for motion pictures and TV films), so did several other big name writers and directors get their starts at WB. Robert Altman started there as an observer as did Hy Averback. Roy (*The Fugitive*) Huggins started there as well.

And the WB television ball was rolling in other places than just the United States, and the foreign business was bringing in additional revenue for the company. Bill Orr says of the foreign distribution: "We had a very big foreign department. We distributed our own. Later, again with the pressures of ABC, they traded off so that they distributed some of our product to syndication, but if I'm not mistaken, we always distributed overseas. I don't think ABC had an overseas distribution set up when they had their original stuff, so I think they gave it back to us to distribute and we'd give them a piece or something if we had a deal. First off, we distributed all of it, and then they asked for co-distribution—where we'd do one, they'd do one, back and forth. It was handled basically by our theatrical distribution offices which were all over the world. They did very well. See, action adventure stuff does better around the world because it's

Bill Orr with Lynn Woolley at Orr's Hollywood home.

more filmatic — not so much nuance and dialogue. So the *77's* and the *Hawaiian Eye*'s and all did great all over the place."

EARLY SERIES

Warner Bros. Presents was made up of three alternating shows: *Casablanca, King's Row*, and *Cheyenne*. It premiered on September 3, 1955, with host Gig Young introducing the show and giving the audience a look behind the scenes and even some interviews with some of the Warners stars. This was a regular feature of the show each week and was used to promote upcoming WB movies. They called it "Behind the scenes at Warner Bros." This five to ten minute tour each week meant that the show featured that week would only be about forty-five to fifty minutes long instead of an hour, but then Jack L. Warner didn't really like television anyway.

Casablanca starred Charles McGraw as Rick Jason in a television

Warners story editor Carl Stucke with Lynn Woolley at Stucke's Bur-bank home.

version of the Warners hit movie. Rick was the owner of Cafe American, located in the port city of Casablanca in Morocco. The era was the time of Nazi occupation and Jason spent his time helping people in need and thwarting the Nazis in any way he could.

King's Row was a medical show, again based on a previous WB movie success, about a young psychiatrist and his dealings with the problems of the people of a small town in the early 1900's. It was a dramatic show wrought with emotional turmoil. The cast included some folks you'd see again later: Jack Kelly as Dr. Parris Mitchell; Robert Horton as Drake; Victor Jory as Dr. Tower; Nan Leslie as Randy; Peggy Webber as Eloise.

Conflict started in 1957 and lasted only one season. It took the place of *King's Row* and *Casablanca* when those shows failed to return for the second season. *Conflict* was an anthology program which presented a new cast of players and a new story line in each episode. The themes of the shows dealt with how people reacted to sudden changes in their lives. Many of the people in this program were later to show up as stars of their own series for Warners. Among these were Efrem Zimbalist, Jr. and Will Hutchins. Jim Garner made several appearances.

Lots of other people who would be big name stars also appeared in *Conflict*. The list includes Elizabeth Montgomery, Jim Backus, Charles Bronson, Natalie Wood, Anita Ekberg, Inger Stevens, Tab Hunter, David Janssen, Dennis Hopper, Jack Lord, and Joi Lansing. One early episode called "Explosion" had the added distinction of having been adapted from a story called "Steel Trap" — written by none other than William T. Orr.

2
Lonely Man Cheyenne

ABC (1 hour) — debuted September 13, 1955
Format: The exploits of a wanderer, Cheyenne Bodie, who assists
*   people in need in the frontier West of the 1870's*
Cast: Clint Walker . . . . Cheyenne Bodie
*   L. Q. Jones . . . . Smitty*
Executive Producer: William T. Orr
Producer: Arthur Silver; Roy Huggins (and a few others over the
*   years)*
Theme Music: "Cheyenne" by William Lava and Stan Jones
Location: Filmed in Hollywood

By the time Warner Bros. was entering the television business, the B Western was declining and was really all but dead as a viable medium for the cowboy. Television had become the new medium for Westerns, and the B really wasn't as solid there as it had been at the theatre. The new television Westerns were being labeled "adult" because of their formatting and their time slots on the tube. Warners entry into this field was *Cheyenne.*

Cheyenne was one of the three original shows that Warners put together for its initial entry into the young medium. It was also the single most successful program in terms of longevity that the studio had in the fifties and sixties. *Cheyenne* lasted for eight years, but during those years the show was put through some changes.

During its first season, *Cheyenne* was teamed up with *King's Row* and *Casablanca* in *Warner Bros. Presents.* Though it was actually the dark horse of the group and was expected not to really make it, *Cheyenne* was the only of the three shows to catch on and gain popularity with the viewers. For this first season, Cheyenne Bodie, played by Clint Walker, had a partner named Smitty, a government map maker, played by L.Q. Jones. L.Q. gave the show its comic relief. Together Cheyenne and Smitty fought all the standard Western badguys — Indians, robbers, and rustlers.

Cheyenne #6102, "Mountain Fortress," was the first television film Warners made, and was shot completely on location about sixty miles north of the studios at Vasquez Rocks. The production crew on this film gave Walker a silver spur to mark his debut as an actor.

When the 1956–1957 season rolled around, the other two shows had folded. *Cheyenne* began to alternate with another WB show called *Conflict*. Bodie lost his sidekick and the format became the one which would last for the life of the series.

Cheyenne Bodie was a throwback to the traditional Western-type hero — a strong, quiet man of action who gave everyone a fair shake and explained exactly where he stood in a situation without wasting a lot of words. Bodie had a realistic, wholesome interest in women, and more than likely, the beautiful woman in the story would fall for the tall, good-looking hero. Cheyenne got kissed more often than the viewers might realize. But most of his kisses ended up on the cutting room floor because the difference between his height and that of his leading ladies was often so great that even with the lady on a stool or box the kiss would not look as natural as it should. So, it would end up being edited out. Also because of his height, Walker's co-stars had to be six feet plus so that they would not be overwhelmed.

Cheyenne Bodie was different from most other Warner Bros. characters in that he had no schtick. He had no weird habits and was not constantly confronted with outrageous characters. His was a simple, straightforward personality. His adventures took him across the American West or often, as in "Border Affair," to Mexico. It was not a fantasy land in some resort city on some beautiful coast, but a rough, rugged land in need of taming and in need of men like Cheyenne Bodie to do the job.

The next season saw *Cheyenne* alternating with *Sugarfoot*. *Conflict*, like so many others, just did not make the grade with viewers and was canceled. When it came time for the 1958–1959 season, Warners found itself without the services of its star; Clint Walker had walked out on his contract. Instead of bowing to Clint's complaints and demands, the studio decided to let him go and brought Ty Hardin in as his replacement to play the part of Bronco Layne. The name of the show remained *Cheyenne* and they even kept the *Cheyenne* theme song instead of giving Bronco one of his own. Incidentally, it was not until its second year that *Bronco* had a song of its own.

For the 1959–1960 season, Walker returned in the role of Cheyenne Bodie; *Bronco* and *Sugarfoot* split off from *Cheyenne* to alternate on the *Bronco-Sugarfoot Hour*, and *Cheyenne* was preempted every third week by *Shirley Temple Specials*. For the 1960–1961 season, the three shows combined to make *The Cheyenne Show*. This would be the last season for *Sugarfoot*.

"Duel at Judas Basin" was made during this season. This episode is of interest because it's the only one in which all three of the stars appeared.

Came the next season, 1961–62, and *Bronco* and *Cheyenne* were left to alternate in *The Cheyenne Show*. This was the fourth and last season for *Bronco*. *Cheyenne*, despite the fact that Walker was disinterested in the series, just kept going on. The next year finally brought the last season for this show as well. In fact it lasted only thirteen more episodes.

The second half of that last season was completed by the new show, *The Dakotas*. *The Dakotas* starred Larry Ward as Marshal Frank Regan and co-starred Jack Elam, Chad Everett, and Mike Green as his deputies. *The Dakotas* was canceled at the end of its half-season run. Story consultant (later story editor) Carl Stucke told about the cancellation: "We had a battle with Metro, which claimed that we borrowed elements from *Bad Day at Black Rock*." Apparently, this dispute killed the series off almost before it really got a start.

In the eight years from 1955 until 1962, there were 108 episodes of *Cheyenne* filmed. *Sugarfoot* had 69 episodes and *Bronco* 68. In popularity, based on audience, *Cheyenne* was number one, followed by *Sugarfoot* and *Bronco*, in that order. Even though last of the three, *Bronco* did manage to average for the four seasons an AA rating of 22.4 and a 35.8 share of audience, according to Nielsen National. That's not too bad. Overall, the three series were extremely successful for both Warners and ABC.

CLINT WALKER

Clint was born Norman Eugene Walker on May 30, 1927, along with a twin sister, Lucille Neoma, in Hartford, Illinois. His parents were Mr. and Mrs. Paul Arnold Walker. When Clint was young, his

Clint Walker as Cheyenne Bodie taming the rugged West.

family moved around quite a bit from river town to river town. Clint's father was a restless man who liked to move. He worked at a variety of jobs including professional wrestling, bartending, and guitar playing.

Clint began his own wandering at the age of sixteen when he quit school to go to work in a local factory in Alton. In school Clint had been a standout football player and the state high school wrestling champion. He also worked on the local riverboats and harvested crops. Then, at the age of eighteen, he joined the Merchant Marine, first working on ore boats in the Great Lakes, then in the North Pacific with the Army Transport Service. Clint returned to Alton at the end of his tour of duty. He told an interviewer for a Warners publicity release, "I became restless and quit in my second year of high school. Soon I joined the Merchant Marine and spent the next three years at sea. I stopped home when I could, but meanwhile I saw fabulous places, had interesting experiences and met all kinds of people."

Back in Alton, Walker again worked at several jobs—everything from truck driving to sales to carpentry. On September 5, 1948, he married his childhood sweetheart, Verna Lucille Garver. On January 31, 1950, their daughter, Valerie Jean, was born.

In November of that same year, Clint decided that there was no future for him in Alton, so packing his family into a $65 Model A Ford, he drove eleven hundred miles through all kinds of weather to Brownwood, Texas, a small town located in the west central part of the state. He had been told his fortune could be made in the oil fields there. This wasn't exactly the case. The only home Walker could find for his family was a run-down old shack outside of town. They had no electricity or running water; instead, they burned kerosene lamps for light and showered from buckets of water. As Walker's luck was going, he didn't fare too well in the oil fields. He had to take on work in construction just to make ends meet. His prospecting did little good either so he finally ended up working the last several months he was in Texas punching cattle on one of the state's larger ranches.

Next, Walker moved his family to Long Beach, California, where his sister-in-law lived. There he worked again as an oil field worker as well as a nightclub bouncer, a private detective, a ship yard worker, and in a saw mill. All this in a period of about a year. Obviously things weren't working out any better than they had in Alton or Brownwood.

Clint heard that he could make good money in Las Vegas, so once again he packed his family up and moved. He homesteaded two and a half acres about ten miles outside of town and put a trailer on the land. His newest job was working as a deputy sheriff at the new Sands Hotel. There he met a great many celebrities, several of whom told him that he should try Hollywood. Van Johnson went so far as to introduce him to agent Henry Willson after they had had a long talk about getting into show business.

Clint began to give the matter serious thought. Finally, in July of 1954, he moved his family to Hollywood where Willson immediately put Clint into dramatic lessons. Walker, however, was not having any luck getting parts; he was just too big! Walker was six feet at the age of fourteen so even at a young age he was head and shoulders above his peers.

Clint commented about this in an early release from the studio: "I can remember how, when at about fourteen, I adopted a slouching, round-shouldered posture. It must have looked terrible, but it was the only way I could think of to make myself look shorter. And that was important." He counsels parents of tall children not to make a big deal of their kids' height, but to compliment it instead. He said that it's good to point out to the children, without making it too obvious, that there are other tall people. This way they realize that they aren't alone in the world.

One day at the Universal-International commissary, veteran actor Fred Somers saw Walker standing by himself off to the side and started a conversation with him. Finding out that Clint was looking for work but was unable to find it because of his size, Fred set up an appointment for Walker with his friend, Cecil B. DeMille. After the interview, Walker was given the part of guard for the Pharoah in the movie, *The Ten Commandments*. Of this picture, Clint said he had only one line, but they took it away from him. "Mr. DeMille gave me a job carrying a spear — the lightest work I'd ever done up to that time," Clint said in a release. But he was practically cut out of the picture. DeMille explained that it was because of his height. Clint did get a six month contract with Hal Wallis. He spent this period studying his new trade.

When the six months was up, the contract's option was not picked up and Clint was again without an employer. But by then, acting was in the man's blood and he was not about to give it up without a fight. He found a job at the Warner Bros. studios as a guard. After several tests for movie roles, the studio tried him for the role of Cheyenne Bodie for the upcoming television series. It had been only an afterthought on the studio's part, and despite the odds and the competition, Walker won the role and a long term contract.

Walker in a typical "Drop it, mister" pose from the *Cheyenne* series.

Clint played the character for seven years and *Cheyenne* only left the air because Walker's contract ran out and he didn't want to continue. He was involved in a very controversial walkout in the fourth year of his contract. Not long after he signed his contract and began filming the new series, Clint said he had a feeling the whole thing was unreal—that there was something else somewhere to appease his hunger. That was 1955. The next year he was saying that the series was just a way of making a living. By 1959 the attitude change was complete with the famous comment, "I feel like a caged tiger." And so he left—meaning to stay away—and even making plans to join his sister back in Illinois in the health food business.

Walker said he could never return to the studio under his old contract. He was willing to stay away until it expired in May of 1962, if that was what was necessary. Walker felt that he had signed a long-term contract to do features because he never thought that the series would do anything. He wanted to do features; he wanted more time off; instead of twenty episodes each year, he wanted only thirteen.

(Walker had had only three weeks off in the previous three years.) He wanted to make more on the reruns—$500 as opposed to the $45 he was then making. Clint also wanted a better deal for personal appearances. He had turned down $40,000 worth because he didn't want to split it down the middle with the studio (that was for about six weeks worth of appearances). Clint felt sorry for Ty Hardin because he knew it was going to be rough on Ty to try taking over the series, so Walker said that he was willing to do the first couple of episodes to help introduce Bronco Layne to the audience if the studio was willing to let him out of his contract.

The studio of course was not willing to just tear up Walker's contract and start over. If it had, it would more than likely have suffered a deluge of walkouts. Bill Orr had a few comments on Clint:

"Clint worked along for X number of years; I forget how many it was, then decided—well first he decided he wanted a big raise as I recall. He wasn't satisfied with the one that was offered and after negotiating around, he decided that if he couldn't get what he wanted, he would walk. I assume he thought that that tactic would put enough pressure on us that we'd come back finally with satisfying offers to him. Our problem with all this was since we had so much television and we had in a sense the same kind of people—everybody under contract—not that Clint wasn't better than the next fellow, but at that moment we had a structure of prices so we knew if Clint got this much, the next guy in the next series would start the escalation. So our aim, of course, was to keep the outlay down as far as we could. It's good business practice. So Clint finally quit and he was out for a year. We talked the network into running reruns during the entire year of *Cheyenne*. We had a big meeting and I said that I had a very strong feeling that the show will sustain its ratings virtually the same with the reruns as it did with the originals. It'll drop, but nowhere near a show that wasn't making it. In fact, I was willing to tie our prices for the reruns to the ratings. We didn't make that deal, but we made a deal [involving the] price we got for whatever the *Cheyenne*s had been costing the year before. I think we got half without expending a nickel except for prints, and I guess the network paid for them. Oh, we had to pay some residuals to Clint and whoever else was in the show. But then he came back after that, and I don't remember the terms of the settlement. I think we picked up an extra year on his contract. Usually when you made this kind of settlement in those days, you'd negotiate for a quick pro quo. If they went a substantial raise, then you'd rewrite your contract so that the contract either tacked on

Bodie dons a headdress with Yvette Dugay in "Gold, Glory, and Custer — Prelude."

a couple of years or you started all over again. You'd get a new contract, depending on where the contract was and what the fee was.

"Clint also did a couple of pictures for us — *Yellowstone Kelly* — Edd Byrnes was in that one, Ray Danton ... listen, we put our people in. Warners always had a history of that. You look back at the old Warners pictures. They had a stock company that today people say, 'What a marvelous group of actors. Aren't they great.' In those days the producers would say, 'Do I have to take Sidney Greenstreet again? or Alan Hale? Oh, is Alan Hale going to be in my picture again?' In fact, you could go to a preview and you'd have Alan Hale in the picture being previewed, Alan Hale in the picture that was playing at the theatre and Alan Hale in the picture that was in the coming attractions. Or another actor, but of course all of them were marvelous personalities."

Of Walker's return to the show, Orr recalled, "I think that he decided that if he performed badly, that we would get disenchanted with having him in *Cheyenne* and would let him out of it. So he would underplay the role. Just kind of slop through the role and he wouldn't stay for offstage lines with people and he quit at six o'clock on the nose, even if we were in the middle of a shot. Since it hadn't worked for him to be off salary for a year, or for a season anyway, he was going to try it another way. So everybody talked to him about it—'Look, Clint, you're up there. If you're lousy, it hurts us, but it hurts you just as much.'"

Walker finally finished his contract in 1963. Suddenly no one seemed to want him. He had had an extremely successful series in *Cheyenne*, and three very successful movies; *Fort Dobbs, Yellowstone Kelly*, and *Gold of the Seven Saints*.

Finally, in 1964, Walker was signed to play the part of Doris Day's old college sweetheart in the movie, *Send Me No Flowers*. It was produced by her husband, Martin Melcher, and starred Rock Hudson as the hypochondriac husband who thought he was dying and decided to find his wife a new husband for after his death. Tony Randall appeared as their next door neighbor who got mixed up in the whole affair. Clint's part was not as big as the three main stars, but as usual he was the largest member of the cast. He was even on horseback in his first scene as he made a daring rescue to save Doris from a runaway golf cart. When the movie had Clint climbing out of a Jaguar XKE, it was obvious he was not fitted well to the car. It was like a grizzly bear climbing out of a tin can.

During the year he was off between Warners and *Send Me No Flowers*, Clint appeared in rodeos to make his living, earning top money for his appearances. After he was signed for the movie, suddenly he began to get offers from everywhere—even from people who had turned him down only weeks before.

The next picture Walker made was another action-filled drama in an outdoor setting called *Night of the Grizzly*, made in 1966. Clint played a rancher in a valley that was being terrorized by a huge grizzly bear. Naturally, in the end, the bear lost. Next came *The Dirty Dozen* in 1967. Clint and his barbells traveled to London to play the part of Samson Posey, a Sioux Indian, in the MGM movie. The picture was about a group of deadbeats that were worked into shape by Lee Marvin and Walker as a commando unit to work behind German lines.

In 1968 came *Sam Whiskey*, another action Western. Then, in 1969, a role that was a little different. It was still a Western, but this time a comedy called *The Great Bank Robbery*. This flick was made for Warner Bros.—Seven Arts and starred Zero Mostel as a master thief

Peter Brown and Clint Walker in "Pocketful of Stars."

and Kim Novak as a carnival cootch dancer, both of whom were posing as evangelists as a cover. Clint played the squarest Texas Ranger possible, but in this movie *he* got the girl! In fact, she leaped from a balloon into his arms. Walker loved it and quipped: "It took a comedy, with me playing the straight man, to get me off the ground with beautiful gals. I hope a precedent has been set."

Clint went back to Western adventure pictures with *Yuma* in 1970, *Hardcase* and *The Bounty Men* in 1972, and *The White Buffalo* and *The Snow Beast* in 1977. Of this group only *The White Buffalo* was not a made-for-television movie.

Walker had another series in 1975 called *Kodiak*. Naturally, it was an action-adventure show set in the outdoors—this time in Alaska. He played the lead role, a member of the Alaskan State Patrol named Kodiak (no first name). The show was shot in Oregon, Washington, and Canada because Clint wanted to show blue skies and clean air which was impossible on a back lot in Hollywood. Also, he thought the scenery was prettier there than in Alaska. Kodiak was another Cheyenne Bodie-type hero — always looking out for the other guy and making the daring rescue just in the nick of time. It was a half-hour series which didn't leave much time for character development or a lot of plot. The show lasted only one season. Walker had a great deal to do with this show — he owned half of it and was responsible even for the title. As he was quoted, "I came up with the name because I thought it sounded Alaskan. Besides, I like short names."

Clint Walker is a polite, quiet man who enjoys the simple life. Once he showed up at a Warners premiere in a panel truck — much to the chagrin of the studio. He rides dirt bikes, prospects, lifts weights, skin dives, enjoys shark hunting so much that he had a thirty-foot boat equipped just for that purpose, and eats only organically grown foods. Even his steak is from specially fed cattle. Clint believes that people *are* what they eat, and when they eat chemical-laden foods, there is no way of knowing what effect the combination will have on them.

"I nearly lost my health before I became concerned about it. I don't say everyone should do as I do or eat as I eat, but I certainly believe everyone should be concerned about the purity of what they eat. I prefer health foods because I've studied them, understand them and believe they are the best for me."

Anyone who has ever seen Clint Walker on television or in a movie would have a hard time arguing that health food is not good for the human body. Many a bad guy in television and movies would agree that it does something for Clint ... he hasn't lost a fight yet.

Cheyenne — Series Index

FIRST SEASON:

Mountain Fortress

The premiere episode: Cheyenne joins a group of white men to drive off Indians attacking a stage, only to find out that the men are robbers. Cheyenne, the robbers, and some soldiers join forces to save themselves from attacking Indians. James Garner guest stars.

Julesburg

Cheyenne, helping lost immigrants recover their stolen cattle, passes himself off as a cattle buyer, in the lawless town of Julesburg. He exposes and kills the guilty party. (Partially based on the film "Colt .45.")

The Argonauts

Cheyenne joins up with two friendly young gold prospectors and watches dissension breed as the gold mounts up.

Border Showdown

Cheyenne chases a gang of bank robbers into Mexico where he finds the gang is holding a small village in a reign of terror.

The Outlander

After he arrives in a new town, Cheyenne is attacked by the foreman of the biggest ranch in the territory. Bodie learns that the rancher's wife is an ex-prostitute he used to know.

The Travelers

When the Marshal is killed, Deputy Cheyenne promises to protect a suspected murderer from lynchers and see that he gets a fair trial.

Decision

Rather than face an Indian war party, a frightened cavalry major orders his company and a party of civilians to march through waterless country. The soldiers, fearing they will all die of thirst, mutiny. James Garner appears.

The Storm Riders

Cheyenne, roughed up by a powerful rancher's gunslinger, hires on as a hand at a small ranch and is instru-

mental in forming an alliance of the small ranchers. Bodie rejects a rancher's wife. She murders her husband, and Bodie is blamed.

Rendezvous at Red Rock

Bodie falls in with a young gunslinger who saves him from a lynch mob. But Cheyenne thinks the gunfighter is a killer and they eventually fight it out.

West of the River

Bodie, leading a small party of cavalrymen, rescues two white sisters from Indians who captured them five years earlier; neither wants to return to the fort. One fears she will be shunned; the other feels she has become more Indian than white.

Quicksand

When Indians trap a group of settlers in an abandoned fort, the true characters of the people come to the fore. Bodie saves the lives of the party by personally challenging the chief of the Indians to a knife fight in quicksand.

Fury at Rio Hondo

Bodie is carrying trade goods into Mexico when he gets mixed up with Mexican revolutionists who are trying to overthrow the government of Emperor Maximilian. Peggie Castle appears.

Star in the Dust

Cheyenne becomes a deputy for a likeable sheriff. But the sheriff falls for a beautiful woman, and keeps some money stolen by bandits so that he may offer her luxury. Bodie is forced to shoot the sheriff in a gunbattle.

Johnny Bravo

Bodie is hired by a Mexican-hating rancher who is trying to find a husband for his daughter, not knowing she loves a young Mexican ranch hand.

The Last Train West

Framed for a murder, Bodie escapes prison and joins colonists bound for California, hoping to find those who framed him. James Garner as Bret.

The Dark Rider

A test show for *Maverick*, this episode pits Cheyenne against Samantha Crawford (Diane Brewster) who will return later to plague Bret and Bart. Bodie becomes involved with Samantha, who, with a group of men, leads a cattle drive to Kansas. They are joined by a padre, and two men are murdered along the way. Cheyenne reveals the padre as a murderer in disguise, whom he has to shoot. At the end of the trail, Cheyenne saves the money due the men by preventing Sam from absconding with the funds. But in true Samantha style, she wins in the end by entering Bodie's room and stealing the money.

SECOND SEASON:

The Long Winter

When winter halts a cattle drive, Bodie volunteers to stay with the herd through the bleak months to come. He blocks an attempt by the

foreman and an outlaw to steal the cattle.

Death Deals the Hand

Cheyenne is travelling to St. Louis with a fur trapper. An old friend of Bodie's, a professional river boat gambler, is forced to cheat the trapper out of his money. Cheyenne recovers the money.

The Bounty Killers

Bodie accepts a job as deputy marshal only to discover that the marshal is a ruthless bounty hunter who always kills his prisoners before they get to jail. Andrew Duggan appears.

The Law Man

Cheyenne, working for the Cattlemen's Protective Association, discovers that his good friend, a former sheriff, is now engaged in cattle rustling. But when Bodie is about to be killed, the ex-sheriff has a change of heart.

Mustang Trail

Bodie hunts mustangs in Mexico with an estranged couple. A brave act by the husband gives the wife new respect. Diane Brewster is featured in a non-Samantha role.

Lone Gun

Much to the resentment of the old hands, Bodie takes over as trail boss on a big cattle drive.

The Trap

Bodie, arrested on a trumped-up vagrancy charge, is forced to work in a silver mine.

The Iron Trail

Escorting a girl who is to marry his boss, Bodie boards a train which is held up by young outlaws who plan to kidnap President Grant. Dennis Hopper, Sheb Wooley and Montgomery Pittman (who wrote the story) appear.

Land Beyond the Law

Falsely accused of a killing, Bodie escapes a posse and joins a robber band. After a few narrow escapes, he finds the real killer. Andrew Duggan and Dan (Hoss) Blocker star.

Test of Courage

Cheyenne, on secret orders, uncovers the army Colonel who has been in cahoots with a gang which raids Army horses, then sells them back to the Army.

War Party

Cheyenne is trying to help a young couple who has discovered gold. It's hoped they can prevent warring Indians from learning of the discovery. There's also a band of outlaws looking for the gold. Angie Dickinson and James Garner star.

Deadline

Cheyenne is plunged into a fight with a land-grabbing politician. It all ends in a gunbattle.

Big Ghost Basin

A mysterious killer terrorizes ranchers and their families. Cheyenne gets the job of tracking down the killer ... but the job is complicated when a young man becomes jealous of Bodie's attention to his fiancee.

Born Bad

Bodie, made sheriff when the old sheriff mysteriously resigns, leads a posse that tracks down a bandit who turns out to be the ne'er-do-well son of the old sheriff and the devoted twin brother of the girl Bodie loves.

The Brand

Bodie finds evidence that a missing pal has been murdered by a young outlaw who is trying to emulate his killer father. When the youth is hanged, Bodie persuades him to go to his death like a coward for the sake of his brother and sister. The youth is Edward Byrnes.

Decision at Gunsight

A crook and his men move into Gunsight and set up a protection racket. Bodie takes over the livery stables in payment of a debt but refuses to make payments. The locals run away, but Bodie shames them into returning. John Carradine appears.

The Spanish Grant

Finding a baby in an ambushed stagecoach, Bodie suspects the child is the real heir to a ranch owned by his new boss. The baby is kidnapped, but Cheyenne comes to the rescue. Peggie Castle appears.

Hard Bargain

Bodie trails Curly Galway, a young bank robber, and captures him. But Cheyenne learns that the young robber needed the money desperately to help his father in a struggle against a neighboring ranch. Richard Crenna stars.

The Broken Pledge

A miner kills his partner and incites vengeance on the Sioux by blaming the murder on them. A newspaperwoman tips off the miner allowing him to ambush the Sioux. Later, the reporter helps Bodie and promises to print the true story in her paper.

THIRD SEASON:

Incident at Indian Springs

A schoolteacher claims a reward for the body of an outlaw. When he later admits he's the outlaw's halfbrother and the claim of killing is false, the townspeople want him to leave. He asks Bodie for help.

The Conspirators

To trap a post war Confederate underground, Cheyenne poses as an actor and passes as a Southern sympathizer. He is nearly killed when his true identity is learned.

The Mutton Puncher

After Thora Flagg plays poker with Ben Creed for Cheyenne's services as foreman and wins, she reveals the stock she is taking to market is sheep, not cattle. Cheyenne is angry at first but helps out. Ben marries Thora.

Border Affair

Mexicans rise against French tyranny, and Cheyenne, returning from a cattle drive, finds lovely Princess Maria who is fleeing from a political marriage with the gross French commander. Sebastian Cabot appears.

Devil's Canyon

Cheyenne's partner, Chip, is murdered when he reneges on a deal to guide treasure seekers. Bodie finds the treasure—a jewelled church altar piece—and gives the reward money to Chip's widow.

Town of Fear

The sheriff, in protecting a prisoner from a lynch mob, accidentally kills one of the mob.

Hired Gun

A gunman, believed hired by a rancher to kill a neighbor, is killed by the sheriff. Bodie, impersonating the gunman, finds the rancher's wife (who is in love with the neighbor) hired the killer to murder her husband.

Top Hand

In a power struggle, three ranchers vie for the services of Cheyenne to ramrod their outfits. Peter Brown stars.

The Last Comanchero

Trailing renegades, Bodie captures their leader, Shep Larkin. But young Benji Taylor frees Shep to exchange him for his fiance who's a prisoner of the renegades. Edd Byrnes is Benji.

The Gamble

Cheyenne helps a widow protect her saloon from encroachment by a crook who threatens to expose her "shameful" saloon-ownership to her daughter if she won't sell out.

Renegades

Young Jed Wayne deserts the Army with his injured horse to prevent the animal from being destroyed. Cheyenne trails him to the camp of Chief Little Elk. Trouble ensues with the Indians.

The Empty Gun

Bodie aids a disabled gunslinger who's trying to give six thousand dollars to the widow of the first man he'd killed. John Russell stars.

White Warrior

Guiding a wagon train of pioneers, Bodie is unaware that the leader is carrying concealed weapons to Apaches. A white youth reared by Comanches is taken into the group by Cheyenne who hopes the boy will rejoin his own race. The boy is finally the means by which the deal with the Apaches is exposed. Michael Landon appears.

Ghost of the Cimarron

To clear himself of a false robbery charge, Cheyenne joins old outlaw Doc Johnson in a hunt for the Kiowa Kid, a turn-coat outlaw. They find him planning a robbery with a boy who is Doc's secret son.

Wagon-Tongue North

Under an assumed name, Cheyenne becomes trail boss for a pregnant young widow whose husband she killed in self-defense. A ruthless rancher tries to stampede the cattle during which time she has her baby.

The Long Search

When an Indian friend of Bodie's is accused of kidnapping a lost boy, Cheyenne learns the boy is adopted and is really the son of the sheriff and a woman saloon owner. The boy is found unharmed in a cave-in. Claude Akins appears.

Standoff

Cheyenne and an escaped criminal find themselves in a town that has been sentenced to death by the Mexican bandit leader Lobos.

Dead to Rights

Investigating the murder of his pal Shorty, Bodie learns that Shorty had info about a missing heir. John Russell and Michael Connors star.

Noose at Noon

When Jim O'Neil refuses to defend himself against a charge of killing a ranger on his land, Bodie investigates and finds the real culprits have threatened to harm Jim's family if he talks.

The Angry Sky

Wounded by a masked outlaw named Black Jack, Bodie is found by a young girl who takes him home with her. Her sister is the wife of a judge who turns out to also be Black Jack. Andrew Duggan is Black Jack.

FOURTH SEASON:

Blind Spot

Trying to re-unite a young Southern boy with his father (who fought for the North), Cheyenne exposes the boy's uncle, who masks greed behind his patriotism in a plot to seize the cotton farms of his neighbors. Bodie corrects the lies and hatred which have been instilled in the youth. Adam (Batman) West appears.

Reprieve

Bodie accompanies Wes McQueen (released from a ten year jail term) to find and return money buried after a stick-up. When McQueen is killed, Bodie agrees to find his son Billy and prevent him from entering a life of crime. Tim Considine is Billy. Connie Stevens appears.

The Rebellion

Cheyenne, hoping to free an American friend who has been captured by Maximilian's forces, joins up with a rebel leader. Bodie learns, almost too late, that the leader is lining his pockets with money for the revolution and has an eye on the presidency.

Trial by Conscience

Cheyenne, trailing the killer of the sheriff, suspects smooth Nick Avalon. Bodie uses Shakespeare to frighten Nick into a confession.

The Imposter

Recovering from an accident that killed his friend Sam, Bodie learns he's heir to Sam's millions unless the latter's son can be found. Meanwhile, another fellow is posing as Cheyenne and is already liquidating Sam's holdings. Bodie finds the son. James Drury and Robert McQueeney star.

Prisoner of Moon Mesa

Bodie aims an ex-foreman to escape from jail when a powerful rancher tries to railroad him for rustling.

Gold, Glory and Custer — Prelude

Cheyenne, working with Commissioner Brady, tries to stop Custer's advance into the Black Hills which leads to the massacre at Little Big Horn. Unsuccessful, Bodie disappears and is listed as a deserter as Custer rides to his death.

Gold, Glory and Custer — Requiem

Part two of the story has Bodie, though being sought as a deserter, returning to tell his eyewitness account of the massacre of Custer and his men. His story of being sent on a secret mission by (now dead) Commissioner Brady and being held and forced by Sitting Bull to watch Custer be led into a trap is believed. Barry Atwater is Custer.

Riot at Arroyo Seco

In drought-stricken Arroyo Seco, Sheriff Cheyenne Bodie holds off a mob bent on lynching an accused murderer. Bodie kills a man in a gun fight and is tried by a hanging judge.

Apache Blood

Bodie helps an Apache-bred white youth and his Mexican wife adjust to the white community. Authorities are notified that the wife is a Mexican national, and so she is forced to return to Mexico. The youth then kidnaps the marshal's daughter to force an exchange of girls.

Outcast of Cripple Creek

As temporary marshal of a wild rail-head town, Bodie saves the town from a conniving cattleman and hypocritical polticians.

Alibi for the Scalped Man

In Emmetsville for the wedding of a friend to the mayor's daughter, Cheyenne learns that his friend is missing. Bodie learns that the bride is not who she appears to be, and later Bodie is accused of murder.

Home Is the Brave

Cheyenne, bringing home the body of Cole Prescott who died an army hero, finds the townspeople hostile, refusing to accept the body of Cole, who was part Indian. Federal troops finally take the body to Arlington — burial place for heroes.

FIFTH SEASON:

The Long Rope

Cheyenne wins the office of sheriff from a ruthless town boss and then has to solve a bank robbery and murder.

The Counterfeit Gun

A dying train robber accuses Bodie of being his boss and Cheyenne escapes to Mexico to catch the real boss, who has a double.

Road to Three Graves

Cheyenne and two others defy cattle-empire despot Loza, who tried to kill them to prevent their carrying equipment to a mine leased from Loza by men dedicated to supporting Civil War orphans. Cheyenne kills Loza and the mine is saved.

Two Trails to Santa Fe

Tipped by renegade Corporal Burch, Apaches attack a gold camp after an Apache girl who married a white man. Cheyenne fights them back, and later Burch is killed by a former wife.

Savage Breed

Cheyenne is guide for a buffalo hunting party which includes crooked Marshal Al Lestrade and a fleeing embezzler, George Naylor. They are cornered by a band of Sioux, who demand their horses. Bodie is ready to comply to prevent bloodshed, but Lestrade refuses and conspires to kill Naylor.

Incident at Dawson Flats

Coming to Dawson Flats to be best man at a wedding, Bodie becomes involved in the framed-up killing of the bride's brother by the groom. Attempts are made on Cheyenne's life before the situation is cleared up.

Duel at Judas Basin

This episode features all three heroes of *The Cheyenne Show* — Bronco Layne, Tom (Sugarfoot) Brewster, and Cheyenne Bodie. Bronco is secretly working for the U.S. Marshal, though Cheyenne doesn't find that out until well into the episode. The three combine to expose an Indian trader and his henchmen as the heavies who are secretly selling Winchester repeaters to the Sioux. Sugarfoot is framed with murder, but

Cheyenne breaks him out of jail. Tom's famed "volume of the law" comes in handy.

The Return of Mr. Grimm

Cheyenne is only performing his duty when he kills an escapee wanted for theft and beating up a dance hall girl. But the boy's father, who owns the mine, shuts it down to starve the town into agreeing to try Bodie for murder.

The Beholden

The townspeople think the marshal is too strict, and that's hurting the town's business. When the bank is robbed and the marshal is wounded, Cheyenne is sworn in as a deputy but barely escapes a trap set by the marshal who is in league with the robbers.

The Frightened Town

Cheyenne helps the marshal and a few men against an attack by the drunken Drovers, goaded into violence by outlaws who are planning a bank robbery.

Lone Patrol

When Indians trap a patrol, an officer sends a cowardly trooper off with a false message, hoping that Indians will torture him into divulging the bogus information. But the trooper dies heroically without giving up the message and the officer leads the patrol to disaster.

Massacre at Gunsight Pass

Escorting an outlaw to trial, Cheyenne and other stage passengers are besieged at a relay station by vengeful Indians after a passenger, Count Nicholas, wantonly kills a peaceful Shoshone.

The Greater Glory

When Roy Wiley is seriously injured in a stampede caused by Rafe Donovan who wants Roy's land, Bodie helps Roy's wife to save her ranch. He accompanies the pregnant woman, who is a Mormon, to Salt Lake City and back.

SIXTH SEASON:

Winchester Quarantine

Halfway Town blockades the market trail after Bodie loses his herd to a malady diagnosed as Texas fever. Then, a Texas cattlewoman picks Cheyenne for her trail boss and personal playmate while moving her herd by another route. Bodie is bitten by the lovebug. Susan Cummings as Helen Ransom; Denver Pyle appears.

Trouble Street

Bodie rides into Colton City after watching a chain-gain fugitive needlessly murdered. Before he can get a meal and a room, he is arrested. In jail, he learns that innocent men are arrested to provide manpower for a chain-gang. Mala Powers and James Coburn appear.

Cross Purpose

Accidental discovery of the remains of Col. Charles DeVier, the town hero, causes Capt. Robert Holman to flee his own wedding to the Colonel's daughter. Bodie brings the fugitive in but doubts his guilt. An old Indian helps expose a phony hero — and save a life. Michael Forest is Holman.

The Young Fugitives

Young Gilby Collins and a carnival trick shot artist's aide are forced to flee the wrath of a mob led by the father of a man killed by Gilby's father. Cheyenne sets out to get the boy to stand trial for an accidental shooting.

Day's Pay

When Billy Fipps is killed spectacularly after taking over as sheriff of Prairie Junction, Cheyenne sets out to take Billy's slayer to trial. But he's intercepted by Emmy Mae who insists that he first save the town from terrorists. Evan McCord is Billy.

Retaliation

When the bank is robbed and a bridge blown up while he's calling on pretty Cora Ainslie and her son, Cheyenne does some fast detective work to find that ex-rebel soldiers are behind a plot to break the town banker.

Storm Center

On the toss of a coin at a crossroads, Bodie rides into the midst of a bank robbery in progress, annexs a $1500 reward, a girl named Kate, and a young cadet who hires Cheyenne for $3 to help him find his father.

Legacy of the Lost

When an old Indian Chief tells Cheyenne he's the long lost son of rich rancher Lionel Abbot, Bodie

tries to settle down and help run the family spread. But Abbot's second son, James, is busy with a scheme to make sure *he* gets the family fortune. Peter Breck guests.

The Brahma Bull

The simple task of buying a yearling bull to replace a kid's pet lost in a barn fire gets Cheyenne involved in a gun duel and set up as a pigeon by a bounty hunter. William Reynolds as Johnny Tremayne.

The Wedding Rings

Trapped by two old enemies, Bodie is about to cash in his chips when a stranger rides up and catches bullets meant for him. Later, he comes upon the dead man's son and vows to do what he can for the family. When he learns the family's town is being terrorized by a dictator, he nearly gets himself hanged pulling off a coup.

The Idol

Cheyenne unwittingly steps into the cross fire of an impending gun battle when he agrees to transport a new teacher and her son to a town terrorized by the Kirby boys. Feared gunslinger Ben Shelby has agreed to clean up the town, but the memory of his last gunfight has done something to him. With counsel from Bodie, he bests the five killers. Jeff Morrow is Shelby.

One Way Ticket

Cheyenne runs into all types of problems while railroading Cole Younger to trial. He prevents one escape, saves Younger's life, and eventually gets him to go to trial willingly. Philip Carey as Cole Younger.

The Bad Penny

Poetic death warnings go to four residents of the town where Bodie is deputy sheriff. Those threatened ignore the warnings. About that time, beautiful Penelope Piper arrives and dazzles the townfolk. When the threatened men begin to die, Ms. Piper is Cheyenne's chief suspect. Susan Seaforth is Penelope.

A Man Called Regan

An unusual episode of *The Cheyenne Show* that actually featured none of the three regulars (Cheyenne, Sugarfoot, Bronco). The show developed into a series, *The Dakotas*: Frank Regan rides into Stark City to see his buddy Johnny Wilson. But cattle king Ben Stark tells Regan that Wilson has vanished—and that Regan better do likewise. Larry Ward as Regan; Jack Elam as J.D. Smith; Chad Everett as Del Stark; Mike Greene as Vance Porter; Arch Johnson as Ben Stark.

SEVENTH SEASON:

The Durango Brothers

When Bodie beats big, brutish Homer Durango in a test of strength, the other brothers decide he'll make a good husband for their sister Lottie. He creates a dangerous situation by refusing to marry. Jack Elam plays Calhoun Durango; Sally Kellerman is Lottie.

Satonka

When Cheyenne stumbles upon the dastardly works of an abominable mountain man and tells his discovery to the frightened citizens of Rope's End, Carol Dana prevails upon him to go back to search for her missing father. The hunt takes Bodie into the shadow of death and the forbidden tombs of the Arapaho dead. Andrew Duggan; Susan Seaforth.

Sweet Sam

Sam Pridemore becomes a hero when he disarms a killer, helps a crippled kid, and wins the heart of a village belle. But Bodie wonders about Sam. Robert McQueeney is Sam.

Man Alone

Young fast gun Terry Brown is suffering from amnesia when Bodie finds him wounded beside the road. Cheyenne helps him recover his memory and helps him find the road to happiness.

The Quick and the Deadly

The murder trial of Jud Ainsley (son of the town banker) backfires into the conviction of sheriff's deputy Harry Thomas for robbing a prisoner. Cheyenne sticks on the side of the disgraced lawman ... and sets up a wedding. Mike Road is Jud.

Indian Gold

There's illness in the tent of White Crow, and he sends for help from the white men for his squaw, offering to pay with gold. When the Indian is accused of stealing the gold, Bodie suspects foul play and stands up for the honor of the red man. Peter Breck appears.

Dark Decision

Cheyenne meets blind singer Constance Mason and her maid Cleo when his cattle stampede and overrun their wagon. Seeking to help them, he is temporarily blocked when Constance falls for the line of Tony Chance, a gambler. Before it's all over, Bodie is facing a murder charge. Diane Brewster is Constance; Peter Breck is Tony.

Pocketful of Stars

Cheyenne and sidekick Ross Andrews find themselves in the cross fire of railroad builders and Indians. Complications set in when Bodie wins Oriental beauty Mei Ling in a lottery conducted by the workers. Peter Brown as Ross.

The Vanishing Breed

When hunters threaten to wipe out buffalo herds, Cheyenne takes the unexpired term of a dead state senator to seek a law against wanton hunting.

Vengeance Is Mine

Ray Masters is out to avenge being double-crossed by Rod Delaplane in a town where Bodie has just been named sheriff. Cheyenne suspects that Rod's gunslinger, Dan Gibson, is the cause of the trouble. Leo Gordon; Van Williams; Denver Pyle.

Johnny Brassbuttons

Cheyenne helps an Indian blood brother prove he did not treacherously arrange the ambush of a wagon train. Tony Young is Johnny.

Wanted for the Murder of Cheyenne Bodie

When Cheyenne happens along just in time to prevent the escape of condemned Pete Walton, he becomes hated by the man's sister, Lenore. Later, the Walton family conspires to engineer Bodie's death. Ruta Lee as Lenore.

Showdown at Oxbend

Cheyenne rides into Oxbend, looking for a piece of property and a place to settle down. But what he finds are a charming female who saves his life and a raging range war. Joan Caulfield as Darcy Clay; Andrew Duggan as Ed Foster.

3
A Rifle and a Volume of the Law

ABC (1 hour) — debuted September 17, 1957
Format: Tom Brewster is studying law through correspondence school and becomes involved in dramatic and/or comic situations in various frontier towns
Cast: Will Hutchins . . . . Tom "Sugarfoot" Brewster
Jack Elam . . . . Toothy Thompson
The Canary Kid . . . . Himself
Executive Producer: William T. Orr
Producer: Harry Tatelman; Carroll Case; Burt Dunne
Theme Music: "Sugarfoot" by Ray Heindorf, Max Steiner, and Paul Francis Webster
Location: Filmed in Hollywood

On September 17, 1957, Warner Bros. premiered a new Western series entitled *Sugarfoot*, starring Will Hutchins as Tom Brewster. Brewster was a law school correspondence student who found that life on the frontier could sometimes be hard to handle. Some of his adventures had a comedic flair while others were deadly serious.

As with other Warners cowboy shows, *Sugarfoot* and its main character, Tom Brewster, had the quality of the human spirit when he struggled to avoid gunplay and violence but didn't hesitate to fight if necessary. Tom would have loved it if the world had just left him alone and let him study his lawbooks, but his luck just didn't run that smoothly. Every week he met someone who needed the services of a lawyer or maybe just a friend to help him out of a scrape.

Hutchins as fun-loving, law-studying Tom Brewster of Sugarfoot.

Brewster was called a sugarfoot — one step below a tenderfoot. He was a peaceful, funloving, laid-back cowboy who, because he was rather idealistic and a bit romantic, was looked upon by the roughnecked cowboys as a gullible coward. It was not unusual that these same cowpokes would wind up with egg on their faces when the sugarfoot displayed his ability to use a knife, rope, fists, or a gun.

His strong sense of justice just wouldn't let him stay out of trouble. Most often his helpfulness got him caught right in the middle of the action so that, whatever the conflict, he had to settle it.

When Tom had trouble, you could just about figure there would be a pretty girl involved. In one episode Brewster got a job at a general store run by two half sisters. The boyfriend of one of the sisters was jailed for murder, and of course Tom took the case. He solved it by finding that the older sister was the actual murderer, and he left town having barely escaped the matrimonial advances of the younger sister.

In another adventure, "Toothy Thompson," Tom met a character by that name played by Jack Elam, who was to become his occasional companion in other stories. Toothy was charged with the murder of a prominent citizen in town and was nearly lynched—if not for Brewster, he would have been. Tom proved that Toothy was innocent and so Toothy decided to make himself Tom's best friend. He followed Tom everywhere and even brought him a gift of a watch that he had stolen. The owner came running to the sheriff's office where Tom was working in the absence of the usual sheriff and began to complain about the theft. Then, seeing Toothy, he began to accuse him of stealing the watch. Tom saved Toothy again by explaining that Mr. Thompson had found the watch on the street and had brought it in hoping the rightful owner would come to claim it. The episode ended with Sugarfoot and Toothy riding off together.

WILL HUTCHINS

It was not by chance that Will Hutchins was given the part of Tom Brewster in the *Sugarfoot* series. In fact, the series was devised specifically for Will by William T. Orr. Hugh Benson told it this way: "We had an idea about *Sugarfoot*, a guy who is studying law. A gentle cowpuncher itinerant who goes from place to place but still has that law book, and someday he's going to be an attorney. We looked around and found this gentle, nice man, Will Hutchins."

Carl Stucke remembers Will: "He was almost the character. I don't know whether he grew into it or whether he already was, but he really was just about the same person. He's another one who wanted to go off and do big things and never really did."

The show was not the only thing Orr provided for his young star. As was his habit to do, he also provided Will's name. Hutchins was born Marshall Lowell Hutchason on May 5, 1932, in Los Angeles, California. He began his career and search for stardom as a young magician in his father's garage in the L.A. suburb of Atwater. In high school, Will distinguished his acting career by walking off with the Best Actor award in a Shakespearian Festival in which he competed with university as well as high school performers. After high school, Will spent four years at Pomona College studying drama and starring in such plays as, "Ah Wilderness," "Of Thee I Sing," "What Every Woman Knows," "Liliom," and others. After "Hutch," as he had become known to his friends, graduated with his B.A. in dramatic arts in 1952, he had just enough time to produce and act in a play for the Ivar Theater in Hollywood, a musical revue titled "Run for Cover."

Hutchins portrays the serious, determined side of Tom Brewster.

It became his fate to receive a letter of greetings from his country's President. Will was drafted for two years which he spent with the Army signal corps in Paris. He was discharged in 1954 as a corporal.

After the army, it was back to college. This time, the theatre arts department at U.C.L.A. to work on his masters degree in motion pic-

Hutchins in another TV role as Dagwood; Patricia Harty as Blondie.

ture production. The term "Hutch style," used to describe his unusual methods, was known to students years after he had left the school.

Albert McCleery, the producer of *Matinee Theatre*, discovered Will when he auditioned for a role in a special all-student production of the series. Will won the lead role and played a man who suffered the experience of accidentally killing a young woman. He hid her body in a closet and tried to remove himself from the terror of what he had done. The show came off extremely well, and McCleery thought that it was because of Hutchins' charm and professional attitude.

After the people at Warners saw the show, they, along with two other major studios, bid for Hutchins to test for a contract. Will chose Warner Bros. because he was interested in doing "The Magic Brew," an episode of *Conflict*. William T. Orr and Roy Huggins decided that Will was definitely contract material and signed him. Will did two more *Conflict*s: "Stranger in the Road" and "Capital Punishment." He was such a standout that Warner Bros. came up with *Sugarfoot* for him from a story they had acquired from the *Saturday Evening Post*. Interestingly, the *Conflict* episode, "Stranger in the Road," played three days ahead of the *Matinee Theatre* episode, "The Wisp End," on December 11 and 14 of 1956 on ABC and NBC, respectively.

In 1957 *Sugarfoot* took the air and lasted for four seasons, ending with the 1960–61 season. *Sugarfoot* alternated with *Cheyenne* from 1957 until 1959, then alternated with *Bronco* for another year before finishing its run by alternating with both. *Sugarfoot* was the first of Will's series and by far the most successful. Two more, *Hey Landlord* for NBC in 1966 and *Blondie* for CBS in 1968, each lasted only one season. Between series Hutch managed to co-star in a few episodes of some other Warners series such as *77 Sunset Strip* ("The Kookie Caper"), *Maverick* ("Hadley's Hunters" and "Bolt From the Blue"), and *The Roaring 20's* ("Pie in the Sky"). He also guest-starred in other shows such as *Gunsmoke, Alfred Hitchcock Presents, Perry Mason*, and *Love American Style*.

Sugarfoot — Series Index

FIRST SEASON:

Brannigan's Boots

Made sheriff by a crooked mayor, Tom defies threats and investigates the murder of the last sheriff. When the mayor's henchman is caught robbing the mail to get a letter that would incriminate the mayor, Sugarfoot kills the mayor in self defense, and subdues his gunman, Billy the Kid. Dennis Hopper is Billy the Kid.

Reluctant Hero

When Tom Brewster saves old Charlie Cade from ambush, Charlie introduces himself as the owner of a nearby ranch and hires Tom as a hand. When Tom sees a cowboy in town forcing his attention on a pretty girl, he intervenes, only to return to the ranch and discover that the cowboy is his foreman.

Strange Land

Sugarfoot, working on Cash Billings' ranch, sees that Cash — a recluse — has let his foreman cheat him and bully the neighborhood.

Bunch Quitter

Taking over the leadership of a cattle drive after the ramrod is murdered, Tom thwarts a plot to steal the cattle; proves the guilt of the ramrod's killer; brings the cattle in safely; and — in a bloody battle — kills the murderer.

Trail's End

Trying to locate young runaway Kathy Larson, Tom finds her working as a bar girl for Clay Horton, who later forces the girl to marry him. Horton kills a cattle buyer, but — though Kathy saw the murder — Horton feels safe because a wife cannot testify against her husband.

Quicksilver

Convinced the mishaps against two mine owners are deliberate, Tom rightly suspects a man who pretends friendship but harbors a grudge. The man is killed in a gunfight which shatters the rock wall and reveals a rich new silver vein.

Misfire

Defending accused murderer Johnnie Wentworth, Tom finds that Johnnie's gun won't fire. At the trial, Brewster accuses Johnnie's foreman, Salt River Smith of the murder. Salt River is played by Pernell Roberts; Connie Stevens also appears.

The Stallion Trail

When the wild horse that Brewster has captured is stolen by his supposed friend, Lon, Tom trails them and finds that Lon has sold the horse and spent the money. Tom gets the horse, Diablo, back, but Lon steals him again.

Small War at Custer Junction

Sugarfoot rescues little Maggie Burke when her father is slain by two men trying to steal his gold mine.

Mule Team

Sugarfoot inherits mules and part of a lost mine. Using the mules to build a railroad track, he crosses the plans of the town's big man, who sabotages his efforts.

Bullet Proof

Because Sugarfoot briefly shared a jail cell with a recently executed bank robber, the rest of the outlaw gang thinks he knows where the money is cached. They try kindness and cruelty to get him to talk. Joi Lansing guests stars.

Deadlock

Serving on a rigged jury, Brewster refuses to vote for the guilt of a rancher who is being framed as a rustler by their own boss. The jury is deadlocked 11-1. Dan Blocker appears.

Man Wanted

When homely Sandy sends Sugarfoot's photo to the matrimonial bureau, pretty Ellie Petersen shows up expecting to marry Tom. Then, Tom is attacked by Deuce, a criminally insane outlaw, who was once Ellie's boy friend. Charles Bronson is Sandy; Pernell Roberts is Deuce.

The Dead Hills

Tom Brewster helps a girl struggle to keep her ranch against the schemings of a woman saloon owner. Ruta Lee appears.

A Wreath for Charity Lloyd

The beautiful wife of an outlaw, anxious for her husband's reform, carries out a hoax in which she pretends to kill her husband so they can make a new life together. Sugarfoot witnesses the fake killing.

Hideout

Tom, Mary and Davey Reader, and an unidentified man are the prisoners of outlaw Ed Roland who's hiding out at the Reader's farm until he can join forces with the notorious

Frank James. Peter Brown plays Davey.

Guns for Big Bear

Tricked by Jasper Monday, Tom is forced to deliver stolen guns to hostile Indians. At the Indian camp, Tom and Monday are imprisoned and condemned to die.

Price on His Head

Outlaws hold a group of stage passengers for ransom while Sugarfoot goes into town for the money. But the money is hard to obtain because the business partner of one of the prisoners would prefer to see his partner dead.

Short Range

Working with a puppet show run by Tania, Brewster learns that Claude Miles is giving guns to hostile Indians. In return, the Indians have killed Claude's brother and promise to kill his young niece so he can inherit a rich ranch.

The Bullet and the Cross

Tom is trapped in a tunnel cave-in with accused murderer Cliff Raven. They blast out. As Raven emerges, deputy Williams shoots him, but the bullet hits a cross he wears around his neck. Charles Bronson is Raven.

SECOND SEASON:

Ring of Sand

Tom and old Job Turner are forced to aid outlaws who have murdered Job's son. Job plans to lead the outlaws to a thirsty death in the desert. John Russell and Edd Byrnes appear.

Brink of Fear

Sugarfoot sponsors the employment of an old friend, an ex-desperado, and has faith in the fellow's supposed reformation. The friend, though, is forced to participate in a bank robbery.

The Wizard

Sugarfoot is implicated in the death of a man—an event which was predicted by Olivia, the hypnotic subject of performer Kerrigan the Great. Olivia accuses Tom, though he knows she is the guilty party. Kerrigan is Efrem Zimbalist, Jr.

The Ghost

Sugarfoot travels to a western town to find a teenaged heir wanted in Missouri. Soon after he arrives, the sheriff is killed in an allegedly haunted house, and the teenager is suspected of murder. Martin Landau stars.

The Canary Kid

The Kid, a desperado who resembles Tom, kidnaps Tom in order to assume his identity as part of a bank robbery scheme. But the Kid enjoys being Tom so much that he decides to destroy his old identity—and Sugarfoot.

The Hunted

Sugarfoot defends big John Allman not knowing that Allman is an army deserter and a psychotic killer.

Yampa Crossing

Tom needs a signature from bad man Galt Kimberly in order to establish the paternity of his son and enable him to collect an inheritance. Sugarfoot catches up with Kimberly at a flooded ford where several people are trapped. Roger Smith appears.

Devil To Pay

Tom goes to an Indian trading post to collect money due a friend for merchandise sold. He finds the latter has been murdered and that someone is cashing in on the Indians' superstition to maintain a false god and collect donations in gold dust.

The Desperadoes

Sugarfoot is visiting the Padre, when three men take control of the Mexican mission. They plan to shoot President Jaurez from the mission bell tower and establish a new republic in Northern Mexico.

The Extra Hand

Tom helps one-armed seaman Alexi Sharlokov overcome treacherous partners through a ruse which makes it seem that Alexi has grown a replacement for his missing arm.

Return of the Canary Kid

The Kid is back for a second appearance, and when Tom impersonates Canary on a train trip — guarded by Chris Colt — he's trying to trap Canary's men into rescuing him, thus leading Colt to their hideout. Canary escapes jail and shows up at the hideout.

The Mysterious Stranger

Tom, working as a clerk in a mine office, learns that a lawyer, trusted by the mine owner, is in collusion with the superintendent in swindling the firm and workers. Adam West appears as Polish pianist Frederick Pulaski.

The Giant Killer

Doreen, whose husband was falsely accused by the crooked town boss, threatens to blow up the hotel with its occupants unless Boss Stoner appears. The bluff works. Dorothy Provine and Jay North appear.

The Royal Raiders

Some of Maximillian's ex-troops, trying to intercept a shipment of diamonds slated to aid the French in the war with Prussia, commandeer an American train. Sugarfoot is a passenger on the train. Jacqueline Beer guest stars.

The Mountain

Tom locates, Vic, an escaped convict, in a mountain hideout with his wife Jean. Tom fails to convince Vic to return for re-trial. Tom and Jean are trapped in a hidden cave, and Vic must conquer fear to save them.

The Twister

Bank robber Garnin holds his brother in a schoolhouse along with Sugarfoot, Alice Fenton and three children. Tom gets Alice and the kids to safety when a twister strikes, But Garnin shoots his brother and is killed himself by the twister as he tries to recover stolen loot.

The Vultures

On the eve of the Apache attack, Capt. Raymond tries to spirit the wife of Col. Starkey away from the fort for her own safety. Jealous, Starkey accuses Raymond of desertion and tries to execute him. Richard Long is Raymond.

The Avengers

Waiting out a storm in a ghost town, Tom discovers a mine full of "fool's gold" guarded by grizzled Zachary, who threatens stage passengers. Dorothy Provine appears.

Small Hostage

In a Mexican village, Tom helps old Col. Craig claim the body of his dead soldier son. Villagers pretend the son has fathered a local orphan boy, Chico. Craig resists the idea, but when Chico is kidnapped, he leads a force to rescue Chico and Tom.

Wolf

Tom defends a shiftless but likeable old loafer, Juf, who's being hounded by a vicious rancher. When Juf dies from eating poisoned beef, his gunman son, Wolf, thinks Tom is responsible.

THIRD SEASON:

The Trial of the Canary Kid

Tom's look-alike cousin is back to cause more trouble — involving several of the WB cowboy stars. Tom is forced to defend Canary against a murder charge. Chris Colt is working with the prosecutor in the case.

Canary's sidekick testifies that Canary couldn't have committed murder because he was robbing a stage at the time. When Canary is back in jail, an ex-gang member helps him break out by starting an anti-Texan riot just as Bronco Layne rides in. Canary breaks out and pulls the identity switch. The crowd thinks he's Tom and attacks him for defending Canary. Chris Colt comes to the rescue. In court the next day, Tom tries to prove he is Tom, but the Kid claims it's just a trick. Just before the jury goes out, Johnny McKay makes a surprise appearance with a letter from Dan Troop saying the Kid was in the Laramie jail on the day of the murder. The Kid is declared not guilty, but as he smiles and prepares to leave, McKay and Colt handcuff him — for the stage robbery.

The Wild Bunch

Accepting a job as a temporary school teacher in Morgan's Ford, Tom learns that his predecessors have all been frightened off by a wild group of pupils led by seventeen-year-old Ken Savage. Troy Donahue is Ken. Connie Stevens appears as Jenny Markham.

The Gitanos

An untamed Romany beauty lures Tom Brewster to a meeting with gypsy law and a showdown with treachery.

MacBrewster the Bold

Brewster, the sheriff of Lodestone (against his better judgment), is rescued from bank robbers by three kilted members of the MacBrewster clan who have come to America to proclaim him their chief.

Canary Kid, Inc.

Tom, posing as a heavily bandaged Guy Yancy, enters a prison to check on escapes engineered by his look-alike fourth cousin. Discovering that inmates are using a funeral wagon for escapes, Tom offers the Kid $20,000 to plot his escape; the Kid bites, and the racket is exposed. Wayde Preston as Chris Colt.

Outlaw Island

Sally Ormond and a prize Arabian, Sultan, traveling under Sugarfoot's protection are abducted by an outlaw and taken to a remote island. Tom finds the island and triggers a revolt of natives against the outlaw and his criminal dynasty.

Apollo with a Gun

Tom spots a bully stealing a famed actress' stallion so that he can collect wagers that she won't do her celebrated riding stunt.

The Gaucho

Tom aids an Argentine gaucho who is gypped by a rancher for delivering a prize bull too late. Robert McQueeney guest stars.

Journey to Provision

Sugarfoot rides into Provision and is mistaken by the crooked sheriff for a government investigator. Tom is threatened with hanging and bribed to leave town, but he remains and breaks the stranglehold the sheriff has on the town. Donald May guests.

The Highbinder

Sugarfoot is hired to escort the ashes of a murdered Chinese youth to San Francisco. The urn also contains the map of a valuable gold strike and an evil Chinese stops at nothing to get the map.

Fernando

A peaceful stone mason at the church decides to enter the boxing ring to raise money to pay for the mission orphanage. But he's helpless in the ring without Sugarfoot in his corner calling out numbers that represent pages in a boxing manual. And Tom is kidnapped.

Wolf Pack

When a friend is killed by a wolf pack, Tom suspects foul play.

Blackwater Swamp

Half breed young Ben Crain, sends for Tom when a villainous rancher, Rome Morgan tries to drive the Mandan tribe away and sell their sacred burial ground to the railroad. Robert Colbert is Ben; James Coburn is Morgan.

Return to Boot Hill

A young fugitive asks Tom to return home with him to establish his innocence. He had been convicted of robbing his father's stage line. Diane McBain costars.

Vinegarroon

Tom is suspected of having murdered a ranch couple and is put in custody of dictatorial Judge Roy Bean.

The Corsican

Tom rescues a trader, his spinster daughter, and a Corsican from Sioux attack. The Sioux capture a giant statue of a Corsican woman — a tie with family tradition. The secret leader of the Sioux is the Corsican's brother who wants him to murder Tom and join the tribe.

Blue Bonnet Stray

On a train trip, Sugarfoot is left with a year-old baby when the baby's mother disappears during a station stop.

The Long Dry

Tom gets involved in a fight over water holes in a drought-stricken town. An elderly man believes the second flood is due and kidnaps Sugarfoot and Anne, a rancher's daughter, to be the twosome for the Ark he's built.

Funeral at Forty Mile

In Forty Mile, Tom traps a murderer and clears the name of a lynched man. Hugh Benson had a hand in writing this one.

The Captive Locomotive

Tom aids a widower and farmers impoverished by drought in combatting the activities of the territorial office manager of the railroad who has stolen railroad tax funds owed the county.

FOURTH SEASON:

Welcome Enemy

Brewster leads Sioux chief Red Wing and daughter White Fawn on a secret mission to Chicago, hoping to secure a protective treaty from President Grant. But Red Wing's assassination is planned.

The Shadow Catcher

As acting Indian agent, Tom tangles with an army officer who is secretly provoking war in order to get the Indians' gold-rich land.

A Noose for Nora

When beautiful Nora shoots a ruthless land company president, Tom acts as her lawyer. But Tom is framed for another murder.

Man from Medora

At 23, future President Teddy Roosevelt goes West for his health, determined to be a cattle rancher. In Medora, he finds a pal in Tom Brewster and obtains half interest in the land-locked ranch of a widow and her pretty daughter.

Toothy Thompson

Simple minded and unethical Toothy becomes Tom's slave after Tom saves him from a lynch mob led by the henchman of the crooked governor. Toothy wants Sugarfoot to become governor and to accomplish this, he kidnaps the governor's wife. She likes the idea; Tom doesn't. Jack Elam is Toothy.

Shepherd with a Gun

Tom helps two teenagers and their crippled father when a power mad land owner tries to take over the father's land and kill his sheep.

Trouble at Sand Springs

When Jimmy and his brother Rance, who is just out of prison, are accused of killing the banker, Tom believes them innocent and defends them.

Stranger in Town

Sugarfoot, mistaken for a professional gunslinger, acts as lawyer for a man whom two immigrants are accusing of cheating them out of a silver mine. When Tom learns his client is a crook, he changes sides in the lawsuit.

Angel

Sugarfoot and Bronco Layne arrive to help Sheriff Billy rid the town of the Ellis gang. They're employed by McTavish, posing as a respected townsman, but who covets rich silver lode property. At the saloon, Tom meets his old pal Toothy Thompson, now deputized and in love with a deaf-mute named Angel. Knowing sign language, Toothy gets information from the girl that exposes the gang. Tom and Bronco overpower McTavish; Toothy and Angel will marry.

4
Show Me a Girl Who's Kissed Him Once

ABC (1 hour) — debuted September 23, 1958
Format: The adventures of a two-fisted ex-Confederate Army captain
  who wanders from job to job and town to town, fighting in-
  justice and outlaws who roamed the West during the post-
  Civil War period
Cast: Ty Hardin ....*Bronco Layne*
Executive Producer: William T. Orr
Producer: Arthur Silver
Theme Music: "Bronco" by Jerry Livingston and Mack David
Location: Filmed in Hollywood

Bronco, like *Cheyenne*, was a Western adventure series. Bronco
Layne was an ex-Confederate captain who, after he was mustered out,
returned home to Texas only to find himself stripped of honor and his
home confiscated. And so began his odyssey. Bronco, like Cheyenne,
was a loner who would have preferred to avoid trouble and conflict,
but who refused to stand by and see others abused and mistreated.

Bronco proved himself to be very much a jack-of-all-trades, working for anyone from the Federal government on a secret mission to a
rancher as a hired hand. His travels led him all over the state of Texas
and other parts of the West. *Bronco* became a hit in its own right
despite the resentment of those dyed-in-the-wool Clint Walker fans
who were upset that Hardin was on their screens instead of Walker.

Bronco was always tied very closely with *Cheyenne* (as was *Sugar-*
foot), and you'll find more information on the show in our *Cheyenne*
chapter.

Ty Hardin appearing as Bronco Layne in the Warner Bros. series *Bronco*.

TY HARDIN

Ty Hardin was born in New York City where his father was attached to the U.S. Army as a civilian engineer. While Ty was still in diapers, the family moved to Texas and he attended schools in both the Houston and Austin areas.

His first stint in college came at Blinn College in Brenham, Texas where he spent a year on a football scholarship. After a four year tour with the U.S. Army, Hardin went back to Texas A&M University — again on a football scholarship to get his degree in electrical engineering. When a severe leg injury took him away from football, he turned to acting, playing his first role in "Ah Wilderness" by Eugene O'Neill. By this time Ty was married and had a son and a daughter.

When his marriage broke up in 1957, Hardin moved to California to work for Douglas Airport in its acoustical research department. While at Douglas, Ty decided to go to a Halloween party dressed as an authentic cowboy. He was looking for the prop department at Paramount to rent some guns (the costume place had only plastic guns), but instead ended up in the office of one of their talent scouts. A script was placed in his hands, he was given a screen test, and a couple of days later he signed a contract that more than doubled his salary as an engineer. (Even at that it was nothing compared to the money paid to today's stars. It was only $300 per week.) At Paramount, Hardin had bit parts in five movies (the first of which was *Space Children*, certainly not a biggie), appeared briefly in a *Playhouse 90*, and was a male model on *Queen for a Day*—for a day.

Ty was unaware that he was to take over for Clint Walker on *Cheyenne* until after Warners had bought his contract. Hugh Benson tells how Ty came to Warner Bros.: "We were in another building, and Ty was outside to see Bill Orr. He came in—our doors were always open to people. Bill Orr screamed, 'Benson,' as he usually did. Our offices were adjoining so I came in. I looked at him and said 'Lock the door.' That was our signal for 'Let's sign him.' We found out that he had been in town a short time. Paramount had signed him to a short six month contract, so we bought the contract from Paramount or traded something; I don't remember. We changed his name to Ty Hardin. [Ty was born Orison Whipple Hungerford, Jr. Ty came from his childhood nickname, Typhoon.] And that's how it came about with him."

Understandably, Ty was a bit nervous about the idea. As he said at the time, "I'm scared stiff, but I do have confidence in the studio." Hardin was at last doing something he really enjoyed. Early on, he had a few problems caused by his basic insecurity that made him a little hard to get along with, but after nearly hitting a director one day, he went home, thought about it, and figured it was time for a change.

Playing the role of Bronco Layne gave Ty the feeling of being somebody. He felt true elation when the kids would ask him for an autograph. Hardin had another problem though—when the fan mail started to come in for his first season on *Cheyenne*, by far the vast majority really got on him for trying to take over for Walker. This hit Ty pretty hard, but instead of giving up, it made him try all the harder to make *Bronco* a hit. So that is just what he did, and by its second year, *Bronco* was an ABC television series of its own, alternating with *Sugarfoot*. Hardin did all his own stunts, being adept at riding, roping, and fighting from his earlier days in Texas.

Bronco carries Anna Kashfi in "Seminole War Pipe."

After his four years on *Bronco* were over, Ty went to Spain to do some work in the movie *The Battle of the Bulge*. He played the part of a Nazi soldier disguised as an American MP guarding the River Ur bridge so that he could mislead the American forces when they came by. He decided to stay in Spain after the film, and did stay for six years. During that part of his expatriation, Hardin owned and operated two saloons on Spain's Costa Brava serving hamburgers, spareribs and chili. One was called the Alamo (strictly Texan); the other, the Fat Black Pussycat.

Ty's other major motion pictures include *PT 109, The Chapman Report*, and *Merrill's Marauders*. He made some forty movies in Europe, but most of them never made their way across the Atlantic. He worked in the London Theatre for a couple of years; in Rome making spaghetti westerns for a few years; and even in Hungary, Israel, and Africa. Hardin never struck it rich, but me managed a living.

Hardin spent the year 1970 in Australia doing the television series *Riptide*, again, shown everywhere but in the United States. His first

Layne with Shakespearean actor Edwin Booth (Efrem Zimbalist, Jr.).

film job back in Hollywood was an episode of *Quest*. Because of his long absence, most casting directors don't remember Ty, so he has had to read for parts like everyone else—despite his experience. Ty formed his own production company, Bookends, to make Westerns. He felt that even though people were making pilots, they weren't selling them because they were not using any good leading men as stars.

Ty, along with Leif Erickson, Alex Cord, and Dan O'Herlihy co-starred in a CBS pilot, *Trapper John, M.D.*, the further adventures of the former *M*A*S*H* character as a civilian surgeon in San Francisco (1979), which featured Pernell Roberts in the title role.

Bronco — Series Index

FIRST SEASON:

The Besieged

Layne comes upon members of a religious sect as they're being attacked by two desperadoes. The badmen want gold that's on the land the sect is about to settle on. Claude Akins and Jack Elam guest star.

Quest of the Thirty Dead

A train on which Bronco and his pal Jim Grant are riding is wrecked by bandits. Grant and 29 others are killed and a former Confederate Army officer gets the blame.

The Turning Point

Layne befriends young John Wesley Hardin and tries to keep him from turning outlaw.

Four Guns and a Prayer

When a Western town is terrorized by the Garnet brothers (and gang), Layne calls in three former desperadoes to help him clean up the place.

The Long Ride Back

Layne rides back home to Texas after the Civil War to marry Redemption McNally, the sister of his dead comrade, Freedom. But Bronco is accused of causing Freedom's death by betraying Southerners in a prison camp escape attempt.

Trail to Taos

Bronco is hired by the Post Office Department (as an undercover agent) to find the brains behind the mob. Posing as an outlaw, Bronco gets in with the mob.

Brand of Courage

Layne is seriously wounded by the two sons of a rancher who's trying to embargo the shipment of cattle and thereby run prices up. Bronco is left on the road for dead.

Freeze Out

Layne hires out to Mary Brown as a guide to take her to a ghost town at the foot of a glacier. Mary is after $70,000 in gold bars stolen from a mine and hidden in the glacier.

Baron of Broken Lance

A powerful rancher tries to get back his daughter who has eloped with Pete Loomis and joined Bronco's wagon train. The rancher has a change of heart when all are threatened by Indians.

Payroll of the Dead

After Bronco helps Major Otis Dameyer reach Chief Sitting Bull, he finds out Dameyer is a bogus officer who lied about being on a secret mission. He wants money the Indians have taken from dead soldiers at the recent Custer massacre. James Coburn stars.

Riding Solo

Bronco is menaced by a mob which thinks he was an accomplice of an outlaw uncle by marriage whose gang robbed a stage and killed the man riding shotgun.

Borrowed Glory

Lloyd Stover steals a dead soldier's Medal of Honor which makes Lloyd a hero and sheriff in his home town. But the "dead" soldier returns and makes demands in return for silence. Robert Vaughn is Stover.

Silent Witness

When Layne is accused of murdering his mining partner, a little dumb girl, whom he taught Indian sign language, clears Bronco with her "sign testimony" and proves the Miners' Protective Association is after the mine.

The Belles of Silver Flat

Layne rides guard on a stage which is carrying $70,000 and a group of dance hall girls. He outwits robbers by having the girls pin the bank notes to their petticoats. Pernell Roberts appears.

Backfire

Deputy Layne finds a slightly crooked sheriff who was in on a "phony" holdup staged by a banker, a gambler, and a store-keeper to keep the sheriff in office. Troy Donahue as Roy Parrott.

School for Cowards

Layne takes on the job of instructor in outdoor survival at a boys' military school and tangles with the strict headmaster.

Prairie Skipper

On a detoured cattle drive, Bronco joins forces with U.S. Naval Captain Carr who doesn't know his beautiful young "wife" is legally married to a rancher with whose money she has absconded. Lorne Greene is Carr.

Shadow of a Man

Bronco rescues a stagecoach robber from quicksand and is arrested by the sheriff as a partner in the theft of the mine payroll the stage carried. When the robber is shot, he tells Bronco to find "Lynn" to clear himself.

Hero of the Town

A payroll is stolen and circumstances make cowardly Tod Biggs look a hero and make Bronco look craven. Later Bronco's best friend in Dusty Flats turns out to be the leader of the outlaws.

Red Water North

Crooked freighter Caleb White knows that if the river boat makes a successful voyage to Benton, it can put him out of business. So he places some people on board to see that it doesn't. Bronco serves as pilot on the trip. Dorothy Provine stars.

SECOND SEASON:

Game at Beacon Club

Layne gets innocently involved with a pretty card sharp who uses special glasses to read the backs of cards. To save his life, Bronco gets the glasses and purposely loses back the girl's winnings. Pat Crowley as Amanda Stover.

The Burning Springs

A Yankee officer, broken in rank, tries to kill Bronco Layne and is courtmartialed. But Bronco defends him. Adam West guests.

Bodyguard

Bronco is hired by Frank Kelton to prevent a stranger, Dan Flood, from murdering him. Bronco learns Kelton had taken Flood's wife when Flood left for the gold rush. Yvonne Craig as Stephanie Kelton.

The Soft Answer

Bronco and Billy The Kid work for Quaker-motivated Spence, a sheepman who rouses the ire of two cattleranchers. Bronco and Billy use violent methods to save Spence's life. Robert Colbert as Arron Running Deer.

The Last Resort

Bronco is framed by conniving Billy Styles as his accomplice in a mailcoach robbery and killing.

The Devil's Spawn

Bronco captures Jeb Bonner, an escaped outlaw, whose bank robbery caused a feud between his brother Pete Bonner and a rival rancher, Rob Maxton. Young hell-cat Bart Bonner fancies that Uncle Jed is his father. Troy Donahue is Bart.

Flight from an Empire

Baroness Illse Von Waldenheim and her handsome son Baron Franz travel through Texas with millions of dollars worth of jewels entrusted to their care by the late Emperor Maximilian. Bronco saves them from an ambush and takes them to Tom Goddard's ranch where Franz falls in love with Marilee Goddard. Mary Tyler Moore is Marilee.

Night Train to Denver

Layne, escorting a "dead" man to Denver, is accused of robbery. The mystery is solved when Bronco proves that the man in the coffin arose and concealed money in the coffin until it reached its destination. Robert Colbert guests.

Shadow of Jesse James

Deputy Marshal Layne tries to capture Jesse James and, at the same time, spare Cole Younger, who rides with Jesse. The plan backfires when Jesse pulls a switch and Cole is badly shot up while Jesse escapes. James Coburn is Jesse; Richard Coogan is Cole.

Masquerade

Four teen-agers, each under pressure of wrong parental influences, are saved from lives of crime by an understanding Bronco Layne.

Volunteers from Aberdeen

Young Tom Fuller's love for married Molly Corley leads him to the brink of destruction, but Tom's saved in time by Bronco Layne who realizes that the woman and her older husband are partners in crime.

Every Man a Hero

Five soldiers—all scheduled for court martial—kill their commanding officer during a Comanche attack in order to destroy charges against them. The five become uneasy when the dead officer's wife arrives (with Bronco Layne) carrying proof of their guilt.

Death of an Outlaw

After the Lincoln County rustling wars, Layne tries to straighten out his friend, Billy the Kid. He is double-crossed by Pat Garrett, who, greedy for reward money, kills Billy. Rhodes Reason is Garrett; Stephen Joyce is Billy.

The Human Equation

Bronco's attempt to persuade harsh Col. Arthur to let Chief Crippled Bear take his tribe to a more habitable place instead of a muddy Oklahoma reservation succeeds when Arthur, dying of cholera, writes a new treaty.

Montana Passage

Framed for murder, Bronco rigs his own death so he can go after his enemies without being hampered by pursuing lawmen. But a schoolteacher convinces him he's wrong to seek personal revenge. He, in turn, makes her aware of her femininity.

Legacy of Twisted Creek

Bronco is charged with bringing a murdering Indian, Char, to trial. But Indian rebels and crooked whites want to create an incident and see to it that Char is killed.

Tangled Trail

Bronco barely escapes being lynched after he spurns a woman and then she accuses him of a murder she committed.

La Rubia

Bronco and beautiful blonde Judith are captured by an ugly Robin Hood style Mexican bandit named Fierro who asks Judith to marry him. She refuses—until she learns he has a million dollars stashed away.

Winter Kill

Powerful Kate Crowley wants to lynch "Pops," who she is convinced murdered her favorite son. Deputy Bronco wants to get Pops to town for trial.

End of a Rope

Deputy Marshal Layne poses as an outlaw to find out why a supposedly hanged criminal turns up alive three years later. He learns that a crooked sheriff and the undertaker are faking hangings—and sending the "dead" criminals off to Mexico.

THIRD SEASON:

Apache Gold

When a number of Apaches are murdered and scalped, the Army sends Bronco to see the Apache chief and prevent an Indian uprising.

The Invaders

An outlaw kidnaps the sheriff's much-loved daughter to insure a lack of opposition while he and his gang await the gold shipment. Bronco saves the girl and the gold.

The Mustangers

Chasing mustang-hunting partner Jimmy Smith for money he's owed, Bronco gets tangled up in the death of a rancher and in a hunt for Mexican treasure.

Ordeal at Dead Tree

Bronco, aided by an ambitious deputy, sets a trap for four vicious Welty brothers who have involved him in a bank holdup and murder rap.

Seminole War Pipe

Bronco saves two Indian friends from a lynch mob ... all bigoted Texas ranchers and Civil War vets. He explains that the two Indians helped save Texas from total destruction during the War.

The Buckbrier Trail

Bronco, taking a killer to Santa Fe for trial, is jumped by the husband of the murdered woman. But the shrewd Marshal is also taking a prisoner to trial. One of them is a decoy.

Manitoba Manhunt

Marlow and Coil kill two lawmen and take over their identities, then join Bronco in a trip to Canada to arrest an embezzler named Powell, an ex-pal of Bronco's.

Yankee Tornado

Bronco and Tom (Sugarfoot) Brewster help young Teddy Roosevelt outwit and jail a ruthless crook who, in hopes of getting control of additional land, tries to provoke an Indian war by indiscriminately slaughtering buffalo.

Stage to the Sky

Bronco helps his old friend Billy, once an outlaw, now a minister, regain $5000 stolen from his flock by his outlaw brother.

Guns of the Lawless

Ex-partners in the ranching business Groves and Munger are feuding, and Bronco sides with Groves. Layne is also murdered by Munger's men without Munger knowing it. When all is out in the open, Bronco saves Munger from his own men and the partners are re-united.

FOURTH SEASON:

The Harrigan

Bronco joins forces with a poetry-spouting Irishman, The Harrigan, to break up a robbery gang. Sean McClory in the title role; Jack Cassidy also appears.

The Cousin from Atlanta

Bronco has his hands full convincing a relative that frontier gunmen are no good for city girls. Anne Helm as cousin Amanda Layne. Gary Vinson and Evan McCord appear.

One Came Back

Layne takes on the job of guiding a quartet of travelers to a border town when pretty Vicky Norton uses her womanly wiles on him. Bronco plans to marry the girl ... but a bank robbery changes his plans. Karen Steele is Vicky; Robert McQueeney also stars.

Prince of Darkness

Patriots discover a plot to raise funds for insurrectionist activities in Reconstruction days and Shakespearian actor Edwin Booth is asked to pretend disloyalty to the Union to learn the plotters' plans. Booth's relationship to Lincoln's killer makes his job easy ... but there's a plot to kill him which Bronco foils. Efrem Zimbalist, Jr. is Booth.

Beginner's Luck

Young Lew Gant is lucky at poker and gunplay but is set up as a pawn in a plot to get the Gant farm. Bronco saves the boy's life when a hired gunslinger challenges him. The kid returns home with a new respect for his father. Buzz Martin is Lew.

The Equalizer

When leaders of feuding outlaw gangs agree to a three day truce for the odd reason that one's daughter is marrying the other's nephew, Bronco draws the assignment of keeping the peace. But look out! Sugarfoot's old buddy Toothy Thompson (Jack Elam) is back and is out to get the gangs shooting again because they ridiculed him and Jim Morgan.

Trail of Hatred

Layne leads a troop of army renegades into Indian-held swamps to capture a deserter.

A Sure Thing

Bronco uses 1000 head of cattle as a bluff in a stacked poker game. He manages to outwit a rancher named Poole who's strangling the town by refusing to permit cattle drives across his land.

Ride the Whirlwind

The return of Dr. Miles Gillis to the town that convicted him of treating enemy soldiers causes four men responsible for his disgrace to shudder in their boots. Bronco is taken in by Gillis' skillful war of nerves against his enemies. But Layne's observation of the strange behavior of deputy Johnny Davis reveals that the deputy is a tool used hypnotically by Gillis. Chad Everett is the deputy.

Destinies West

While on an army assignment to find a million in gold and a renegade ex-Union soldier who stole it, Bronco encounters a beautiful lady gambler Belle Siddons, a sometimes nun with several aliases and very winning ways. Kathleen Crowley as Belle; Robert McQueeney and Leo Gordon also appear.

The Last Letter

Heading up a dangerous ragtail band of Rebel prisoners of war pledged to help the Union fight Indians after the Civil War, Layne sets out to deliver a fortune in gold to America's friends during the Mexican Revolution. While on the mission, he learns of the assassination of President Lincoln, under whose secret orders he is working. Robert Colbert appears.

Rendezvous with a Miracle

Bronco unfrocks a harlot in a nun's clothing and sees a hoodlum converted to religion. Mike Road appears as Mike Bestor.

One Evening in Abilene

While Civil War hostilities still burn, Layne is forced to hire fast gun Clay Farraday (a Rebel gunman) to help with a cattle drive into Kansas. But in Abilene, Marshal Wild Bill Hickok is conducting a vendetta against Southerners. Jered Barclay as Clay; Jack Cassidy is Wild Bill.

Until Kingdom Come

Mexican revolutionaries chase Duchess Eugenia and her charge Prince Philip across the border where Bronco helps them find asylum. An ex-newspaperman forms an alliance with a crooked sheriff to steal away her crown jewels. But he decides that love is more important than money. Philip Carey is the crook-turned-lover; Jackie Beer is the Duchess.

Moment of Doubt

Masquerading as a disgraced army officer, Layne infiltrates an organization of post Civil War subversives operating in New Orleans. Aided by an ex-slave undercover man, he manages to see behind every mask at Mardi Gras.

A Town that Lived and Died

Emily, a pretty writer, gets Bronco to guide her to a ghost town. There, Bronco finds himself facing a Kangaroo court held by Yankees who plan to hang him for activities as a Rebel spy. A series of flashbacks by people involved in a key gold shipment brings events up to date, including the reason why young Emily tries to help Layne escape the hangman's noose.

The Immovable Object

When Tom Christopher sits tight on his land and blocks construction of a dam, neither the Army, the Governor, nor Bronco can move him. William Fawcett, Mike Road, and Maggie Pierce.

Then the Mountains

Revenge because Bronco Layne presided over a court-martial which ordered his execution is the motive Bohannon has for marking Bronco's wagon train for extinction. Layne has Bohannon's number but the wagon-master's troubles are compounded by Julie Mae, who provides refuge for a Union soldier wanted for desertion, robbery and murder. Gerald Mohr as Bohannon; Susan Seaforth is Julie; John Dehner also appears.

5
The Legend of the West

ABC (1 hour) — debuted September 22, 1957
Format: Adult-Western series with mixture of drama and humor
about a couple of roving gamblers who, together or separate-
ly, meet their share of villains and charming damsels while
trying to make a decent, semihonest living
Cast: James Garner . . . . Bret Maverick
. . . . Pappy (Beauregard
Maverick)
Jack Kelly . . . . Bart Maverick
Roger Moore . . . . Beau Maverick
Robert Colbert . . . . Brent Maverick
Diane Brewster . . . . Samantha Crawford
Efrem Zimbalist, Jr. . . . . . . Dandy Jim Buckley
Richard Long . . . . Gentleman Jack Darby
Leo Gordon . . . . Big Mike McComb
Kathleen Crowley . . . . Melanie Blake
Mona Freeman . . . . Modesty Blaine
Arlene Howell . . . . Cindy Lou Brown
Peter Breck . . . . Doc Holliday
Executive Producer: William T. Orr
Producer: Roy Huggins (first three seasons, 57–58, 58–59, 59–60)
Coles Trapnell (fourth season, 60–61)
William L. Stuart (fifth season, 61–62)
Theme Music: "Maverick" by David Buttolph and Paul Francis
Webster
Location: Filmed in Hollywood

"Maverick"

The legends of the West—Hickok ... Dalton ... Earp ... Holiday ... Maverick....

Maverick?

Sure, Maverick! Even the last line of the Maverick theme song attests to the fact: "Maverick is *the legend of the West.*"

To those who can remember the anticipation of 7:30 P.M. (CST) on Sunday night, Maverick—all *five* of him—dealt his way into our hearts and into video legend forever. Besides, whoever said that a legend has to be heroic, gallant, and always willing to fight for what he believes in? The legendary Maverick shot down that premise when he first recalled his Pappy's most revered proverb: "He who fights and runs away lives to run another day" (not exactly the Cheyenne creed).

Although Maverick was not a likely candidate for the Medal of Honor, he won enough audience respect and devotion to capture the Emmy Award as Best Western Series, dethrone Ed Sullivan as the king of Sunday night, and set a trend of humor and wit in an historical period usually associated with drama. Even those viewers who were not Western fans could find delight in *Maverick* in the same fashion that viewers in later years who were not especially fond of war pictures could enjoy the timeless humor of *M*A*S*H.*

The Maverick family was conceived in the office of Warner Bros. Executive Producer and Vice President William T. Orr, under the guiding hand of Producer Roy Huggins (later to create the 60's hit, *The Fugitive*, and the 70's hit, *Rockford Files*).

"I wanted to see how many rules we could break and get away with it," admitted Huggins, referring to the classic Western plot: a rugged, courageous, principled, white-hatted cowboy fighting relentlessly with blazing guns against the fiends who would do evil to the moral, upright, peace-loving individuals of the American frontier.

And break the rules he did; but it was a gradual process. In the first few episodes Bret was a little tougher and more ethical than he had appeared on paper.

In the premiere episode, "The War of the Silver Kings," Bret tackled the town tyrant, Phineas King. While successfully accomplishing that task in the allotted sixty minutes, he still managed to help rehabilitate an ex-judge turned alcoholic. This was definitely not the Maverick that was born in the mind of Roy Huggins. In fact, in its five-year run *Maverick* never had the cowardly soul that it purported to have. There were definitely moments of indiscretion and quasi-cowardice but not enough to live down to the reputation heralded by ABC in the summer of 1957.

As the season progressed and Bret Maverick moved from town to town (and poker game to poker game), it was clear that an additional family member was needed. After all, when it takes a week and a day to film a weekly series, something has to give. Thus, Bart (Jack Kelly) was brought onto the scene.

Multiple leads had been considered for other shows in addition to *Maverick*. Until *Maverick* came along, the standard video season consisted of 39 original episodes and 13 reruns. "The Legend of the West" broke that mold with 27 originals the first year, 26 thereafter, and the remainder of the year filled with reruns and preemptions. But even with a trend toward a less grueling production schedule, a series could still get into trouble if the sole lead character became ill or met with an accident. From the beginning of shooting *Maverick*, the idea of a co-star had been floating around.

"We had always told ABC that Maverick would have a brother," relates Orr. ABC suggested that the brother be a supporting character, but Orr told them that the public would think of the brother as a lesser role if he was not given co-star status. ABC agreed and almost all was well.

It so happened that the exclusive sponsor of *Maverick*, Henry Kaiser, was not aware that another brother was in the making. He loved Jim Garner as Bret, and the thought of bringing in a co-star enraged him.

Warner Bros. set up meetings with the Kaiser organization in Hawaii and San Francisco with hopes of securing the sponsor's blessings for the addition of Bart. The studio finally won out but agreed to have both of the Brothers Maverick together in as many episodes as possible. This would allow the audience to become accustomed to Bart before weaning them totally from Bret for some of Bart's solo appearances. After difficult and tedious labor pains, Bart Maverick was born and pronounced a legitimate member of the Maverick family.

The chemistry of Kelly and Garner moved the show toward its original Western-comedy claims. The scripts turned from the more serious straighten-out-the-crooked-town routine to an even more successful mixture of drama and comedy.

Warner Bros. had a host of writing talent at its disposal with such men as Howard Browne, Coles Trapnell, Marion Hargrove, Douglas Heyes, and writer-producer Roy Huggins. One of Huggins' stories made it to the screen twice: "Lovely Lady, Pity Me," the premiere episode of *77 Sunset Strip*, was reworked into a Bart Maverick episode entitled "The Lass With The Poisonous Air." Just the reverse happened to the second episode of *Maverick*, "Point Blank," which appeared later on as the *77SS* episode, "Perfect Setup."

Many of the teleplays were based upon stories recorded in the book, *Yellow Kid Weil*. Orr explains: "He [Weil] was a famous conman at the turn of the century who operated mostly out of Chicago. Yellow Kid Weil was like the men in *The Sting*. Out of that book we got quite a few stories for *Maverick*." The rights to *Yellow Kid Weil* were bought by Warner Bros. for a period of two years, June 30, 1958 to June 30, 1960, with option to renew.

One of the memorable episodes with both brothers was "Shady Deal At Sunny Acres," based on a *Yellow Kid Weil* story. Bret, upon winning $15,000 in a late-night poker game, saw the local banker, John Bates, working late and decided to deposit his winnings until morning. The banker took the money, gave the victorious gambler a receipt, and upon Bret's arrival at the bank the next morning, declared that he had never laid eyes upon Maverick before. Bret promptly displayed the receipt but was told that it was not an official bank receipt. Bret, keeping his cool, warned Bates that he refused to leave town without his money. For the remainder of the show Bret could be seen leaning back in a chair outside the bank either whittling or resting his eyes with his hat pulled over his face in true cowboy style. All of the town's people joked with Maverick about how he was going to get his money back; nobody *really* believed Bret's story. Every time he was asked, Bret answered, "I'm working on it." Each time he answered with this statement the surrounding citizens rolled with laughter. But while Bret kept sitting in his chair, taking it easy, and replying. "I'm working on it," Brother Bart arrived in town under another identity and proceeded with an elaborate scheme to "legitimately" swindle the banker in a fake stock deal with the aid of several comrades. In this episode John Bates had a most memorable, often repeated maxim: "If you can't trust your banker, who can you trust?"

The cunning and genius of beating a crook at his own game was not exclusively a talent of the Maverick brothers. They learned to fend for themselves while dodging the lovely Siren of the West, Samantha Crawford, played by Diane Brewster.

Samantha, commonly known as "Sam," was a beautiful, intelligent, avaricious dealer of the deck who would stop at nothing to take your last dollar. Her appearance on a *Maverick* episode meant trouble for Pappy's boys. Using her feminine charm to its fullest (complete with fake "Southern Belle" accent), Sam could make anyone her

James Garner (top) as Bret and Jack Kelly (bottom) as Bart Maverick.

puppet. But the only "strings" in which she was interested in pulling were those attached to one's purse.

Bret first came within her clutches when she beat his straight with only a pair of nines, costing him $20,000. She was sly enough to lure Bret into agreeing to play "According to Hoyle" (the title of the episode). [*Hoyle's Book of Games* was popularly followed in the latter nineteenth century although it included some variants on the game (i.e., a straight can be beaten by a pair of nines).]

Brother Bart also later got mixed up with Sam. In "The Savage Hills" episode of *Maverick*, Sam accidentally awakened Bart while sifting through his clothes' pockets in the middle of the night in his hotel room. Actually, Sam had gotten the wrong room. She thought the room was occupied by a Mr. Gunnerson who allegedly had stolen treasury plates for which there was a $10,000 reward. Agreeing not to turn her in to the sheriff for illegal entry and promising to give her back her clothes (you'll have to see the show to see how he managed that), Bart made a deal to get half of the reward money.

To make a long story short, Mr. Gunnerson turned out to be a United States Secret Service agent. Bart ended up in jail for assault on a federal officer but was released when Sam sweet-talked the judge, a Southern gentleman from Atlanta who fell hook, line, and sinker for Samantha's heavy accent. But Sam made up for her good deed by picking Bart's pocket while kissing him goodbye at the train depot.

The importance of Samantha cannot be overstated. She was the *original* Maverick.

On the *Cheyenne* segment of *Warner Bros. Presents*, Samantha debuted as the Maverick prototype in an episode entitled "Dark Rider," which aired September 11, 1956. Owing Cheyenne Bodie some money, Sam gave him the slip. Cheyenne finally caught up with her, only to have her get away again. Said Huggins, "*Maverick* really started with Samantha."

During its five-year run on ABC *Maverick* also had a host of other characters who popped up now and again: Big Mike McComb, the giant Irishman (played by Leo Gordon) who was ordered to kill Bret in the very first episode but didn't because he had a heart of gold, became a loyal comrade to the Maverick clan; Dandy Jim Buckley (Efrem Zimbalist, Jr.) and Gentleman Jack Darby (Richard Long), two fancy-dressed gamblers with a lavish love of money who occasionally allied with Bret or Bart to make a fast buck or get out of a sticky situation usually without regard as to how the Mavericks extricated themselves; Doc Holliday (Peter Breck), who helped fill the gap after Jim Garner left the series and helped bail Bart out of some tough spots with his fast gun and macho nature; Melanie Blake (Kathleen Crowley), Modesty Blaine (Mona Freeman), and Cindy Lou Brown (Arlene Howell), lady friends of the Mavericks who seemed to always turn up at either the perfect or imperfect time flaunting their feminine charms; and the one and only Pappy, who was seen in only one

Roger Moore as the polished Beau Maverick.

episode, "Pappy," but was omnipresent in his often repeated aphorisms. (The one-time-only appearance of Pappy was played by James Garner, who was grayed up to look about thirty years older.)

Pappy's proverbs became an established part of the *Maverick* scene. After a miraculous win at the poker table Bret could be heard to mutter, "As my pappy used to say, 'Hell hath no fury like a man who loses with four of a kind.'" Or maybe when Bart was asked to give up gambling and settle down, he remembered his dear old dad's admonition: "Work is right for killing time, but it's a shaky way to make a living." In "Shady Deal At Sunny Acres" Bret remarked to "Honest John" Bates, the crooked banker, "As my old pappy used to say, 'You can fool all of the people some of the time and some of the people all the time — and those aren't bad odds!'" Another popular one was, "No use crying over spilled milk; it could've been whiskey."

These constant references, or "Pappyisms," were enjoyed especially by Jim Garner's real-life father, a carpet layer. Jim's dad used to call up his son after the airing of a particular episode and brag about how funny he (Dad) was. But Jim would always counter by telling him to remember that all of those clever sayings were from the mythical Pappy, not the real Dad Baumgarner. No doubt Jim's dad really enjoyed kidding his son.

The character of Pappy did a lot to aid in his sons' lack of interest in Western heroism. When the Civil War broke out, the elder Maverick gave fatherly advice to his gray-clad sons: "If you either one gits back with a medal, I'll beat you to death."

Bret and Bart didn't disappoint their dear Pappy. Both were captured by the Union army. To escape rotting to death in a Yankee prison or — worse yet — becoming martyrs, they volunteered for service in the Union forces in the West keeping the Indians under control. Bart spoke of this part of their past as their days as "galvanized Yankees."

There was one story about an ongoing joke of drawing on each other with prop guns. Whenever one ran into the other on the Warner Brothers lot, the one drawing first would call "bang" and the other would have to drop whatever he was doing. It was rumored that Kelly caught Garner at the studio commissary and Brother Bret had to drop his complete lunch.

Many of the tricks floating around were strictly fictitious, but Kelly admitted that there was some truth to them like the time he caught Garner trying on a new set of threads and Jim had to drop his pants.

But even with all of the jesting and comaraderie of the *Maverick* cast and crew, the bottom fell out in December of 1960 when the courts decided in favor of Jim Garner in his suit against Warner Bros. to be released from his contract.

Bart Maverick with Pat Crowley in "A Tale of Three Cities."

During a writers' strike Warner Bros. kept on shooting television series. Scripts were procured from various sources for other Warners shows, but there was a shortage of available scripts for *Maverick*. The studio then put Garner on *force majeure* which exonerated Warner Bros. from liability for strikes, fire, wars, lockouts, delay in a performance, or any other acts beyond their control. In other words, James Garner was placed on suspension until such time that *Maverick* scripts could become available. Garner went to court to press for release from his contract on claims that the studio was still "active," being able to keep other series shooting. The court ruled that the studio had no right to put him on *force majeure* and James Garner was released from his contract, freeing him to pursue feature films which paid more for less hours than did television.

With Bret gone, Brother Bart was joined by Cousin Beau (Roger Moore). Roger was brought over from *The Alaskans* which had been canceled.

Beauregard Maverick (namesake of his "Uncle Pappy") was a

A trio of Mavericks—Jack Kelly (left) as Bart, Roger Moore (center) as Beau, and Robert Colbert (right) as Brent.

disgrace to the Maverick clan. He was a war hero. Pappy considered Beau as the "white sheep" of the family and had banished him to England. After five years of crooking up his straight path, Cousin Beau returned to America in the premiere episode of *Maverick's* fourth season, "The Bundle from Britain."

Actually, Cousin Beau explained that he wasn't the hero people proclaimed him to be. He really didn't capture a Yankee general single-handedly. After being captured by Union forces, Beau was found out to be the only man in the camp who could play poker well, and the general (an avid poker player) invited the prisoner into his tent for a friendly little game. Completely engrossed in the table action, neither man was aware of the action taking place outside. The Confederates had made a surprise nocturnal attack on the Yankee camp. Just as the general laid down his hand in disgust and exclaimed, "I give up," the Confederates entered the tent. Beau was assumed to be the captor of an enemy general rather than the winner of a poker hand. Everyone accepted his true explanation as a modest attempt to decline glory.

Beau lasted one season. His character was believable and entertaining, but as Hugh Benson reflects, "*Maverick* was on a slide after Garner left. We knew it was going to go off, so we put Bob Colbert in place of Roger Moore and he [Moore] went off to do features."

Robert Colbert was the last of the Mavericks for the award-winning series. He played the part of Brent, Bret and Bart's never-before-discussed younger brother. But Brent never stood a chance with the show in decline and also being moved by the network to an hour earlier—an undesirable time slot—to lead into a new ABC show, *Follow the Sun*, which itself lasted only one season. Colbert guest starred in many TV shows of the era and finally got a starring role in the series *The Time Tunnel*. Later he became Stuart Brooks in the daytime soaper, *The Young and the Restless*, on CBS.

Maverick was canceled at the end of its fifth season. It had been an innovative series that had projected an unknown into stardom. James Garner went on to success in movies and the long-running series, *The Rockford Files*. However, *Maverick* was too good an idea to die a lonely death at the hands of Nielsen.

The hands of fate resurrected the original Mavericks, Garner and Kelly, in a 1978 made-for-television movie on ABC, *The New Maverick*. The film introduced Cousin Beau's son as the newest Maverick, Ben (played by Charles Frank). Ben went on to play his solo Maverick role for one unsuccessful season in *Young Maverick*. That was followed by a final attempt to recapture the original Maverick magic with *Bret Maverick* (starring James Garner), but it, too, failed in the ratings.

JAMES GARNER

"It was sure good to see Jim back on the lot," remarked the secretary in the West Coast legal department for Warner Bros. Productions. Garner had returned to the Warners lot in 1978 for the first time since his departure from *Maverick* in 1960. The reason for his return was the filming of the made-for-television movie, *The New Maverick*. It was a happy reunion. There was never any animosity caused by the lawsuit to release him from his contract. As most people associated with Jim Garner will tell you, "He's a prince of a guy!"

. Garner's personality off-screen is the same as on-screen. His easygoing, Oklahoman manner is appealing and responsible for his tremendous success in movies and television. An old friend of his commented in 1959 that Garner had everything it took to be a success in show business including a ready sense of humor and a strong enough constitution to not let people take advantage of it.

His friend could not have been more correct. The "ready sense of humor" is what made Bret Maverick and Jim Rockford such welcome guests in the living rooms of American viewers. Although the two characters are a century apart in setting, the demeanors are identical because both are in reality one-in-the-same with the *real* James Garner.

He admitted not having to act, insisting that he was only playing himself in the role of Bret Maverick.

As any drama coach will emphasize, "If you want to be considered a great actor, don't ever get caught acting." At first paradoxical, this statement gains credibility when witnessing a performance by someone like Garner. Perhaps that naturalness is what attracted attention to him in the first place. His *real* discovery parallels that of the *mythical* discovery of Lana Turner.

Bill Orr explains that Richard Bare, a Warners director, spotted Jim in a restaurant bar. Bare walked over to Garner and asked him if he was an actor. Garner said that he was but that he hadn't done a lot other than one of the members of the board in *The Caine Mutiny Court Martial*.

"Dick said we were in the television business and were looking to do more shows and liked his looks and said why doesn't he come over to Warners and meet us."

Garner did follow up on the offer. While meeting with Orr, Jim revealed that he had a test at 20th Century–Fox which had not been screened by Darryl Zanuck, producer-director at Fox. The people at Fox had asked Garner for an extension on his test because Zanuck was in New York and it would be a while before he was back at the studio.

Orr knew that he wanted Garner: "I liked him very much. We told him that the minute he heard whether he was going to get the job at Fox, let us know."

For some reason 20th Century–Fox did not pick James Garner up. Fox's loss was Warner's gain."

"We made a test of him and put him under contract immediately," says Orr. "He did several roles in *Cheyenne* and some other things. Then we came up with *Maverick* and he was our thought for *Maverick* instantly. So, we put him in a pilot."

"We talked to Josh Logan, who was doing *Sayonara*, and there was another role in that of a young captain. We exposed him to Josh. Josh liked him and gave him the role. He [Garner] went off to Japan to shoot [the movie] and when he was gone, the pilot [of *Maverick*] was bought. We were going to go on the air with it and wanted to start with the series.

"Well, he was still over there. So there was a little worry that we weren't going to get him back in time."

Fortunately, they did get Jim back in time to begin production of *Maverick*.

Just who was this soon-to-be new star? What was his story before being "discovered" in a restaurant bar?

Jim Baumgarner grew up in Oklahoma and then moved with his family to Hollywood when he was a teenager. But living in the "Celluloid City" did not whet his appetite for a career in acting.

After working for a while as a gas station attendant, oil field worker, and carpet layer (his dad's vocation), Garner was inducted into the army and went off to Korea for fourteen months of combat as an infantryman.

Upon his return in 1952 Garner looked up an old friend, Paul Gregory, who had been a Hollywood soda jerk when Garner was pumping gas. But Gregory had forsaken his milkshake-making for the more glamorous life as a producer. At the time of Garner's return, Gregory was rehearsing his stage production of *The Caine Mutiny*

Court Martial. Wanting to help out his old buddy, Gregory gave Garner the job of cueing the star, Lloyd Nolan. Jim Garner received a whopping weekly salary of $40.

Not willing to settle for very long into such an unchallenging job, Jim landed his first acting role just before the play's opening as one of the six judges. He had no lines, but better pay — $150 a week.

Jim managed to bear up to the boredom of his role through 512 performances. The monotony finally got to him and he quit when he decided that any producers or directors wouldn't be impressed by a guy who hadn't been given any lines.

Jim Garner had finally been bitten by the acting bug and was determined to win a role that superseded that of a mute judge.

Not much else happened in Jim's acting career before being spotted by Dick Bare in the restaurant bar. By the way, no one knows for sure what Garner was doing at the bar because it later became widely known that his strongest drink was soda water.

In 1956 he married Lois Clark and became stepfather to her nine-year-old daughter, Kimberly. The couple had their first child in December of 1957 during the first season of *Maverick*.

With Garner's return from Japan came the filming of *Maverick*'s first season. ABC promoted the new series ahead of its premiere with vigor and enthusiasm; it didn't take long for the audience to build. The fans immediately took Jim Garner to heart. When Roy Huggins was asked about William Orr's casting of the unknown Garner in the lead role, Huggins responded, "How right Bill was."

Garner said that he thought Maverick really emerged as a comedy after its fourth or fifth show. One reason he saw for its transformation was the unique style of writer Marion Hargrove's stage directions, commonly referred to as "the beady-little-eyes bit."

After observing Garner's clowning around between scenes with outlandish expressions and mimicry, Hargrove got the idea of spicing up the episodes by spicing up the scripts. In one script Hargrove wrote, "Maverick looks at him with his beady little eyes." Other directions might specify, "He looks as if he has lost his place in the script," or "Cousin Lonnie is an early Rotarian type with a hearty handclasp and a big mouth."

With stage directions nearly a riot themselves, the free-style humor poured over into the actual lines. Garner then began to innovate with much of his improvisational madcap antics. As Hargrove wrote in an article for a major American magazine, "Writing for *Maverick* is never dull."

James Garner, as Bret, and Louise Fletcher in "The Sage of Waco Williams" episode.

With quality dramatic and tongue-in-cheek scripts Bret Maverick was a major contender for top spot in the Sunday night ratings. Garner probably got tired of people asking him about being opposite Ed Sullivan so he answered them by saying that if people liked Westerns, they'd watch *Maverick*; if they liked variety shows, they'd watch Ed Sullivan.

Jim not only got fed up with repetitious questions, but directors also. He couldn't stand the Hollywood philosophy of determining what prompted an actor to say a particular line or make a particular move. To Jim, if the script said exit—he would exit, regardless of what subconscious motivations came into being.

He didn't care for taking his work home with him either. Hoping to keep his work life and family life separate, Garner never took a script home to study.

One thing about a Western which generally throws a monkey wrench into the works is that the star must be able to ride a horse. Fortunately, that proved to be no problem for the boy from Oklahoma.

Jim kidded about wanting to ride a *real* horse in the show and not a Hollywood nanny. Director Bud Boetticher put in a call to his private stable and had a *real* horse sent over to the lot.

With the addition of being able to ride a horse was the necessity of being somewhat able with a deck of cards. It just so happened that one of Garner's buddies in Korea had been a dealer in Reno and taught Jim some slick tricks with the pasteboards. This experience enhanced the credibility of the character of Bret Maverick for the poker table shots. Of course, for the extra fancy stuff the camera would zoom in to frame just the hands which belonged to a real professional card dealer.

Looking back on his childhood experience with cards, Garner recalled a lesson well learned from his dad. Jim lost a $5 bet to his dad on a card trick at the tender age of 12. Don't worry about Jim losing his hard-earned money; after recalling how he had to mow lawns for weeks to pay for his gullibility, Jim finally found someone to play his dad's card trick on to recover his loss: Jim's nine-year-old daughter.

Well, Garner could ride a horse and deal a game of five card draw and pull the wool over the eyes of an innocent little girl. But next came the real challenge for an actor—could he get along with his co-star?

Jim and Jack had a fine personal and professional relationship. They got along extremely well, but Garner never missed an opportunity to poke friendly jabs at Kelly. He said he didn't want to admit that Jack's episodes were boring, but every time he tried to watch one he fell asleep. Jim also kidded Jack about putting on weight and not being able to buckle his gunbelt.

Getting a straight answer out of Jim Garner was like pulling teeth from a grizzly bear.

Actually, he and Jack Kelly got along very well and had a high mutual respect for each other—but you could never get Garner to admit it without a good-natured jab at his TV brother.

After the judicial emancipation from his Warner Bros. contract, Garner happily stated, "I'm a free man." He admitted wanting to do movies and doubted that he would soon return to the tube.

Once away from *Maverick* Jim spent plenty of time on the golf course while contemplating his upcoming attempt at some new movies. But he didn't mind reflecting back on his *Maverick* years.

Said Jim, "I loved Bret Maverick. *Maverick* made me." But he knew that the series wouldn't last forever and felt that it was best for his career to bow out at the time he did.

Beauregard Maverick in love with Kaye Elhardt in the "Pappy" episode.

However, it was also well-known that Garner had ideas of departing after the *Maverick* creator, Roy Huggins, left Warner Bros. for greener pastures at 20th Century-Fox.

Jim's evaluation of *Maverick* in its final two seasons was that it didn't have the humor of Huggins' years on the scene. He felt that the show moved from genuine humor to slapstick, and this was moving away from the original intent of Huggins.

After some relaxation and a few good rounds of golf, Jim settled down to making movies: *The Thrill of It All* (1963), *The Wheeler Dealers* (1963), *Move Over Darling* (1963), *The Art of Love* (1965), *The Skin Game* (1971), *Support Your Local Gunfighter* (1971), and *The Castaway Cowboy* (1974). During his *Maverick* years he managed to squeeze in two movies between shooting seasons: *Darby's Rangers* (1958) and *Up Periscope* (1959).

Although Jim Garner vowed never to return to a TV series, he relented and appeared in NBC's *Nichols* in the 1971–72 season. The show died from low ratings after a single season.

Jim decided to try TV one more time with *The Rockford Files*, debuting on the NBC network Friday the 13th, September, 1974. Apparently he was influenced by the fact that the show was being produced by his old friend, Roy Huggins. *The Rockford Files* proved to be almost as good a showcase for his talents as *Maverick*. But Jim Rockford outlasted Bret Maverick in total seasons on the air and was also considerably better paid.

As his popularity proves, Jim Garner is a star of the highest caliber. And, in addition to that, he's a really nice guy!

JACK KELLY

Jack Kelly and Avis Car Rental had a lot in common: they tried harder, but it seemed they were destined to be Number Two. Top billing for Kelly was long in coming and, once it arrived, was short-lived.

Show business was in the Kelly blood. When his mother took her baby son for an Ivory Soap modeling job, Jack was already playing catch-up with his older sister, Nancy. At age six she was an established model and her success overshadowed her baby brother's.

By the time Nancy was 15, decade-old Jack had fallen farther behind. On the Broadway stage Nancy reaped success in *Susan and God* with Gertrude Lawrence. This set the stage for a career in the cinema. Jack had just begun his stage career, appearing in five plays, when his family moved to Hollywood.

Jack still had second billing in the Kelly family when Nancy received the Antoinette Perry Award plus an Oscar nomination for her part in *The Bad Seed*. Jack had the talent but never seemed able to catch up with his sister's success in show business.

Jack departed from the world of acting to help keep our shores safe from the Japanese by serving as a weather observer somewhere between the Aleutian Islands and the Arctic Circle. He toyed with the idea of studying law at UCLA while having plenty of time to think. But after the war he drifted back into acting making appearances on *Studio One*, *Kraft Theater*, and *Philco Playhouse*.

In 1955 he got a big break by landing the leading role in the Warner Bros. television production, *King's Row*, but his first taste of stardom was fleeting. *King's Row* flopped, lasting only seven episodes. However, two years later when the producers of *Maverick* realized that another good-looking, chicken-livered gambler was needed to meet the production schedule, someone remembered Kelly from *King's Row*. Several other actors had been screened as possible co-stars with Garner, but Jack Kelly seemed to fit the role much better than anyone else. As William Orr tells it, "We never made a whole test of Jack Kelly. We took him down, had him stand with Jim and improvise: chat back and forth and do a kind of improvisational scene. So, from that we cast him." According to Orr, Kelly was not a counterpart, but "he fit in well."

With the landing of the role of Bart Maverick in the promising new series, Jack found himself back in a familiar setting: again he was Number Two, this time playing second fiddle to Jim Garner. But by now Jack had gotten used to living in the shadow of another. Kelly's wife and sister claimed that he was never bothered by being second billing, and he remained as amiable and congenial as ever.

"Frustration simply is not there," he insisted. "I'm in business for the profit. And that's where my deeper interest lies."

If profit is what he was looking for, then he wasn't disappointed. *TV Guide* reported that Warner Bros. paid him $2,000 per week to be Bart Maverick.

At first it was thought that the viewers might not accept another Maverick just when they were getting used to the first one.

"It was a tough spot," recalled Kelly. "Garner had already made half a dozen shows and it was a success before I ever got there. Jim sensed that I was walking into a tough thing and made me feel like a brother right away.

"We play well together and the result is a very happy thing. The peculiar part is that the audience — or a lot of it anyway — seems to think we really are brothers."

Because of a carefully planned integration of Brother Bart into the script, Jack caught on as a welcome addition.

Kelly initially appeared with Garner in "Hostage," followed by two more episodes with both brothers: "The Jeweled Gun" and "The Wrecker." Bart Maverick's solo debut was "The Naked Gallows" in which he attempted to clear the name of a friend who had escaped from jail after being falsely accused of murder. This and following Bart episodes during the first season were prologued by Bret just to insure a smooth acceptance by the viewing audience.

Jack's personality and acting ability soon overcame the letters of complaint from fans who could not picture anyone as Maverick other than James Garner. Some viewers even wrote to voice support for Kelly in belief that Garner was favored in the scripts. The Warner Bros.

production staff explained that the scripts were tailored to fit the personality of each Maverick brother. Women fans seemed to enjoy the sexy nature of Kelly; thus the more romantic stories were directed his way. When Pappy got engaged to a young girl of 18, Bret admitted, "This type of thing—dealing with girls—is more in Bart's line than mine."

Kelly objected to Warners bosses' idea that only Jim Garner could handle the comedic stories. Jack felt that he, too, was equipped for humor and that it was ridiculous for typing him in just the romantic stories with only light comedy.

Jack saw the characters as having much possibility for development, but the heavy production schedules limited taking each script to its fullest. He complained about the delivery of new scripts the night before shooting and protested that more time was necessary to properly examine and develop fully his characterization within the episode. Kelly wished for time to work with a dramatic coach for intensive work before shooting. That way he could go into each episode with some solid ideas for the director. He may have claimed that profit was his major interest but doing an exceptional job of acting was a noticeable priority. Jack took his job seriously and displayed a strong sense of conscientiousness.

When Garner went on strike against the studio and filed suit in 1960, Kelly elected to hold to his contract. Had he walked out, there would have been the possibility of getting much more money out of the studio. But Jack, knowing he didn't have the strong bargaining position that Garner might have, played it safe and inherited the starring role of *Maverick*. At this point he had finally shaken being overshadowed by another and enjoyed the satisfaction of top billing.

Looking back on his first three years of *Maverick*, Jack said that he never fancied himself as a cowboy before the series but after the experience he found it very satisfying: "I wouldn't mind playing Bart forever."

But *Maverick* with Jack Kelly as the star lasted only two more seasons (1960–62). Jack was proud of his work as Bart Maverick and felt very fortunate to have been able to have played the part. The last show aired July 8, 1962.

Television gave Jack Kelly the chance for security. It enabled him to make a good salary, get public exposure, and satisfy his creative talent. With the demise of *Maverick* Jack could take consolation in what he had left: a happy marriage and home life, good friends, and an excellent financial situation.

Jack's wife, Donna (who used to act under the name of May Wynn), and he enjoyed their time together that was very limited during shooting of *Maverick*. Much time was spent by Jack in the kitchen where he was constantly trying out new recipes. In addition to his culinary interests he spent a great deal of time outside playing golf or sailing. A favorite seasonal pastime was Christmas shopping which, for him, began months in advance.

With all of his hobbies, one might think Jack Kelly spent quite a lot of money; actually, it was the contrary. Frugality was a constant practice. Kelly's weekly salary from *Maverick* was almost entirely invested. He even claimed that he couldn't afford a particular sailing ship he wanted because it was too expensive and beyond his budget. Kelly became quite an authority in real estate and held properties valued in the six figures. Other investments included a successful nursery business catering to the horticultural needs of large hotels. His business manager, Louis Berke, and three lawyers aided him in overseeing all of his varied business interests, making sure that he didn't spend money on anything which wasn't tax deductible.

With his life financially and emotionally secure, Jack Kelly retired from being a series star to occasionally guesting on other shows: *Bob Hope Chrysler Theatre*, *Batman*, *Name of the Game*, *Alias Smith and Jones*, and *Ironside*. In 1978 Jack appeared rather briefly in the made-for-television movie, *The New Maverick*. Other screen credits include *Where Danger Lives* (1951), *Drive a Crooked Road* (1954), *To Hell and Back* (1956), *Hong Kong Affair* (1958), *Love and Kisses* (1965), *Young Billy Young* (1969).

Maverick — Series Index

FIRST SEASON:

War of the Silver Kings

The premiere episode: Bret Maverick arrives in a silver mining town and ends up leading independent miners against the deceitful and conniving Phineas King, a powerful silver magnate. In the process Bret also helps an honest but drunken judge sober up and get elected.

Point Blank

Bret becomes the prey of a beautiful girl when she and her boyfriend plot to rob the local bank and make the townspeople believe that Bret's body is that of the robber. The body is to be made unrecognizable by shot-gunning the head.

According to Hoyle

Bret makes his initial encounter with the foxy Samantha Crawford. After fleecing him at poker, Samantha turns on the tears and counterfeit Southern accent (complete with overwhelming charm) to convince Bret to go into partnership against a crooked gambler. Samantha, being Samantha, pulls a series of double-crosses and Bret has to extricate himself from her clutches, as he will have to do in various episodes in the future. Diane Brewster co-stars as Sam.

Ghost Rider

A young wife, supposedly dead, and her lover mistake Bret for a killer who is after the stolen money the couple has hidden. Edd Byrnes is featured.

The Long Hunt

Bret discovers from a dying outlaw that an innocent man is in prison for a bank robbery the outlaw actually committed. Bret promises to do all he can to free the innocent captive. But complications arrive when Bret runs into the dead outlaw's gang, one of them the boyfriend of the jailed man's wife.

Stage West

Bret learns the location of a gold mine but is taken prisoner with a widow by a gang who want to know the site. With the help of a hidden gun, Maverick overtakes the gang and offers to sell them the map for $15,000. Bret knows the mine is worthless, but the outlaws don't.

Relic of Fort Tejon

When he tries to expose a crooked gambler, Bret gets into trouble. His trouble is compounded when thrown into jail for a shooting that was actually committed by the crooked gambler. Bret breaks jail and follows the no-good into the desert.

Hostage

This is the first episode with Brother Bart. The Maverick boys try a bit of uncharacteristic chivalry when they attempt to rescue the kidnapped daughter of an aristocrat. Actually, the brothers' real motive is to get the aristocrat's approval and invitation to board an elegant new steamship which is loaded with wealthy, second-rate cardsmen.

Stampede

Bret teams up with Dandy Jim Buckley to find loot taken in Wells Fargo robbery. They turn it in for the reward money which is promptly bet on a boxing match. All goes well until their boxer walks out just before the match and Bret becomes the unlikely substitute.

The Jeweled Gun

Always willing to assist a beautiful young lady, Bart Maverick accepts the job of accompanying Daisy Harris through the Badlands and posing as her husband. But Bart doesn't realize that the whole thing is a scheme to kill him and cover up the as-yet-undiscovered murder of Daisy's real husband by her and her lover.

The Wrecker

The Maverick brothers are the high bidders at an auction for the wrecked brig, "The Flying Cloud." Their curiosity soars when it appears someone else was bidding frantically against them for the ship and its contents. This episode is based on a story by Robert Louis Stevenson.

The Quick and the Dead

Bret is accused of bank robbery but gets away in hopes of finding the real culprit. When Bret breaks up a gunfight with the man for whom he is looking and Doc Holliday, Doc threatens to kill Bret for interfering.

The Naked Gallows

Bart tries to clear the name of a friend who has been falsely accused of murder and has escaped jail.

Comstock Conspiracy

Bret kills a man in self-defense, but the body disappears. It soon becomes clear that the body was hidden by the dead man's railroad partner who is trying to conceal business troubles. Werner Klemperer is featured.

The Third Rider

Bart is mistaken for the third member of a bank-robbing threesome. After escaping from the marshal who has captured him, Maverick trails the trio's leader.

Rage of Vengeance

Hired by a beautiful woman to accompany her to Montana and to protect the $200,000 she has in a suit-case, Bret becomes curious. The situation becomes more confusing when he discovers the money is counterfeit. John Russell co-stars.

Rope of Cards

Sitting on a cowtown jury hearing the murder case against a young rancher, Bret is the only juror who votes not guilty. Through persuasion and an ingenious card trick, he convinces the rest of the jury to his way of thinking. William Reynolds is featured.

Diamond in the Rough

After Bart is robbed and shanghaied in San Francisco, he returns to settle up with the man responsible by exposing the man's scheme of selling worthless stock. Jacqueline Beer appears.

Day of Reckoning

Bret and a cowardly town printer must defend a town from being torn apart by a rancher and his men who already gunned down the marshal.

The Savage Hills

Bart Maverick meets his nemesis— Samantha Crawford. They team up to find stolen treasury plates but run into complications from a secret service man and Indians. As is the usual situation for the Maverick boys, Samantha comes out the winner.

Trail West to Fury

In a flashback episode, Bret and Bart return to their Texas ranch after the Civil War only to team up as trail bosses for a lovely lady rancher who must get her cattle to an Arizona army post. But the boys soon find that someone doesn't want the herd to get to its destination.

The Burning Sky

After their stagecoach overturns, Bart and five other passengers are besieged by bandits who are after money carried by one of the passengers. But Bart knows that once the money is turned over to them, the bandits will finish them off.

The Seventh Hand

Bret still has not learned his lesson about staying away from business deals with Samantha Crawford. This time she stakes him in a poker game, but the game is robbed by two gunmen. The rest of the players suspect Bret set them up for the robbery. He and Samantha set out to find the robbers to save Bret's future in the poker business.

Plunder of Paradise

Bart, Big Mike McComb, and a lovely damsel set out to find a long-lost Mexican treasure but are being followed by a group of Mexican banditos.

Black Fire

Bret takes on the identity of one of the group of relatives who are summoned to the home of a wealthy, aged rancher to determine who is to receive his fortune when he dies. The plot thickens when the relatives begin to be murdered one by one. Hans Conried and Will Wright are featured.

Burial Ground of the Gods

Bart catches up with a no-good who robbed him and ends up joining the crook, a young lady, and her suitor as they search through Indian country for the lady's missing husband. Claude Akins guests.

Seed of Deception

When Bret and Bart are mistaken for Wyatt Earp and Doc Holliday, they play along and enjoy the town's hospitality. However, their fun produces problems when the town marshal almost forces them into a fight with a tough gunman and some bank robbers move into town.

SECOND SEASON:

The Day They Hanged Bret Maverick

Bret faces the gallows when he is framed by the real culprit of a Wells Fargo robbery and murder. When Maverick discovers that the sheriff and coroner are money-hungry, he convinces them to fake the hanging for a piece of the stolen loot. Then he sets out to find the killer himself and clear the Maverick name.

The Lonesome Reunion

A pretty young woman asks Bret to guard her hatbox which she says contains valuable papers. But Bret is held up by a man who claims there is $120,000 inside. When the robber opens the box, he finds a hat. Bret then trails the woman and an accomplice to the town of Lonesome where Maverick temporarily ends up in jail on a murder charge. John Russell is featured.

Alias Bart Maverick

Bart discovers that teaming up with Gentleman Jack Darby is a rotten idea when Gentleman Jack relieves him of $1,000. Bart then is involuntarily coupled with dance hall girl Cindy Lou Brown, and together they must fight off Indians and badmen while tracking down Jack.

The Belcastle Brand

Bret is befriended by an aristocratic family on their Wyoming ranch and agrees to act as guide on their bear hunt. Their group is robbed and stranded on the desert by outlaws.

High Card Hangs

When Bart and two others face hanging for a mining camp robbery-murder, they decide to cut cards to see who will confess to the foul deed. In reality, Bart has a scheme to flush out the true culprit.

Escape to Tampico

Bret is offered $6,000 to go to Tampico and see that a wanted man is returned to the U.S. When Bret becomes friends with his prey, he warns the man that his girlfriend may be proceeding with the mission that Bret has abandoned, but the man does not believe Maverick. The Tampico set is the same one used for Rick's Cafe American in the Oscar-winning Warners movie, *Casablanca*.

The Judas Mask

Bart's investment money is stolen by a dance hall girl, and he pursues her into Mexico. She explains that she took the money to keep Bart from going into the saloon business with the man responsible for her sister's suicide. All seems well until the would-be business partner shows up.

The Jail at Junction Flats

Bret becomes the unwilling partner of Dandy Jim Buckley in a horse-selling game which makes them a fast $10,000. As usual, Dandy Jim makes off with his half (and Bret's) but is jailed in Junction Flats for shooting the sheriff's nephew. Bret is now faced with breaking Dandy Jim out of an impregnable jailhouse that is the pride and joy of the sheriff. Dan Blocker makes a brief appearance as Hognose Hughes.

The Thirty-ninth Star

After Bart mistakenly gets an identical suitcase to his own, he is pursued by roughnecks. The suitcase is then stolen from Bart, and the search for its mysterious contents begins.

Shady Deal at Sunny Acres

This episode is a classic of wit and cunning. Bret employs his horde of gambling associates and his Brother Bart in carrying out the "sting" of a bank owner who has fleeced Bret out of $15,000. Honest John Bates is played by the masterful Warners contract player, John Dehner.

Island in the Swamp

Bret stumbles onto a bayou island full of backwoods smugglers and becomes their prisoner. He decides he had better devise an escape soon before it is decided he isn't needed anymore. Edgar Buchanan and Arlene Howell co-star.

Prey of the Cat

As guest of a rancher, Bart takes part in a hunt for a mountain lion in which the rancher is the victim of an apparent accidental shooting. When the rancher's wife becomes extra friendly with Bart, ranchhands suspect that Bart murdered their beloved boss so he could carry on a relationship with the wife. Life becomes difficult for Bart until he discovers the real murderer.

Holiday at Hollow Rock

Bret Maverick knows the sheriff of Hollow Rock is as crooked as they come and sets out to expose him through a horse race at the Fourth of July celebration. William Reynolds is featured.

The Spanish Dancer

Bart allies with Gentleman Jack Darby and a beautiful Spanish dancer to take on a conman who has cheated Bart out of a mine.

Game of Chance

Bret and Bart run into a couple of con artists — a French beauty and her uncle — who have an ingenious scheme involving a valuable pearl necklace which can be switched very easily for a valueless necklace.

Gun-shy

Another one of the classic episodes. This one was a favorite of James Garner because it parodied the perennial number one television show, *Gunsmoke*. The story revolves around Marshal Mort Dooley and his efforts to keep Elwood, Kansas, a decent place to live. This includes ridding the town of no-good gamblers like Bret Maverick. But Bret has to stay in town so he can locate buried Confederate gold before two other treasure hunters beat him to it. Other characters include Deputy Clyde Diefendorfer, Doc Stucke, and saloon owner Amy Ward.

Two Beggars on Horseback

Bret and Bart race each other to Deadwood, each hoping to be first to cash his $10,000 draft on the Gannet Express Company which has closed down all of its offices except for the Deadwood office. But it is soon to close when the messenger steps off the stage and gives notice that the company cannot cover its debts. However, the Deadwood branch has at least $11,000 on deposit — only enough for one of the drafts. The boys are slowed down by a conniving female who demands a commission from whichever brother makes it to the office on time.

The Rivals

A handsome young millionaire trades identities with Bret so as to win the affections of a wealthy young lady who despises wealthy young men. Roger Moore stars in his first episode, but as the wealthy young Jack Vandergelt rather than as Beau Maverick.

Duel at Sundown

Upon request from an old rancher friend, Bret breaks up a romance between the rancher's daughter and a worthless gunslinger. The gunman challenges Bret, but Brother Bart arrives in town to take on the gunman under the assumed identity of a notorious fast gun. Edgar Buchanan and Clint Eastwood co-star.

Yellow River

Bart Maverick gets involved in a cattle drive by a Samantha-like confidence woman. Robert Conrad appears.

The Sage of Waco Williams

Bret Maverick is shadowing Waco Williams in order to catch Willams' outlaw friend, Blackie Dolan, and collect the reward money. But Bret and Waco make enemies of a wealthy cattleman and his son, causing complications in apprehending Blackie. Wayde Preston stars as the fearless Waco Williams.

The Brasada Spur

Bart plays up to a wealthy widow so he can gain admittance to an exclusive poker game made up of millionaire railroad men. He gets into the game and wins big, but he is tricked by the widow into staying in town.

Passage to Fort Doom

Short of money, Bart Maverick takes on the job as a guide for a wagon train headed to Fort Brader. Several situations develop among the passengers on the journey. When the group arrives at Fort Brader, it learns a cholera epidemic has wiped it out. But that doesn't stop the Indians from attacking to add to their troubles.

Two Tickets to Ten Strike

Bret arrives in the town of Ten Strike with a fellow passenger, a pretty young girl, who soon finds herself held for murder of a man whom Bret discovers was her long-lost father. Connie Stevens guest stars.

Betrayal

While trying to find the two men who robbed him of $1,500, Bart watches a scheming female try to steal her cousin's fiance. Then the woman helps free the two thieves Bart had captured and confined to the local jail.

The Strange Journey of Jenny Hill

Big Mike McComb is accused of murder and Bret must find the real culprit, a man McComb has identified as an outlaw believed dead. Bret follows a beautiful singer, the outlaw's wife, from town to town, concert to concert, hoping she will lead him to her husband. Things become less simple when Bret falls in love with her.

THIRD SEASON:

Pappy

The whole Maverick clan gets together when Pappy decides to marry a girl young enough to be his granddaughter. Bret and Bart believe there is something stronger than love involved, namely greed. Bret impersonates Pappy in order to find out the truth from the bride-to-be's suspicious relatives. At the end of the episode, Bret and Bart run into their Uncle Bentley, who bears a strange resemblance to Bart. Troy Donahue and Adam West appear.

Royal Four-flush

Bart runs into a con man who owes him $4,000. The man claims he doesn't have the money right now, but Bart doesn't believe him. While following him, Maverick learns of a plot to take a wealthy mine owner.

The Sheriff of Duck 'N' Shoot

Bret is framed into taking the position of sheriff in the wild town of Duck 'N' Shoot. Learning of a plot to rob the bank, Bret removes the money and hides it, but someone steals it from him — landing Bret in jail. Bret sends for Brother Bart to help get him out of the mess.

You Can't Beat the Percentage

Bart Maverick becomes involved with a scheming female who will stop at nothing to get what she wants — not even murdering her husband.

The Cats of Paradise

Bret makes a big mistake when he goes into business with Modesty Blaine selling cats to a town overrun with mice. She conveniently pockets all the profit and keeps Bret at a distance by charming both the mayor and the superstitious sheriff. Buddy Ebsen and Richard Deacon are featured.

A Tale of Three Cities

No offense, Mr. Dickens. Bart gets held up by a young lady who needs to pay off her father's gambling debt. Maverick later catches up with her, hears her sad story, and offers to help combat the men who are threatening her father.

Full House

Bret is mistaken for the criminal mastermind, Foxy Smith. The men called together to hear his plan include Billy the Kid, Cole Younger, Belle Starr, Jesse James, Black Bart, Ben Thompson, and Sam Bass. They become suspicious of Bret — especially Cole — and our gambling hero has to come up with an ingenious plan before it is discovered who he really is.

The Lass with the Poisonous Air

When Bart falls in love with a beautiful girl, he also falls into a scheme to frame him for murder.

The Ghost Soldiers

Bret and two soldiers watch the Indians massacre the inhabitants of Fort Burnside and return to the fort where Bret comes up with a plan to stop the Indian uprising by appealing to the Indians' primitive superstitions.

Easy Mark

Bart innocently switches identities with the son of a railroad president who is on his way by rail to an important board meeting. It becomes obvious that Bart is the target of unscrupulous fiends.

A Fellow's Brother

After a Wells Fargo agent is murdered in a holdup, Bret is arrested. The slain agent's brother shows up and claims that Bret is innocent, leading Maverick to wonder if he has fallen into a frame designed for someone else.

Trooper Maverick

Bart Maverick is enlisted by the Army to work undercover in trying to discover how Army guns are getting into the hands of Indians.

Maverick Springs

Bret becomes mixed up with Melanie Blake and some worthless land. However, he employs Bart to help him sell back the land for a profit.

The Goose-drownder

A stagecoach with some suspicious individuals arrives and Bart finds himself and Gentleman Jack Darby being held captive by a wounded outlaw and his girlfriend.

A Cure for Johnny Rain

Johnny Rain is a "black-out" drunk who cannot remember what he did while under the influence of strong drink — even if it is holding up a few stagecoaches. Actually, Johnny is unknowingly controlled by a dance-hall girl who takes advantage of his problem. Bret tries to work out a cure.

The Marquesa

Is she or is she not an imposter? That is what Bart must find out before his saloon, recently won in a poker game, is closed down. Not even the Marquesa knows for sure!

Cruise of the Cynthia B

Bret is one of eight suckers who have been sold the same boat. But if they can get her to Memphis, the paddlewheeler will bring $20,000 from a wealthy shipper. The problem is that the owners are being murdered one by one.

Maverick and Juliet

Unknowingly Bret and Bart are pitted against each other in a poker game to decide an ongoing feud between the Carteret and Montgomery families. Each brother is threatened with death if he doesn't come out the winner, which puts Pappy's boys in a bit of a predicament.

The White Widow

A woman bank president has been receiving death threats and hires Bart, needing money desperately, to act as her bodyguard.

Guatemala City

A beautiful female disappears from San Francisco after romancing Bret. He soon learns that she has fled with a gentleman accomplice after heisting some jewels. Three months later Bret finds that she was seen in Guatemala City, and he goes after the pair in hopes of collecting the $25,000 reward.

The People's Friend

Bart finds himself running for State Senator on the Reform ticket after breaking up an assassination attempt. As the election nears and tensions build, Bart knows that if he wins the election, he loses his life.

A Flock of Trouble

Bret wins "three thousand head" in a poker game. Assuming his spoils are cattle, he is shocked to find that he is the proud owner of three thousand sheep. What makes matters worse is that there is a war on between sheepmen and cattlemen.

Iron Hand

Bart joins the cattle drive headed by a young lady, her brother, and her foreman, a man who looks strangely familiar. While Bart makes a deal with Indians to pass through their land, the lady owner sells her herd. However, the money turns out to be counterfeit and Bart suspects the foreman has something to do with the misdealings. The part of the woman's brother is played by a little-known actor by the name of Robert Redford.

The Resurrection of Joe November

Bret is hired to have a casket legally moved from a cemetery in New Orleans. He discovers that, instead of a body, the casket contains a missing jewel collection.

The Misfortune Teller

Someone has been using Bret Maverick's name in taking businessmen in a phony development company scheme. Bret is arrested and thrown into jail, but Melanie Blake helps him escape. Together they search for the culprit who is using his name.

Greenbacks Unlimited

This is one of the all-time great comedy classics. Bret's old friend, Foursquare Farley, reveals that he has unlimited funds for playing blackjack because he has a secret door leading to the vault of the Denver State Bank. Foursquare impresses upon Bret that he always pays the bank back out of his winnings. When Bret learns the bank is about to be robbed by Big Ed Murphy and his henchmen, he and Foursquare remove all of the money from the vault. This is just the beginning of a series of hilarious incidents. John Dehner stars as arch criminal Big Ed Murphy.

FOURTH SEASON:

Bundle from Britain

Cousin Beau Maverick makes his debut as he agrees, for a sum, to impersonate the son of the Marquis of Bognor. It seems innocent enough at first but soon gets Beau kidnapped by a gang of crooks.

Hadley's Hunters

Sheriff Hadley is a well-respected legend in his own town because of his successful hunts for infamous criminals. Bart Maverick finds out firsthand that the men the Sheriff hunts down are innocent men set up to further the Hadley legend. This episode contains hilarious cameo appearances by Clint Walker, Will Hutchins, Ty Hardin, John Russell and Peter Brown, Wayde Preston (in absentia), and Edd Byrnes.

The Town that Wasn't There

An unprincipled railroad land agent tries to con townspeople out of their land for a very unfair price, but Beau convinces them to move their town, literally, to a sheep ranch. Land agent realizes that the land is worth nothing without a town on it, so he agrees to buy at a fair price.

Arizona Black Maria

Bart is saved from scalp-hunting Indian by two ragged outlaws. The outlaws then steal his water and leave him to die.

Last Wire from Stop Gap

Bart and Beau stumble onto a racket of diverting all bullion and cash in Stop Gap into the safe of the Hulett Western States Telegraph Company.

Mano Nera

Bart finds plenty of trouble after arriving in New Orleans — a suspect of murder by the police and a figure of harassment by a secret organization, Mano Nero — Black Hand.

A Bullet for the Teacher

An entertainer, posing as a school teacher, accidentally shoots a man who is in business partnership with Beau Maverick. The partner's brother blames Beau for the shooting death so he can own the saloon which his brother and Beau own.

The Witch of Hound Dog

Bart arrives in the Tennessee mountains to collect a gambling debt and finds himself involved with a witch and her vicious brothers. Wayde Preston guests.

Thunder from the North

Beau Maverick is framed for murder of an Indian by men who desire a war with the Indians.

The Maverick Line

Bret and Bart inherit a dilapidated stagecoach line but the lawyer acting as executor hires a man to kill them so ownership will fall to him.

Bolt from the Blue

Beau is falsely identified as horse thief and seducer, Benson January. Before he is hanged, he escapes to find the real Benson January and his partner, Bolt. Will Hutchins is featured.

Kiz

Beau guards a lovely heiress who believes her life is in danger. He learns that her cousin and an attorney are trying to have the heiress judged incompetent. Max Baer, Jr. guest stars.

Dodge City or Bust

A spoiled, arrogant woman gets Bart to escort her to Dodge City so she can get married — for money.

The Bold Fenian Men

Irishmen, known as Fenians, are plotting to invade Canada and thus force England to grant independence to their homeland. Beau is caught in the big middle.

Destination Devil's Flat

A minister's chest of gold is constantly switched in contents for rocks to keep a thieving sheriff and others guessing. Peter Breck co-stars.

A State of Siege

Bart stops at a hacienda for a night's sleep but stumbles upon a plot to revolt against the United States and a planned execution. Ray Danton guest stars.

Family Pride

Beau feels that he is a disgrace to the Maverick name when he is swindled several times by two conmen and a pretty girl. However, the Maverick name comes out the winner when it is discovered that the girl's grandmother had been a Maverick.

The Cactus Switch

Bart Maverick takes on a couple of swindlers in a game of who can outswindle the other.

Dutchman's Gold

The popular top ten hit, "Dutchman's Gold" by Walter Brennan, was the inspiration for this episode. Beau runs into an old prospector who has discovered gold—but it is cursed and leads to several deaths.

The Ice Man

A gubernatorial race becomes hotter when a twenty-year-old corpse is discovered in a glacier and one of the candidates tries to blackmail the other on a murder charge. Andrew Duggan is featured.

Diamond Flush

Beau Maverick is outwitted by a couple of genteel, middle-aged con artists into replacing a valuable diamond with a fake one when Beau believes he is doing just the opposite. Beau discovers he has been taken and tries to set things right.

Last Stop Oblivion

Bart and other stagecoach passengers spend the night at an isolated way station run by a family who specialize in killing and robbing wealthy travelers. Buddy Ebsen co-stars.

Flood's Folly

After a blizzard forces Bart to take refuge in a mountain hotel in Colorado, he learns of a plan to have a girl committed to an institution so her relatives can gain control of her inheritance.

Maverick at Law

Bart becomes a hunted figure of the law and outlaws when part of the loot taken in a bank robbery turns up in his saddlebags. He gathers evidence to prove his innocence and the guilt of an embezzling banker.

Red Dog

Beau finds a nice cave in which to escape the cold weather. However, this cave happens to be the meeting place of outlaws planning a bank job.

The Deadly Image

The Army captures an ex-con and Bart Maverick, whom they have mistaken for a nefarious outlaw. They escape and take up residence in a mountain cabin owned by the ex-con's daughter who is also the girlfriend of the man for whom the Army mistook Bart.

Triple Indemnity

Big town-boss George Parker loses $800 to Bart in a poker game, but has two of his thugs beat up Bart and recover the money. Bart teams with old friend Doc Holliday to get back at Parker, who owns almost every business in town—including the Western Insurance Company. Doc and Bart heavily insure Bart with the company and, wanting to protect Maverick at all costs, Parker has to practically give Bart the run of the town.

The Forbidden City

This is Brent's debut. Brent Maverick, younger brother of Bret and Bart, arrives in the sinless town of Sunburst. He soon discovers that the town is not as wholesome as it seems. Three of the town's leading citizens have committed murder to cover up a twenty-year-old crime.

Substitute Gun

A sheriff forces Bart to take on the identity of a professional gunman who has been killed so as to find out who hired him. Bart gets involved in a romantic quadrangle that almost costs him his life.

Benefit of Doubt

Brent Maverick is accused of having loot dropped by bandits after robbing the American Mail Company. A dance hall girl comes to his rescue to save him from the posse and reveals she knows where the money is.

The Devil's Necklace (two parts)

Bart must save the West from an Indian uprising spurred by the gift to a belligerent chief of a necklace that makes the wearer invincible to bullets.

FIFTH SEASON:

Dade City Dodge

Crafty Pearly Gates and a female accomplice take $5,000 from Bart at the races, and Bart must pose as a bounty hunter to get financially square.

The Art Lovers

Bart is forced into servitude to a railroad tycoon after heavy poker losses but cures both his and the railroad's financial ills by having a little knowledge of human gullibility. Jack Cassidy guest stars.

The Golden Fleecing

Bart turns temporarily from the poker table to the stock market when asked by a kindly farmer to help set up a gold mining company. He must keep up his guard against a wealthy intruder and his glamorous daughter.

Three Queens Full

An obvious spoof on *Bonanza*. Bart is saddled with guarding three beautiful brides for Joe Wheelwright's sons: Moose, Henry, and Small Paul. Jim Backus co-stars.

A Technical Error

Bart is puzzled when he wins a bank in a poker game and the loser doesn't seem that upset. It doesn't take long to find out that the bank is short $20,000 and to prevent a run on the bank, Bart's buddy, Doc Holliday, is enlisted to help.

Poker Face

A contemporary Robin Hood type of bandit detains Bart Maverick and others. Even though his fellow travelers do not care for Bart's gambling ways, their fate depends on his luck and talent in a high stakes game for their freedom.

Mr. Muldoon's Partner

An Irish leprechaun brings Bart anything but good luck when one of Bart's five wishes turns out to be stolen money. Bart is faced with being jailed, murdered, or married.

Epitaph for a Gambler

When Bart accepts a $10,000 I.O.U. at the roulette table, he also becomes involved in blackmail.

The Maverick Report

A newspaper is being sued for libel by an influential senator, and Bart has just won the paper in a poker game. He and Doc Holliday try every way imaginable to get out of a sticky situation.

Marshal Maverick

A gambling debt forces Bart to become marshal of a town threatened by a killer.

The Troubled Heir

Pearly Gates and the beautiful Marla take Bart again for some loot and when Bart tries to get back at them, he unwittingly sets up Pearly to be killed.

The Money Machine

It's a battle of wits when Bart becomes involved in the purchase of a money machine by his niece who borrowed $10,000 from him. Bart sets up a swindle of his own to get back his money. Andrew Duggan guests.

One of Our Trains Is Missing

Bart gets involved in one of the biggest thefts in history after encountering Modesty Blaine, Doc Holliday, and the betting of some manufacturers out to prove who is superior in locomotives.

Efrem Zimbalist, Jr., as Stuart Bailey.

6
The Street That Wears the Fancy Label

ABC (1 hour) — debuted October 19, 1958
Format: Private investigators in a mystery-adventure series who
operate out of Hollywood to trap the lawless
Cast: Efrem Zimbalist, Jr. . . . . . . Stuart Bailey
Roger Smith . . . . Jeff Spencer
Edd Byrnes . . . . Gerald Lloyd Kookson III
(Kookie)
Richard Long . . . . Rex Randolph
Louis Quinn . . . . Roscoe
Jacqueline Beer . . . . Suzanne Fabry
Brian Keith . . . . Lt. Roy Gilmore
Robert Logan . . . . J.R. Hale
Joan Staley . . . . Hannah
Executive Producer: William T. Orr
Producer: Howie Horwitz
Theme Music: "77 Sunset Strip" by Mack David and Jerry Livingston
Location: Filmed in Hollywood

Like the song says — "you meet the highbrow and the hipster" on Sunset Strip in Los Angeles, California. You also meet Stuart Bailey (private eye extraordinaire) and partner Jeff Spencer (ditto) who woo beautiful women, solve all kinds of hidden clues, and always get bumped over the back of the head while fulfilling their roles as modern day Sherlock Holmeses. *77 Sunset Strip*, the first of Warner's private eye shows, set the pace for those to follow: a glamorous

97

location, flawlessly handsome heroes, mystery, and beautiful but treacherous females. *Strip*, as the prototype, begat *Hawaiian Eye*, *Bourbon Street Beat*, and *SurfSide 6*, all cast from the same mold.

During the first season, Efrem Zimbalist, Jr. and Roger Smith shared star billing and had the limelight more or less to themselves. As Bailey and Spencer, they solved their mysteries in alternating episodes, occasionally working together or with their jive-talking buddy Kookie (Edd Byrnes) who parked cars for a living next door at Dino's Lodge. Kookie was at first a supporting character, but, as often happens, he became more and more popular and eventually began showing up as the lead character in many episodes. By the time the show's fourth season rolled around, Kookie stepped off the parking lot, became Mr. Kookson, and was installed as a partner in the firm of Bailey and Spencer.

Kookie wasn't the only supporting cast member in the early episodes. The first person you'd meet inside the office was the lovely Jacqueline Beer, who played the French telephone operator Suzanne. Those viewers who looked carefully could see by the sign on the door that she actually worked for the "Sunset Answering Service" rather than for the detective firm itself. But she was loyal to Stu and Jeff and helped them out of many a mess.

There was one other major supporting cast member, and call him a stool pigeon, snoop, or whatever—it was often Louis Quinn as Roscoe who supplied the needed information to crack a hard case. Roscoe also served as the show's comedy relief with his racetrack antics.

As to the origins of the series, associate producer Hugh Benson, who's now with Columbia remembers, "The idea for *77SS* came up through an episode of the *Conflict* series that we were doing in 1956. The format was discussed among Roy Huggins, Bill Orr and myself." That *Conflict* show was called "Anything for Money," written by Huggins, and starring Zimbalist in a solo adventure as Stu Bailey. That laid the groundwork for the 90 minute film done later called "Girl on the Run." That's the show that also featured Edd Byrnes, but as Benson says, "He played a killer. Naturally, we changed his character and made him a parking lot attendant."

So how did Kookie end up at Dino's, an actual restaurant on the Strip? Benson says, "Driving along the Strip one day, I think it was Bill Orr who said 'Why not have Kookie working in a parking lot and we'll use Dino's as their hangout.' I looked at him and I said, 'That's a great idea; let's do it.'"

But Benson says not much actual shooting was done at the actual site. "We built a replica of Dino's on a stage. We built the driveway, the overhang, the entrance, the canopy next door [it was a model agency then; now it's a movie theatre], and we built the interior of Dino's." No actual scenes were ever shot there.

Bill Orr still contends that Dino's became so famous that a chain of restaurants using that name could have made a fortune. But Orr says no one ever followed up on the idea.

At any rate, "Girl On the Run" hit the airwaves on October 10, 1958. The regular season premier on ABC was a few days later on October 19th. The first regular episode in the series was "Lovely Lady Pity Me."

It might also be noted that there was somewhat of a legal squabble over 77SS involving the studio and Roy Huggins. Huggins apparently wanted financial recognition for having a part in the creation of the series. Warners studied the first ten episodes of the show and concluded that "Lovely Lady Pity Me" was the first to really present the characters and format of the show. The "Anything For Money" episode of *Conflict* had been taken from a Huggins story called "Death and the Skylark" that appeared in *Esquire Magazine* in 1952. Other elements of the series may have come from another Huggins story called "Point Doom" that was in the *Saturday Evening Post.*

Warners prevailed in the case and took steps to keep the same thing from happening again. "We'd try to adapt as much as we could from short stories," says Benson. "Especially the first episode of every series. That way, we didn't have to pay royalties to the writers for creating — the creation would be in the book itself." The legal complications never affected the public's attention for the show.

As the seasons rolled by, 77SS grew in popularity, and finally, in 1960, the powers-that-be decided to expand the show. In June of that year, it was revealed that Warner Bros. was making 77SS the busiest set in Hollywood by starting a shooting schedule of 43 new episodes, instead of the normal 39. That made four new shows, and as Roger Smith explained in one press report: "When you realize that six days of shooting are required to produce an hour program, and we work on a five day week, this 43-segment schedule actually means more than a year of work." It also gave 77SS a bit of an edge because the show could feature new episodes well into the re-hash schedule of competing series.

The expanded schedule meant either longer working hours for the already overworked team of Bailey and Spencer, or a new detective. Kookie was still a season away from becoming a junior partner,

Bailey, Kookson, and Spencer team up against the forces of darkness.

and by that time *Bourbon Street Beat* was on the rocks ratings-wise, so Richard Long was able to transfer his Rex Randolph character to the Strip. As Roger Smith told one Hollywood reporter: "Shooting 39 programs with just two principals is hard enough. With 43, it was just impossible. We had to expand the firm. Now we can shoot with any two or any one of the three appearing to keep the continuity."

The first *Strip* featuring Rex was filmed in the "swamp" on the Warner Bros. back lot. Long and Smith were dressed as peons in an unidentified Latin-American country to save an innocent girl from a dictator. The segment was called "The President's Daughter."

Another early Randolph episode was called "The Laurel Canyon Caper," in which Rex took the assignment of protecting a rising star (Jock Mahoney) from a blackmail artist. Rex got bumped over the head and socked in the stomach in this one, and Kookie took a few lumps too. Randolph played a major role in "The Hot Tamale Caper" in which he was kidnapped and presumed dead. Richard Long also showed up in a few episodes playing characters other than Rex

Randolph. He was in "The Fifth Stair" early in the series, and appeared in a final season, Bailey-only episode called "The Fumble."

Lest we forget, there was another reason for expanding the detective firm—to allow Zimbalist some time off for movie making. With Rex on board, Stu skipped the first three shows of the third season.

Some mention should be made of the attempts to keep the continuity among the four private eye shows that Warners was producing. When Rex Randolph transferred from Bourbon Street to the Strip, they still talked now and then of his days in the Crescent City. And guest appearances happened frequently. It was Tracy Steele (*Hawaiian Eye*) who got Spencer involved in "Perfect Setup." Tom Lopaka, also of *Hawaiian Eye*, got Stu onto a case in the 50th state in "Only Zeroes Count," while setting up Jeff with another case in "Who Killed Cock Robin." (By the way, trivia buffs, that's the episode that featured Fay Wray of *King Kong* fame.) Cal Calhoun of *Bourbon Street Beat* made an appearance on the Strip in "Upbeat," while Sandy Winfield and Ken Madison of *Surfside 6* lent a hand to Stu and Jeff in "The Hot Tamale Caper." In "Double Trouble," one of the gangsters takes time out to watch *Hawaiian Eye* on TV. Some of Warners cowboy stars showed up in *77 Sunset Strip* from time to time in other roles.

Bill Orr says all the guest shots caused a bit of controversy among sponsors. He explains, "Eventually somebody called and said, 'Listen, I don't think you ought to put all those guys in all the shows all the time.' I said, 'Why? It spruces them up a little bit. If you have somebody that likes them here, they like them over here and you get an audience.' But the sponsors who were paying this for that show—and maybe our rates weren't the same for another because of a different time slot—got mad because a guy they're paying a better price for will show up on another show." Orr says the studio was asked to "cool it" on the guest shots, and so finally they were held down a bit.

Another change in *77SS* came in the fourth season when Kookie pocketed his comb and left the parking lot to try his luck as a member of the firm. Actually, Kookie never left the restaurant for good. As Hugh Benson puts it: "Kookie was never a full-fledged detective. He still ran the parking lot of Dino's and was a detective on the side. We had a contract dispute with Edd in which he decided it would be to his advantage not to play Kookie any more and we put Bobby Logan in the role." Byrnes was a little smoother that season—a little more debonair—but he never quit being Kookie.

"Kookie-talk" gave way to "initial-ese" those last couple of seasons with Logan trying to establish his own identity separate from what Byrnes had done.

In the fifth season, the firm of B & S was sporting larger offices. In fact, Dino's was even bigger so the Frankie Ortega Trio could register some time on camera whenever our heroes were dining or meeting a client in the restaurant.

77 Sunset Strip went through many changes over the years, but the biggest change of all came in the sixth season. The announcement came in July 1963 that the show's format would change, the cast would be pared down, and even the headquarters of Bailey and Spencer (now just Bailey) would relocate. The studio press releases summed up the new format this way: "Mystery melodramas following the adventures of private investigator Stuart Bailey in contemporarily themed actions of wide scope; a 'new look' featuring prominent guest stars in trenchant characterizations amid adult appealing stories."

Prominent guest stars, yes. But the old familiar faces, no. Gone were Roger Smith (who ironically had parodied *Dragnet* way back in the initial episode of *77 Sunset Strip*, "Just routine, you understand"), Kookie, J.R., Roscoe, and Suzanne. Gone were Dino's, the Sunset Answering Service, and the snappy, finger-poppin' theme song.

Credit (or blame as the case may be) for the new look goes to the new producer brought in that year by Warner Bros.—Jack Webb. Webb moved the office from the Strip to the century-old Bradford Building in downtown L.A. Supposedly, the old dignified building was to add to the drama, scope, and adult appeal of the revamped series.

Webb's entrance on the scene meant goodbye for the old crew of producers—Bill Orr, Howie Horwitz, and Hugh Benson. Benson commented: "The format change during the last season was made by Jack Webb and his group after Bill Orr and I were asked to depart the hallowed studio, and I really don't know how the old cast and crew felt about what Webb did. All I know is that a year later Bill Orr and I were brought back and we did *F Troop, Mister Roberts*, and *Hank*. I really don't know how long *77SS* might have lasted [without the format change]. I think it was getting tired."

Zimbalist, as the only returning cast member, was said to favor the new concept of the show. He had not been too happy for the past couple of seasons under the old format, wishing instead to do feature films.

The first episode of the new *Strip* certainly had the feel of a

Efrem Zimbalist, Jr. (left) as Stuart Bailey and Byron Keith as Lieut. Gilmore.

feature. Filmed in five hour-long segments, the episode was simply called "5" and it took Bailey across three continents searching for clues to murder and treasure, with a dramatic climax in New York City. In the show, Stu is hired by an art collector, seeks a hit-and-run killer, learns that the victim had a bundle of enemies, and runs into an international smuggling ring. The episode's long list of star-studded guest actors included Luther Adler, Richard Conte, Wally Cox, George Jessel, Diane McBain, Burgess Meredith, Peter Lorre, Ed Wynn, and Clint Walker.

On July 26, 1963, Fairfax Nisbet wrote in the *Dallas Morning News* of a visit to the set of the new look *Strip*: "We found Mr. Zimbalist the same charming gentleman of whom a Hollywood actress once said, 'he's the only man in Hollywood who can kiss a woman's hand and make it seem like a fine old American custom.'

"When we visited they were making one of the episodes of the five-parter. Big Clint Walker and Ed Wynn were the guest stars.

"Zimbalist was trying to buy a gun from Walker, a Texas cowboy who had inherited a pawn shop and was trying to get rid of the whole stock so he could hit the trail. But he was giving Efrem trouble over allowing him to buy a gun, which the latter sorely needed.

"On the sidelines, waiting for his scene was Ed Wynn, the delightful veteran of stage, screen, radio and television, who has forgotten more show business than some of the rising young stars will ever know."

The producer-director for the new *Strip* was William Conrad (radio's Matt Dillon, and later TV's Cannon) who handled the "5" episode before moving on to another series, *Temple Houston*, on NBC. Jim Lydon was waiting in the wings to take over.

The new theme song, played over stock openings that showed Bailey's silhouetted profile or the detective riding down an elevator, was written by Bob Thompson and will never be remembered like David and Livingston's original theme.

Following "5" the series settled into hourly segments, most of which were told in the form of flashbacks. After the tease and the stock opening, Bailey would persuade his secretary to stay late at the office and take notes on his latest case. While Stu talked and tried to make time with the lady, the scene melted away and thrust us into the middle of the adventure. Stu and the chick were back at the end of the show to close up the office and tie up any loose ends. (The secretary was Joan Staley.)

Unfortunately for the new crew, the revamped format turned off *77 Sunset Strip*'s old fans, and failed to produce many new ones. There was never a seventh season.

EFREM ZIMBALIST, JR.

The biographical names section of Webster's Collegiate Dictionary identifies the name Efrem Zimbalist as a Russian-born violinist born in 1889. No—that's not the man who played Stu Bailey, but rather his father. That's why the name "Junior" was tacked on. (For equal time purposes, Efrem's mom was also in show business—opera star Alma Gluck.)

Once you know about Ef's unlikely set of parents, perhaps the most surprising thing about him is how badly he wanted out of *77 Sunset Strip*. When someone once told him that *77SS* would fall apart without him, Zimbalist groaned, "That's the most depressing thing I've ever heard."

Fact of the matter is, Zimbalist wanted to be a movie star. He was in his late 30's to mid 40's during the run of the series, and he always felt a TV show was for actors 25 and under—people who could still find work after the series died.

Ironically enough, it was a feature movie that got Zimbalist his long term contract with Warner Bros. He came to Hollywood from the New York stage in 1956 to star with Natalie Wood in *Bombers B-52*. The movie fared only so-so, but Efrem's performance got him in with Warners.

Early in life, Efrem had things pretty easy. He spent much of his boyhood in New York City, where he was born, attending fashionable prep schools. That apparently didn't prepare him too well for college. He enrolled at Yale at age 16 but was soon bounced. He tried enrolling as a freshman again but still the grades were lacking, so he quit.

In 1940 he took a job at NBC in New York as a page boy, and he soon became interested in acting. He enrolled in the Neighborhood Playhouse where other young actors like Tony Randall and Gregory Peck were also studying. It was there he met Emily McNair, who had come from Washington, D.C. hoping to make it on Broadway. Two short years later, he was private first class Zimbalist, and she was Mrs. Zimbalist. They had two children before she died of cancer five years later at the age of 29.

Zimbalist, by the way, did appear in seven Broadway shows, including *The Rugged Path* with Spencer Tracy and *Fallen Angels*.

Efrem had a hard time adjusting to his wife's death. He gave up acting and took his children to Philadelphia where he worked for his dad who was director of the Curtis Institute of Music. He stayed there four years, studying and composing music. (Writing classical music has always been a favorite pastime.)

In 1954 Efrem decided to try acting again, so he headed for California. After making *Bombers B-52*, he appeared in about six other features before being signed to do a private eye series for television.

But Efrem, try as he might to stay in the movies, could not escape his destiny, so along about 1958 entered Stuart Bailey, a Ph.D. from the Ivy League who prefers danger, mystery and excitement (and women) to philosophy.

The series was much panned by critics, but Zimbalist himself was rarely criticized along with it. One *TV Guide* critic wrote in 1958, "As eye Bailey, Zimbalist has a refreshingly speculative look about him." Richard Boone once remarked that Zimbalist might be "the best actor

Left: Grace Lee Whitney; right: Jacqueline Beer.

in series television today." About the nearest thing to a pan one can find is the comment of an unidentified Hollywood producer discussing Efrem's well-known wish to be out of TV and in movies: "Zimbalist is a decent actor, but he hardly figures to make the world forget about Barrymore. He should be happy he's working steadily."

Working steadily was *not* one of Ef's problems in those days. In fact, one thing that really bothered him was that Warner Bros. turned down jobs *for* him. He was once offered a role in MGM's *Butterfield 8* opposite Elizabeth Taylor. But Warner Bros. said no on the grounds that Efrem (a) was not to be loaned out to a rival studio, (b) was tied up with 77SS, and (c) was about to become involved in the WB production of *The Crowded Sky* starring Dana Andrews. When Universal-International wanted to borrow Efrem for *Portrait in Black* with Lana Turner, the game rules came into play again. Something just always seemed to throw a monkey wrench into those big movie roles.

During much of the shooting of 77SS, Zimbalist lived out in the country near Encino with his second wife, Stephanie Spaulding, along with their daughter Stephanie and his two older children, Nancy and Efrem Zimbalist III. Animals played a big role in their lives with Efrem once putting up a sign that read: "Chickens at play, please drive carefully." Efrem also had a dog, a pony, some doves, and fooled around with a 1934 Packard touring car which he bought back in '49. Mrs. Zimbalist had her guppies. Hundreds of them to hear Efrem tell it. And she absolutely *hated* it when the big ones would eat the little ones.

After they lived together for awhile, Efrem and Stephanie split up, and he built her a house several hundred yards away saying, "It's a simple matter of chemistry. We are unable to reside under the same roof."

Back on the set, in later years, Zimbalist became totally bored with *Strip*. He admitted to never studying his lines, saying they never changed much anyway, and once commenting that it was a tribute to the writers that audiences are able to watch the show without losing their dinners. Toward the end of the series, he speculated that feminine appeal was all that kept the show going: Robert Logan (J.R.) for the teenagers, Kookie for the young marrieds, Roger Smith for women a bit more mature, leaving Efrem for "grandmothers, derelicts, and nonwalking patients."

But bored or not, Zimbalist and Smith always seemed to get along fine on the set; in fact the horseplay often got so bad that one would often have to leave the soundstage while the other delivered his lines. Smith once said that it was hard for the two of them to look at each other during a serious scene without laughing. In Roger's words, "He crosses his eyes while I'm delivering lines, and breaks me up."

For a guy totally bored with a show—and wanting out so badly—Zimbalist managed some *fine* performances. Probably the best remembered was the episode called "Reserved for Mr. Bailey" in which Zimbalist was the only actor on screen. The episode was originally aired on January 8, 1961, with the ABC-TV publicity release describing it as "a haunting, hour-long teleplay depicting Stuart Bailey's fight to save his life and sanity in a restored desert ghost town." The plot developed this way: A mysterious phone call in the night brings Stu to the office; then, he's whisked away to the ghost town where a voice from nowhere tells him he's marked for death. He finds his name in the hotel register, a reservation and a key. Out near the street is a gallows with a note, "Reserved for Mr. Bailey," attached to the noose. All through the hour, Bailey is taunted with guns with no firing pins, a working pay phone (but no change to use), three wax figures around a card table with a vacant spot for Bailey, and the ever-present voice. The teleplay was written by Montgomery Pittman from a story by Charles Sinclair and Bill Finger (the man who wrote most of the Batman mysteries for National Comics in the early and mid 50's).

Another notable Bailey episode was "Double Trouble" in which Bailey took the role of an underworld hitman who happened to be his double. The acting job on the part of Zimbalist was incredible with him playing not only Bailey, but also the hitman, and then Bailey disguised as the hitman. And it's really not confusing when you see it.

Bailey was involved in some fine mysteries including "Genesis of Treason" adapted by Charles Sinclair from Holly Roth's "The Sleeper." The story had Bailey working undercover for the government to probe the treacherous murder of a high Air Force official. When the murderer committed suicide, Bailey had only a Bible scripture as a clue to why the crime was committed. It was a Communist plot, by the way.

Zimbalist's versatility also showed through as he played a down-and-outer, publicly disgraced on a phony charge of sedition in "Downbeat," and when he investigates a strange cult in "Mr. Paradise." More interesting roles came in "Mr. Bailey's Honeymoon" in which Stu was in Oklahoma, being claimed as a bridegroom by a hillbilly waitress, and Roger Smith's "Once Upon a Caper" in which Stu played a rare comedy role on the series.

Ef also put in a superlative acting job in *Strip's* second two-part show, "The Hot Tamale Caper," in which Rex Randolph was presumed dead in a plane crash. As Bailey, he gathered up the forces—Jeff, Kookie, and Roscoe—and went to a Latin American country to pull a coup and save Rex. It was one of the series' finest efforts.

What was probably the low point for Stu (not necessarily Efrem) came in the first episode when Bailey fell head-over-heels for a chick who wouldn't even tell him her name. The plot of "Lovely Lady Pity Me" had Stu being set up by the treacherous lady, who got him accused of murder, then split. Jeff bailed him out.

As we've mentioned, Bailey appeared as the lone star in the series' closing episodes after the format change, with the only notable episode being "5."

Finally, the show wore out its welcome. So on to movies for Zimbalist? No, if you'll recall, it was right into another TV series—the very successful Quinn Martin/Warner Bros. show, *The FBI*, on ABC.

Currently, Zimbalist shows up at an occasional pro golf tournament and appears in films. One of the latest was called *Terror Out of the Sky*, a 1978 sequel to an earlier TV movie about killer bees. He also appeared in a 1979 TV movie, *The Best Place to Be* with daughter Stephanie.

ROGER SMITH

Roger Smith's first reaction to 77SS was total dislike. He hated his character name. He hated the show's producer, Howie Horwitz. Nothing went right for him on the series. The show was a hit; Efrem Zimbalist, Jr., Edd Byrnes, and the gang were all getting interviews and hundreds of fan letters each week, but Roger was getting only about sixteen. Warners was seriously thinking of replacing him.

Then, something happened. Smith was introduced to dramatics instructor Paton Price by his wife, Victoria Shaw. Price taught him that the key to acting was to act naturally and be yourself. After the "Hong Kong Caper" aired around Christmas time in 1958, Roger's fan mail began to pour in. He was finally accepted by the ABC viewers and even developed a friendship with Howie Horwitz.

Roger's show business career began at age seven as a member of the Meglin Kiddies. He spent three years dancing and singing with this group and was known as a child comic. At the same time, he worked with other theater groups and appeared in plays in the L.A. area.

Roger Smith as Jeff Spencer makes a fast getaway.

His acting career was broken up at the age of twelve when his father opened a western clothing manufacturing company in Nogales, Arizona and moved his family eastward. There, Roger forgot his aspiration for the stage and concentrated on school, becoming the president of practically every social club in the system. His hard work on the football team won him the honor of being the first player from his high school to ever win an athletic scholarship to the University of Arizona.

In college, after Smith had played the lead in a fraternity play, his drama coach persuaded him to major in drama. While at the university, he took up the guitar and was soon accompanying himself to Mexican, Spanish, and Calypso songs. He developed such a talent, in fact, that he was soon winning first prizes on the Ted Mack, Horace Heidt, and University of Arizona talent shows. He also came in first on the *Talk of the Town* show in Tucson.

Roger and a friend made an eight millimeter movie, a comedy about adult situations in teenage style that won him recognition on a tour through the Southwest. At that time, Roger was still planning to join his father in business back in Nogales.

After two and a half years on campus, the naval reserve put Roger's university life to an end. He was stationed in Hawaii as a link trainer instructor, and while there, he and friend Bob Shane (later of the Kingston Trio) began singing at parties. It was at one of these parties that James Cagney heard Roger and was impressed by both his voice and stage abilities. Cagney told him that he should go to Hollywood when he was discharged.

In March of 1955 Smith received his long awaited release, and after a short stint home in Nogales, headed to Hollywood. After discouraging efforts to find Cagney, he struck out on his own. He was in and out of various casting directors' offices, changed his name to Smith Rogers and back again, and finally ended up singing at the Cabaret Concert Theater. Roger met a girl there who was up for a contract at Columbia who asked him to help her with her reading. He agreed and off they went; however, it was Roger and not the girl who ended up with a contract. He made three films for Columbia and even starred in the first one that he made, *No Time to be Young*.

Soon after, Cagney arrived back in Hollywood. As he had promised in Hawaii, Cagney got the young actor parts in two of his pictures: *Man of a Thousand Faces* and *Never Steal Anything Small*. Roger thought himself "lousy in both," but Morton Da Costa, directing *Auntie Mame* for Warner Bros., thought otherwise. He was given the part of Rosalind Russell's nephew and Warners bought his contract from Universal which had borrowed him from Columbia and later signed him to their own contract.

While still at Columbia, Smith met Victoria Shaw in an acting class. One day the class leader assigned the pair a scene at the beach so Roger suggested to Victoria that they go there to rehearse. She agreed, but instead of the beach, they ended up at Disneyland. The next date was to the movies, and a few weeks later they were buying furniture. They were married July 28, 1956. Their daughter, Tracy, was born in July of 1957, and their son, Jordan, was born in October of 1958.

Roger wrote "The Down Under Caper," a story set in her native Australia, for his wife. After writing the script, he had to convince Victoria to do the show. Roger wrote several other scripts for 77SS.

One show he wrote called "The Silent Caper" is highly unusual for TV because, as the name indicates, not a word is spoken for the entire hour. The strange thing about it is that the viewer has absolutely no trouble following the goings-on as Jeff woos women, solves clues, fights criminals, rescues "Jingle-Bells" (a glamour girl kidnapped by gangsters), and ends the episode with a spectacular chase and fight atop a water tower. The episode stays tense all the way through with cliffhanger after cliffhanger taking the place of dialogue. There are some funny moments in it as Smith's script calls for the audio to malfunction on a TV set—just to make sure there's no dialogue. Bill Orr's reaction to the segment is: "Give me more 'Silent Capers.'" You see, Warners was able to ship the film to overseas markets without hiring foreign actors to dub in dialogue in other languages. Saved a *lot* of money.

Another story penned by Roger is "Once Upon a Caper"—for the true 77SS buff, an episode not to be missed. It's the story of the birth of the firm of Bailey and Spencer as seen through the eyes of Jeff, Stu, and Kookie. Rex Randolph gets Jeff to relate the story of how Jeff and Stu joined forces to combat crime and mystery. Jeff tells a very interesting and convincing story about how *he* was doing rather nicely in his Beverly Hills office, but poor Mr. Bailey was struggling to make ends meet and attract cases on "the other side of town." Through chance they manage to be working on the same case: Jeff, to return a favor to young Gerald Lloyd Kookson III: Stu, at the much-regretted request of an insurance firm. The case is concluded and, of course, Jeff Spencer is the grand hero.

Rex then runs into Bailey and mentions that Jeff has told the story of their beginning. Stu agrees that it really is a good story. As Stu tells it, he was set up pretty well in his Beverly Hills office while poor old Jeff was new and struggling on "the other side of town." As the story turns out this time, Mr. Bailey is the super sleuth and saves the day with his masterful abilities.

Puzzled by the differences in the two stories, Rex asks Kookie for the straight story. Would you believe *both* of our heroes were struggling this time? *Kookie* is of course the suave, hip, and totally unbelievable mastermind in bringing the caper to its finale. Rex, visibly shaken by all that he has heard, turns to Roscoe for a little advice on who is to be believed. But when his racetrack buddy begins with, "You know, if it wasn't for me, those two would never have gotten together," Rex tells him to clam up and quickly exits—a crazed look in his eyes.

Smith wrote "Mr. Goldilocks," and "The Common Denominator," in collaboration with a close friend, writer and director Montgomery Pittman. He also wrote an *Hawaiian Eye* script. In addition to scripts for television, Roger wrote two American folk songs which were introduced during the 1959–60 season.

Of Smith's writing abilities, story editor Carl Stucke says: "Roger used to come into the office and scream (about) scripts; he always figured he could write better than what he was getting. It's funny— some of the scripts he wrote were good but not brilliant; they were interesting, but nothing really special. But you couldn't tell him that— you had to be very careful."

Stucke says Smith would occasionally wish that a particular Stu Bailey script could have been written for Spencer instead. Zimbalist apparently never made such suggestions: "No—Zimbalist was a gentleman (not to be interpreted that Roger was not; but Smith was sometimes outspoken in contrast to Efrem's quiet, reserved nature). His father was the violinist, and he was raised right. He was a gentleman at all times."

Roger left the show in the 1964 season when Jack Webb took over and the format changed. His next series, *Mr. Roberts*, was also done for Warners. It was based on the play by Thomas O. Heggen and Joshua Logan and dealt with life on a cargo ship, the *USS Reluctant*, serving behind the lines in World War II. Smith played the title role of Doug Roberts, an officer stationed on the ship. His ambition was to be reassigned to a fighting ship.

Between series, Roger starred in the road company of *Sunday in New York* and made personal appearances in other countries promoting *77SS*. He also found time to perform in his own nightclub act and even participate in a flying circus.

Roger is now retired from acting, working instead as manager for his present wife, Ann-Margret.

EDWARD BYRNES

77 Sunset Strip had plenty of action and mystery, but it also had something new: an idol for the mass, newly-emerging teenage crowd. With Bailey and Spencer holding the plot worshippers on the edges of their chairs while they cracked case after case, Kookie kept the teeny-boppers glued to the tube by merely opening car doors and running a comb through his golden locks.

Kookie (nickname for Gerald Lloyd Kookson III) won the hearts and passions of thousands, if not millions, of teenage girls. His hot rod (a customized Model T roadster), acrobatics, and smooth way with the chicks secured the attention and admiration of the teenage guys. He quickly became the most popular parking attendant on record.

The man who brought Kookie to life and molded him into an institution was Edd Byrnes (changed from Edward Breitenberger). And, to the surprise of many, it *was* acting. In real life Edd was nothing like his hep-talking character on the Friday night scene.

"I had absolutely nothing in common with the character," Byrnes explained. "I didn't like sports cars or rock 'n' roll and I never parked cars for a living or ran a comb through my hair off camera."

He sure fooled us on the screen. Critics had no idea that Edd Byrnes was probably doing the heaviest job of acting of anyone on the set.

77 Sunset Strip producer Howie Horwitz backed up this claim stating, "Efrem is playing Efrem. Roger is playing Roger. But Eddie is creating a character that's almost his opposite."

Just what was Edd Byrnes like if he wasn't Kookie in real life?

Edward Breitenberger grew up in New York and was somewhat less than the model student. After dropping out of Haaren High School, Edward got a job driving a truck. But his burning ambition was to be an actor.

"I always wanted to be an actor. Maybe it was because everybody said I could never do it. I was a skinny little kid. We lived in a medium-nice little neighborhood in New York, and I knew nobody was going to help me break out of it except myself. I went to a gym and worked a lot on the parallel bars and the rings. Got to be pretty good at it. It built me up. I was driving a truck, and I just didn't figure to spend the rest of my life driving a truck at $85 a week."

And he didn't. After getting some acting experience in off-Broadway and Eastern stock companies, Edward bid farewell to his mother, older brother, and younger sister (his father died when Edward was 14), and headed for Hollywood. That was in 1956.

He managed to break into television playing an Indian in a skit with Joe E. Brown on the *Buick Circus Hour*. The future car-parker pulled in a whopping $125 for that one, but it was better than the $5 he made carrying a spear in the Ziegfeld Theater's production of *Hamlet*.

Times began to look up for Edward. He soon came under contract to Warner Bros., enabling him to secure appearances on *Cheyenne, Jim Bowie, Oh! Susanna* and several others.

It was also about this time that he received a name change. Breitenberger didn't have quite the impact of Bogart or Gable, so Edward opted for his mother's maiden name, Byrnes. The studio was not too enthusiastic over the first name Edward, so a compromise was made and Ed added an extra "d" to add a little uniqueness to his new title. Thus, Edd Byrnes was born.

Edd's big break came with the opportunity to play an assassin in *Girl on the Run*. It was nothing but success from then on.

Edd Byrnes, the former truck driver for $85 a week, was now basking in the prestige of being a star in an extremely popular prime-time television series. His fan mail soon began to average 15,000 letters a week and in one month appeared on the covers of 26 magazines. Edd became a very wealthy 26 year old; his newly-acquired possessions included a Beverly Hills mansion, complete with a swimming pool in back and a Rolls Royce parked in front (one car Byrnes didn't mind parking himself).

"I could give lessons on spending money. I went to Italy to buy $500 tailored suits and $100 shoes. I traveled around the world first class. Eventually I had a home in Rome and two in Beverly Hills.

"I'd been a poor kid and suddenly I was turned loose in the candy store. I wanted to taste everything in life and I did. I enjoyed fine wine, fine women, fine automobiles, and fine clothes."

Edd Byrnes was not the only party cashing in on the success of *77 Sunset Strip*. Warner Bros. and the ABC Network did all right for themselves too. The show was one of the biggest ever on the air. And

Edd Byrnes as Kookie in *77 Sunset Strip.*

it took a lot of hard work to keep it there ahead of any kind of competition the rival networks could send up against it.

To keep a tenacious hold on its ratings, it was arranged to write Kookie into every script. Two full crews were employed so as to enable the filming of two episodes simultaneously. Stu Bailey might be on the trail of foreign spies on one set, while Jeff Spencer was closing in on a blackmailer on the other set. Kookie was kept busy running back and forth from one set to the other. In all there were seven stages and one outside location. Kookie, that is, Edd, got plenty of daily exercise. (Producers were so anxious to have Byrnes appear in each episode that when Jeff Spencer traveled abroad in "Hong Kong Caper," Edd appeared in a cameo role as a ricksha boy. A similar trick was later used with Louis Quinn in "Vacation with Pay.")

The constant action on the set didn't slow down Edd's schedule. In one three week period he submitted to 49 interviews. If that wasn't enough, he recorded a hit single, "Kookie, Kookie, Lend Me Your Comb," which was a gold single and a gold album.

Everything was going Edd's way. His parts became larger and more important as the *Strips* moved along into the 1960's.

One of the several episodes which featured him as the lead was "The Canine Caper," in which Kookie was entrusted with the care of a French poodle belonging to a visiting princess. After recovering the lost dog, Kookie followed up on his romantic relationship with Her Highness and helped to recover some stolen gems smuggled into the U.S. in her canine's collar, unknown to the princess.

After leaving Dino's parking duties to J.R., Kookie shed his jacket and comb for the more mature look of a sport coat and tie, taking up vocational residence with Bailey and Spencer as an associate private investigator. In this new role, Mr. Kookson left the novelties behind and joined the ranks of the adult world.

One of his most memorable appearances was in "Terror in a Small Town." While on a trip to pick up an important dossier, Kookson picks up a hitchhiker who pulls a knife on our supersleuth and makes off with his car and clothes. Unjustly accused of attacking a local woman and unable to identify himself (a storm knocks down the telephone lines to L.A.), he is grabbed by an angry crowd of townspeople after an exciting chase through town. Just before the mob has a chance to tighten the noose around his neck in the town square, word comes that Mr. Kookson is not the culprit, but that the real offender was arrested by police in Kookson's stolen car. "Terror in a Small Town" never lets up in action and suspense.

Even though *77 Sunset Strip* matured throughout its run, as all quality shows eventually do, it ran its course. Edd Byrnes, accustomed to steady work, became unemployed and found that getting another acting job was not so easy. The character that he so skillfully created on the screen followed him everywhere he went. Nobody wanted to hire him because he was too easily identified as Kookie and would not be accepted by audiences in other roles.

"It was tough to find work in Hollywood after the show went off the air. Producers thought I was totally the character I played in *Sunset Strip*, not an actor playing a role."

On being identified with Kookie after the show's demise, Byrnes explained, "Total identification with a character only happens in television, not movies. I suppose it's something of a compliment to play a role so well that even professionals mistake the actor with the part."

Where does a gifted actor go when he is unemployable in Hollywood? Overseas, of course.

"I went to Europe where the series was widely televised. European producers aren't as naive as the local variety. They appreciated the fact that I was an actor. I did eight movies over there — in England, Yugoslavia, Germany, Spain, and Italy."

"I lived in London for a couple of years. Some of the movies were good and some were never shown in this country. But the money was terrific!"

Now Edd Byrnes is back in the U.S.A. and available to American viewers once more. The latest film and television roles have been in *Grease, Fantasy Island*, and his NBC series, *Sweepstakes*, which had a very brief run. Edd Byrnes is back with us, and he is a very welcome sight.

LOUIS QUINN

Hate to shatter your illusions, but in real life he doesn't play the horses, and he doesn't like cigars. On *77 Sunset Strip*, though, you'd never see Roscoe doing much else. In fact, Louis Quinn, as the lovable ex-Broadway horse player and stool pigeon, became so well known for betting on the nags that viewers used to send in money to be placed on "sure things." The money, of course, had to be returned. You may wonder why *Strip* fans were willing to take the gamble with Roscoe since his horses rarely finished in the top ten. The fact is, the show's scripters were warned to keep his nags way back.

That provided the comedy, but Roscoe had another important function: to gather inside information for Stu and Jeff which his background and sources could best provide. Many a time Roscoe eked out the info that broke the case or maybe even saved the hero's life. Roscoe also provided some identification for the older crowd. He was referred to as their "Kookie" with a style and a rap just as distinctive.

Quinn wrote much of his own dialogue for *Strip*. He had been a gag writer for radio and had written one-liners for fifteen Warner Bros. feature films before the war. He got his shot on the series when Howie Horwitz handed him a one-page part and told him to work on it. Quinn came up with literally pages of Roscoe-type patter. He got the part and kept writing the gags. He says he modeled Roscoe's mannerisms after an old idol of his — vaudevillian Ted Healy. The clothes and the railroad-style telephone by his bedside were developed by taking a look at all the horse race types he'd known.

Louis Quinn and Roger Smith: "Elementary, my dear Roscoe."

Louis Quinn Frackt was in his mid 40's during the run of *77 Sunset Strip*. He was the baby in a family of seven kids and began working nightclubs early in Chicago. In '38 he was in L.A. writing for radio and throwing a paper on the side. In 1950 he made the Copacabana. Later he went under contract to NBC but never made it. Then it was back to Los Angeles as emcee of an afternoon show on KHJ-TV in Los Angeles. L.A. became home when he was tapped for the part of Roscoe, and he and his second wife, actress Christine Nelson, lived only two blocks from Dino's Lodge on the Strip.

Quinn is still active, having made an appearance in a 1978 episode of *Fantasy Island* guest starring with Edd Byrnes.

ROBERT LOGAN

Beginning with the October 13, 1961, episode of *77SS*, Kookie began sporting a coat and tie and driving a rather conservative Ford

Falcon. His Model A and job as Dino's parking attendant were willed to the heir of the teenagers' dreams—J.R. Hale.

J.R. Hale was the character name for Robert Logan, oldest of seven children from Brooklyn, New York. He came to the attention of 77SS producer Howie Horwitz via Henry Willson, a Hollywood agent who spotted Logan eating a hamburger in a diner near the UCLA campus. In fact, so pleased was Horwitz with the tall, good-looking athlete from Brooklyn (now living in the L.A. suburb of Gardena after his father's transfer as a bank executive) that he signed Logan without a screen test.

Logan didn't originally intend to be an actor, but an athlete. He was successful in track and baseball in high school and had been offered a baseball scholarship to the University of Arizona. However, a D in high school geometry postponed his entry into the U of A. To make up his grade for eligibility Logan entered Los Angeles City College for a semester. He kept up his baseball practice and also served as a ski instructor near Big Bear. But a contract with Warner Bros. brought an end of a prospective professional baseball career.

Logan let it be known from the start that he was not to be pushed around. After discovering that his newly-created character name was to be Junior, he promptly put his foot down exclaiming, "Nobody calls me Junior!" The powers-that-be relented and renamed him J.R. Apparently Logan never forgot his high school jock indoctrination. He commented on acting from a macho view, "A lot of it is sissy."

In time, he came to enjoy the role—sissy parts and all—and found himself a welcome addition to the crew at Bailey and Spencer. J.R. became a valuable asset to the firm of Bailey and Spencer, as Kookie had been in the earlier episodes. He helped Stu fight communist agents in the "Catspaw Caper," and stole the show in "To Catch a Mink."

J.R. talk (initial-ese) was Logan's gimmick in the same way that Kookie talk was Edd Byrnes'. J.R. talk consisted of abbreviations, nicely complementing his use of initials instead of a first name. A few examples of J.R. talk would be B & S (for Bailey and Spencer), U.A.M. (for Unknown At Moment), N.T.I. (for Nothing To It), etc. Through most of the episodes in which J.R. appeared, Jeff, Stu, and company would sometimes have to stop for a minute to translate J.R. talk. At any rate, even with another difficult-to-understand parking attendant, the 77ers never failed to get their man for the remaining seasons.

Logan now works in feature films such as the *Wilderness Family*.

JACQUELINE BEER

It's a long way from the Champs Élysees in Paris to the Strip in L.A., but Jacqueline Beer made it. Working for the Sunset Answering Service, Suzanne evolved from message-giver to girl-Friday. Because of her strong French accent, Jacqueline wasn't given many lines in the earlier episodes, but as her English improved so did her part. She went from featured to co-starred billing.

Jacqueline was selling perfume at Oberon's in Paris until 1954 when a delivery boy sent her picture to a local motion picture magazine. The magazine sponsored Jacqueline, and she became Miss France and represented her country in the Miss Universe contest. The contest was held in Long Beach, California, where Jacqueline fended off all Hollywood agents who came to her door, intending to return directly home after the contest was over. But when the contest came to its conclusion, Jacqueline decided to remain (she stayed at the home of some friends she had met in Paris). Now however, the agents could not be found.

Her accent *did* lead to a job for Universal, publicizing a new film. This job got her some free drama lessons and ultimately an audition at Paramount which promptly placed her under contract. Jacqueline was soon loaned out to TV. Her first work for Warners was free-lancing in *Sugarfoot* and *Maverick*, which led to her being cast as Suzanne.

77 Sunset Strip—Series Index

FIRST SEASON:

Lovely Lady, Pity Me

Stu becomes interested in pretty Ann Melville, and finds himself involved in a blackmail scheme and accused of murder. Kathleen Crowley is Ann.

A Nice Social Evening

Stu is engaged by a government agent to keep an eye on a wealthy Latin American playboy while he's in Hollywood. After Bailey is almost murdered, he exposes the killer who's after the playboy. Dorothy Provine appears.

Casualty

Jeff is retained by a woman who has seen her supposedly dead husband alive. He undercovers an insurance fraud racket operated by the husband — among others.

The Bouncing Chip

Bailey is hired by Las Vegas hotel men to find out who is passing counterfeit chips in their casino.

Two and Two Make Six

Spencer is approached by a fashion designer who wants him to save her husband (an ex-con) from a mysterious assassin. Jeff discovers the husband holds a piece of evidence that would convict the vengeance killer of several men. Whitney Blake and Adam West star.

All Our Yesterdays

Lucinda Lane, aged ex-silent-screen actress, spends huge sums of money remaking an old success, "Foolish Girl." Her relatives, meanwhile, greedy for her money, try to get evidence through Stuart Bailey, proving her incompetent. John Carradine appears.

The Well Selected Frame

Sexy Valerie Stacey hires Jeff to get divorce evidence against her husband, then frames Jeff as his killer. Peggie Castle is Valerie. The Frankie Ortega Trio appears.

The Iron Curtain Caper

Stu is hired by a newspaper to go to Germany and bring correspondent Larry Hilton back from captivity in the Red zone. He locates Hilton in an East German hospital and fends off the Reds to bring him home.

Vicious Circle

Lou Catto, a reformed gangster, vows to wreak vengeance on hoods who kidnapped his lawyer son, who, not wanting his dad to commit a crime, informs the police and hires Jeff Spencer. Bert Convy as Blake Catto.

One False Step

A Washington lawyer comes to Stu with a story of a young man who approached him on a plane trip with an offer to swap murders. Richard Long and Connie Stevens appear.

The Court Martial of Johnny Murdo

Murdo, a cadet at a fashionable military academy, is convicted of stealing a $757 student fund. His mother hires Jeff to see if Johnny is really guilty ... but someone doesn't want Jeff to investigate.

Hit and Run

Kookie borrows Stu's convertible for a date and gets arrested for reckless driving.

Not an Enemy in the World

Jeff has reason to believe that Marcel Fabry, Suzanne's missing brother, fell in love with Elaine Lamson and killed her husband. But the search for Marcel reveals that it was he who died in a murder-for-insurance plot.

The Secret of Adam Cain

Fred and Venice Cain hire Stu to recover a stolen vase. Stu is kidnapped and wisked away to Algeria. The vase is lost at sea.

The Girl Who Couldn't Remember

A pretty amnesia victim who has $10,000 in cash, but no identification papers in her purse, comes to Jeff for help. Spencer learns she was a murder witness. John Vivyan appears.

Dark Vengeance

Stu promises to help a news commentator in a crusade against racketeers who have blinded him. Stu becomes a murder target.

Conspiracy of Silence

Jeff is hired to protect his client's coed daughter from an unknown killer. Pat Crowley appears.

Eyewitness

Little Timmy's estranged parents think he's making up stories when he says that through his telescope, he saw a hunter kill a bear. But what he saw was the accidental killing of a fur-coated wife of a doctor. Stu saves Timmy's life. Jay (Dennis the Menace) North is Timmy.

Lovely Alibi

When Lt. Bird tries to pin Ed Fuller's murder on racketeer Vic Gurney he gets nothing but trouble. Gurney frames him and he's kicked off the force. Bailey helps him get reinstated. Claude Akins is Bird.

In Memoriam

Disturbed by "crackpot" reports of his death, playboy publisher Noel Reynolds hires Stu to find out who's needling him.

The Fifth Stair

Tony Wendice, unjustly suspicious that his wife Margot is having an affair with Jeff Spencer, hires a killer to murder Margot. But Margot shoots the killer and she and Jeff are charged with murder. Richard Long is Tony.

Pasadena Caper

Stu, hired to find the missing Peter Baker, dredges Peter's car out of the bay along with a decomposed body. It turns out that Peter's mother and her housekeeper have tried to pass off the body of the housekeeper's son (who died in a fall) as the heavily insured Peter.

The Hong Kong Caper

Paul Nolan shows Jeff a note from his late Army pilot son, and a lucky piece marked "Candy's Hong Kong—#84." So Jeff is off to Hong Kong for a run-in with Oriental villain Run Run Lee played by Reggie Nalder.

A Check Will Do Nicely

Stu goes to Paris with his client to find his daughter who has been kidnapped.

The Grandma Caper

Jeff, Kookie, and the gang pit their wits against a grandmother who stages a one-woman crime wave to the horror of her wealthy family. But Grandma's bank robbery results in the capture of a famous criminal gang. Frances Bavier is Grandma.

Honey from the Bee

Kairos realizes that an ancient tapestry, now decorating a Beverly Hills restaurant, conceals diamonds. A chain of events is set off that results in three people being killed. Stu investigates. Ruta Lee and Connie Stevens appear.

Abra-Cadaver

Investigating a murder-for-insurance ring, Jeff becomes a prospective victim. Jeff gets evidence, and relays it to Stu. Stu arrives with the police just in time to save Jeff after his true identity is learned by the crooks. Robert McQueeney and Pernell Roberts appear.

A Bargain in Tombs

Stu heads for Rome in search of a missing heiress. He finds the girl is posing as an archeology student and is unwittingly helping loot a hidden Roman tomb.

The Widow Wouldn't Weep

Sexy Margie hires Jeff to prove that her husband's suicide was murder.

Downbeat

Though Stu is cleared on a sedition charge, he loses his private investigator's license and goes on a big drunk. A former OSS buddy, who sells government secrets, finds Stu and offers him a job. It was all a plan to get the goods on the OSS man. Dorothy Provine appears.

Canine Caper

Six rubies, stolen in Amsterdam, are hidden in the collar of a poodle which belongs to a starlet wooed by Kookie.

Mr. Paradise

Stu is hired by relatives of Cyrus Blanton to investigate a cult which Blanton joined. Stu learns the cult leader, Mr. Paradise, exploits elderly members for their wealth. Blanton grows suspicious of Paradise, who then plans to kill him. Stu is captured and almost killed ... but he's rescued by Jeff and Roscoe. Andy Duggan is Paradise.

Strange Girl in Town

Jeff and a girl are innocently involved in murder when she witnesses a killing.

Only Zeroes Count

In Hawaii, Stu helps the government trace phony bills by courting a girl who knows the girl friend of an imprisoned counterfeiter. Robert Conrad appears as Tom Lopaka.

The Kookie Caper

Kookie befriends a cute teenager, Carrie, who's believed to be a runaway heiress. Jeff and Stu become involved in kidnapping and murder before the real heiress turns up. Will Hutchins as himself.

SECOND SEASON:

Six Superior Skirts

At a charity bazaar, Bailey, protecting a fabulous jewel collection, uncovers a conspiracy. Part of the conspiracy is to replace the Moorfield Diamond with a phony. Diane McBain and Will Hutchins appear.

Clay Piegon

Bailey is hired by a deejay to locate four people he knew years ago. No sooner has Stu found two of them than they are murdered.

Thanks for Tomorrow

Spencer helps his friend, Lonnie Drew, a good guy, but a born gambler, who has become innocently involved in a race-fixing scheme and a $100,000 robbery. Adam West is Drew.

Sing Something Simple

Stu is hired to guard opera star Zina Felice who is receiving threatening notes.

The Treehouse Caper

Jeff promises a dying convict that he will give the convict's daughter half the reward for stolen diamonds. But Jeff is double-crossed by a crooked insurance investigator. Kookie makes an appearance — bald.

Out of the Past

Bailey goes to Hamburg to buy top secret papers from an Army deserter and falls into a trap set to catch a scientist. Stu saves the scientist and kills an ex-Nazi in a shootout. Adam West appears.

The Widow and the Web

Jeff is hired to investigate an accidental death in which Jerry Shannon toppled off a high ladder. But Jeff discovers a murder plot with himself as an intended victim.

Secret Island

Stu and jewel thief Pierre D'Albert are en route from Manila to the States when a typhoon downs the plane. The two, along with several others, reach an island which Stu finds is a target for an H-bomb test. Tuesday Weld and Kathleen Crowley appear.

The Texas Doll

When a handsome gigolo is murdered, Chris Benson, a lovely teenage heiress found in his bedroom, is a prime suspect. Spencer proves her innocent. Sherry Jackson is Chris.

Vacation with Pay

On a trip to Paris to guard a millionaire's daughters against fortune hunters, Stu and Kookie learn that the girls' uncle is in league with smooth, young Pierre to force a rich marriage.

The Jukebox Caper

Jeff poses as a singer to investigate the death of a singer. He gets a contract with the dead man's old boss, the racketeer head of a record company.

Created He Them

Suspected of the murder of her invalid husband, innocent Dr. Mary Adams resists advice to plead guilty of a mercy killing, and hires Stu to investigate the case.

Collector's Item

Jeff is hired by a countess to deliver a supposedly rare piece of sculpture to New York. But Jeff learns the countess is part of a spy ring attempting to steal the formula for a top-secret plastic. Jim Backus and Joanie Sommers appear.

Switchburg

Stu is checking on the chances of buying a long deserted hotel for an eccentric client, and he discovers the building is being used for the counterfeiting of silver dollars.

The One That Got Away

Jeff is hired by an insurance company to confirm the death of a man, whose widow is to collect $200,000. But the dead man turns up alive in Mexico with a girl.

Ten Cents a Death

After several girls at "Danceland" have been murdered, Stu, Jeff, and Roscoe are hired by girls to find the killer. Stu gets Suzanne to take a job at Danceland. Robert Colbert appears.

Who Killed Cock Robin

Jeff accompanies blind director Wilson James to a reading of the will of an eccentric Hollywood genius. Through film, the dead man directs a varied group to participate in a treasure hunt for $1,000,000. Jeff is brought into the case by Tom Lopaka of Hawaiian Eye. Fay Wray as Clara.

Condor's Lair

Teenage novelist Kitten Lang calls on Stu when a mysterious person starts blackmailing her. Troy Donahue as Star Bright. Tuesday Weld is Kitten. Robert Lowery appears.

The Starlet

After losing an award, an actress apparently kills herself. But Jeff is hired to prove it was murder. Diane McBain stars.

Safari

An egotistical tycoon, who suspects attempts are being made on his life, hires Bailey to go with him on a safari. Richard Coogan and Robert Colbert star.

Blackout

Jeff is hired to protect pearls during a store demonstration. Crooks cook up a plot to nab the jewels and head for South America. They kidnap Suzanne. Warren Oates, Donald May appear.

Return to San Dede (The Desert Story)

The first of two two-part episodes of Strip. Stu is hired to escort a girl, heiress to her father's political throne, safely to her Latin American homeland, San Dede. He becomes involved in a game of power played with deadly intent.

Return to San Dede (Capital City)

Part two: Stu returns the girl to the capital city of San Dede only to find the government in the hands of her enemy.

Publicity Brat

Stu is asked to find a valuable necklace belonging to a woman, but is handicapped by the cooperation of her mother and her daughter. Both are actresses with overactive imaginations. Mousie Garner appears.

The Fix

Jeff gets involved in a fight fix episode when he is hired to dig into the past of a fighter. Jeff is nearly killed, and Roscoe takes some lumps. Mary Tyler Moore plays Laura Chandler.

Legend of Crystal Dart

Bailey goes with glamorous ex-Folies Bergere star Crystal Dart to a ski lodge to evict her estranged spouse. Then, a murder is committed. Marilyn Maxwell is Crystal.

Stranger Than Fiction

Jeff enlists the aid of Roscoe to help him solve the murder of a beautiful ex-chorus girl married to a wealthy older man. She was killed by her lover after they faked her kidnapping and collected $200,000 from her husband.

Genesis of Treason

When an Air Force lieutenant is convicted of being a spy, Marta hires Bailey to prove he isn't. Bible quotes used by the lieutenant provide the clues. Donald May is Lt. Francis B. Holister.

Fraternity of Fear

A man whose son was killed in a college fraternity hazing gag arranges for Jeff to live in the frat house as a student to learn the truth. Diane McBaine appears.

Spark of Freedom

In Budapest on an intelligence mission, Stu, with the help of Hungarian Freedom Fighters, tries to rescue a young scientist. The scientist is executed, but Stu, disguised as a priest, gets some important data. Also produced as "Blind Drop: Warsaw" for the *Conflict* series.

Perfect Setup

This Roy Huggins teleplay was also produced as "Point Blank" on *Maverick*. In this version, Tracy Steele (Anthony Eisley) gets Jeff involved in a case on a small Hawaiian Island where he's set up as a "pigeon" by a man and his sweetheart. The idea is murder Jeff and pass the body off as his own. Connie Stevens appears as Cricket and does a song with Jeff on the plane. Warren Stevens as Mel Dixon.

Sierra

Also seen as "Big Ghost Basin" on *Cheyenne*. Summoned to a man's mountain home to help solve the mystery of his daughter's strange behavior, Stu ends up matching wits with a man-killing animal and a gang of criminals. Sherry Jackson as Ella.

The Silent Caper

Probably the most unique of all the WB episodes, because this one had no dialogue. The Roger Smith script, also called "Much Ado About Nothing" featured a stripper kidnapped because she is about to testify before the Crime Commission. Spencer rescues the drugged Jingle Bells (changed from Lolly Pop) and she squeals on schedule.

Family Skeleton

When a businessman is kidnapped for ransom, Stu reveals the culprits are neither his wife nor her underworld friend.

THIRD SEASON:

The Negotiable Blonde

When a businessman's blonde secretary flees to Acapulco with half a million dollars in negotiable bonds, he hires Spencer to bring her back. But Jeff learns that the businessman is head of a dope ring.

Attic

Jeff trails a woman to an abandoned farmhouse and is captured by the very crooks he was hoping to find. They tie him up and leave him to die in the attic. Jeff's efforts to escape are slowed down when a rattlesnake joins him in the attic. Kathleen Crowley, Robert Colbert, and John Dehner are gang members.

The President's Daughter

When a dictator took over his country, Presidente Alonso of Pinacaro fled to the U.S., but was forced to leave his daughter behind. Rex Randolph and Jeff are hired to find her and they rescue her from a firing squad.

The Fanatics

Stu acts as bodyguard to a U.N. mediator in North Africa. But when the mediator is shot and must be operated on, foreign agents arrange to bomb the operating room. Bert Convy and Tris (Rocketman) Coffin appear.

The Dresden Doll

Dolly Stewart asks Roscoe to kill her husband; but she also hires Jeff to protect him. When she holds Jeff at gunpoint, Rex arrives in time.

The Laurel Canyon Caper

The bunch at 77 Sunset Strip is thrilled when singer Barry James is offered a motion picture part. But Barry becomes a suspect when the publisher of a blackmailing scandal sheet is murdered. Randolph goes to work for his friend. Jock Mahoney is Barry James.

The Office Caper

Stu is a witness against a racketeer, and is a target for death by his henchmen. The hitman rents the office right above 77 Sunset Strip. Robert McQueeny is one of the crooks.

The Duncan Shrine

Randolph runs into trouble when he investigates the disappearance of a statue from a cowboy star's grave. Richard Deacon appears.

The Widescreen Caper

Stu takes on the assignment of keeping watch over a film festival marked for tragedy by an astrologer. Stu assigns each of the gang—Jeff, Rex, Roscoe, Suzanne, and Kookie—a client to watch during the festival. Ruta Lee appears.

Trouble in the Middle East

In backward Scythia, tourist Jeff is caught in a battle between rebels and the pro-modernization government. He tries to rescue the daughter of the head-of-state.

Double Trouble

A government official hires Stu to impersonate an underworld hitman he resembles in order to gain evidence against mobster Silk Cipriano. Stu gets the evidence on tape, but when he has to make out with "his" old girlfriend, she exposes him. Bruce Cabot is Silk.

The Affairs of Adam Gallante

Jeff is hired by Alice Gallante who says someone has been trying to kill her ever since her husband Adam disappeared. The trail to Adam leads to several other Mrs. Gallantes and a killer.

The Valley Caper

Rex pretends to be an actor to learn why a charming movie star is being blackmailed by her ex-con ex-husband. Kathleen Crowley and Tris Coffin appear.

The Antwerp Caper

In Antwerp, Stu investigates the claim of a stage magician that his pretty protégée Gabriella is the daughter of a prosperous couple who lost their small child in a Nazi concentration camp.

The Rice Estate

A young widow hires Stu to find out who's behind threats and attempts to keep her from selling her dead husband's huge old mansion. Montgomery Pittman, who wrote the story, appears.

The Double Death of Benny Markham

Finishing up a case in Liverpool, Jeff is about to return home when he gets a visit from Benny Markham, a lovable cockney who has done some professional safe-cracking for him. Benny offers Jeff a tidy sum to find *his* killer. You see, Benny was hired to steal a metal bottle. As he later found out, the contents of the bottle were radioactive and Benny will die of radiation sickness in two weeks.

Tiger by the Tail

Guarding a visiting maharajah, Stu exposes wife Lada and an aide as hirelings of a foreign agent later shot by Stu. The princess is kidnapped but Kookie comes to the rescue. During this episode, the maharajah's party takes a tour of the Warner Bros. Studios. His Highness breaks up a scene, cheering Roger Moore in a clinch with an actress. Roger Moore and Merry Anders as themselves.

The College Caper

A gangster's son, an All-American football player, thinks his dad is dead. The gangster hires Stu to protect the college student from a vengeful criminal. Chad Everett appears.

Once Upon a Caper

The origin episode of the 77ers as written by Roger Smith. Rex makes the mistake of asking Jeff, then Stu, then Kookie how the eyes got together. He gets frustrated when he gets three different stories. Superb comedy.

The Hamlet Caper

The question "to kill or not to kill" comes up for the *Hamlet* company. And who to kill may well be actor Derek Fielding played by Andrew Duggan. Rex is hired to protect him.

The Positive Negative

Rex and Kookie recover a diamond tiara stolen from the mistress of a tycoon. They learn that a friend and guest of the tycoon is in reality a former Nazi SS man — and a killer.

The Man in the Mirror

Jeff frees a retired broker client from fear of suicide by proving it was not his other personality who was trying to kill him — but a real murderer. Robert Colbert; Tris Coffin.

Mr. Goldilocks

By Roger Smith and Montgomery Pittman: Jeff is shot trying to capture a jewel thief and pursues him into the desert where he is ambushed and severely wounded. Sue Anne Langdon appears.

The Corsican Caper

After a charming lawyer convinces Suzanne she's heir to millions, she learns he's told the same story to others — for a fee. He is murdered, Suzanne arrested, and Rex must solve two murders. Max Baer appears.

Strange Bedfellows

Jeff solves a case involving theft of jewelry and love letters of professional beauty Maritza Vedar (Kathleen Crowley). She kept the letters for blackmail purposes. Ty Hardin plays the part of Drew Dekker, a cowboy actor.

Face in the Window

Rex is hired by a fading Western star to put a stop to a prowler menacing his starlet fiancee. Rex uncovers an embezzlement and murder scheme as Kookie moves the chick into a "peeper-proof-pad." Peter Breck and Merry Anders.

Open and Close in One

Old time comic Baxter Kellogg's good luck charm is missing and Stu is hired to find it before Baxter does an act on a 50 foot platform. Buddy Ebsen is Kellogg.

The Space Caper

To aid a scientist friend who works as an undercover agent for the government, Jeff poses as a scientist at a missile center. He exposes a spy who tries to kill him in a rocket test chamber.

Old Card Sharps Never Die

Rex gets involved in frontier week celebration of a town run by a businessman named Henning, and manages to save the life of 70-ish card sharp Notch McConnell. Notch has been pegged for murder. Robert Colbert appears.

The Legend of Leckonby

Jeff is hired to find Stanley Leckonby, an ex-con, and the stolen money he never spent. Kookie and Roscoe help Jeff solve the case. Richard Carlyle in the title role.

Vamp 'Til Ready

Melissa asks Stu to find her missing husband David, a pianist. Stu locates David, but also uncovers a plot to murder him. Kookie and Roscoe help in the case. Bert Convy is David.

The Common Denominator

Spencer helps Lt. Gilmore find the killer of four beautiful women by looking for a common denominator which seems to be boats. But later, Gilmore reveals that all the victims were French. Suzanne is used as bait and she subdues the killer.

The 6 Out of 8 Caper

At Santa Anita, wealthy Barbara Wentworth sends a companion to check on her strangely lucky neighbor who's been picking 6 winners out of 8 horses each day. Stu is hired to find the answer, and naturally, Roscoe becomes involved.

The Celluloid Cowboy

Numerous "accidents" endanger the life of Western movie star Flint Dakota, so his wife hires Jeff. Andy Duggan is Flint. Donna Douglas appears.

The Eyes of Love

Bailey solves one murder, and the killer falls prey to the trap he set for a wealthy wife who was to be his second victim.

Designing Eye

Jeff is hired by Mark, Pop and Ellen, owners of a fashion house, to discover how rivals are "pirating" their new designs. Suzanne hires on as a model to help in the case.

Hot Tamale Caper — Part 1

The second two part episode of *Strip* — this one written by Fenton Earnshaw. Rex Randolph is reported killed in a plane crash ... but Stu and Jeff learn that the corpse is not that of Rex. Clues lead to Miami, and Stu calls in the SurfSide 6 agency to help out. Ken Madison and Sandy Winfield learn that Rex is a dead ringer for Miguelo, the late President of Ylapa, a Latin American Country. Stu and Jeff meet with Roscoe and Kookie to make plans for a trip to Ylapa. Van Williams and Troy Donahue appear briefly.

Hot Tamale Caper — Part 2

In Ylapa, the 77ers learn that Rex is being forced to substitute for the dead President Miguelo. Rex is to be assassinated as part of a political plan. They engineer a dramatic rescue.

Caper in E Flat

Rex is hired to investigate attempts on the life of country crooner Billy Boy. Rex enlists the aid of Kookie and Roscoe. Cloris Leachman appears.

FOURTH SEASON:

The Rival Eye Caper

A fly-by-night detective agency solves case after case and attempts to take over the 77 offices. Stu learns the rivals are pulling robberies, then solving them to build a reputation. Chad Everett appears.

The Inverness Cape Caper

Stu tries to find a missing uncle for a young girl and learns the missing man has been on the lam for fifteen years after supposedly being killed by a gangster.

The Desert Spa Caper

Suzanne wins at the track, but Roscoe goes broke. She decides to take a vacation at an exclusive women's health spa. An actress there is in danger, and Suzanne (along with Jeff) gets the job of protecting her. Kathleen Crowley appears.

The Man in the Crowd

By Montgomery Pittman and Roger Smith: Psycho R.E. Venge tries to kill Jeff who he thinks collaborated with Commies during the Korean War. Jeff finally takes on Venge in hand to hand battle in a swamp. Robert Colbert is Venge.

Big Boy Blue

Jeff discovers that a trumpet player is on the run after a talent scout brings him to L.A. from a jail in Mexico.

The Chrome Coffin

A rich hotrod enthusiast is the object of an extortion attempt against his uncle. Stu, Kookie and Roscoe investigate. Max Baer appears.

The Missing Daddy Caper

A nurse's shapely legs in high heels figure in a case involving Jeff, Kookie and a gangster who wants to kill a fugitive father. Grace Lee Whitney appears.

Turning Point

Stu does a good turn for a friend who is a minister, and takes a misguided youngster under his care.

The Navy Caper

Jeff is called on by the Navy to test security measures; Suzanne becomes a society journalist; Roscoe becomes a cloak and dagger man; and Kookie helps in the case. The object is to crash the gate of a Naval base under heavy security.

Reserved for Mr. Bailey

The most talked-about Stu Bailey episode: Stu gets a mysterious phone call in the night, and then finds himself all alone in a ghost town. A voice out of thin air tells him he's marked for death. A gallows bears the message: reserved for Mr. Bailey.

Twice Dead

Bailey draws an ex-convict (jailed for killing his wife) for a client.

The Lovely American

Jeff gets a big reception while on assignment to deliver some money to the people of an Italian village. But he's also the object of a scheme to ruin the image of all Americans.

The Lady Has the Answers

Beautiful Lally turns up in Jeff Spencer's bedroom, and gets him involved in a case having to do with a body on a patio in Bel Air, a sleep walker, and thousands of dollars in jewelry. Merry Anders is Lally.

The Cold Cash Caper

Robbers grab $400,000 from a chemical plant office. Stu gets a clue while dating the secretary of the plant's boss.

The Deadly Solo

Gandy Waters' wife solicits Jeff to protect her husband following attempts on his life.

The Unremembered

Kookie provides a clue that solves a case involving thefts of jewels from Hollywood moguls by a thief in screen disguises. The clue leads Bailey and Kookson to a silent film star.

Mr. Bailey's Honeymoon

A hillbilly waitress in a little Oklahoma town claims Stu as her bridegroom. William Windom appears.

The Down Under Caper

Written by Roger Smith for wife Victoria: Spencer delivers jewels to Sydney, Australia and becomes involved with a beautiful sheep ranch owner. Victoria Shaw as Margaret Hughes.

The Diplomatic Caper

Stu gets Kookie, Suzanne and Roscoe to help squelch foreign agents' plan to pressure a delegate to the United Nations. Chad Everett.

The Bridal Trail Caper

A wedding is upset when an ex-rodeo star turns up and threatens to expose an incident in the bride's past. Diane Cannon and Jack Cassidy appear.

Dress Rehearsal

Kookson solos as he takes on the job of protecting the life of a rich lady. John Astin appears.

The Bel Air Hermit

Squatter relatives are worried that an heiress is blowing her wealth on bad investments. Stu looks for the source of her tips.

The Parallel Caper

Jeff and Kookie go their separate ways as they investigate a case involving a fisherman's death and a society girl's concerns about her brother.

The Brass Ring Caper

Kookie stars again as he takes on the case of a young man who's accused of murder. Kookson is personally involved because he gave the man a ride into Hollywood.

Ghost of a Memory

They're having a funeral for teen-age singing idol Johnny Main—but Main's voice and image appear in the air, causing panic.

Bullets for Santa

An attempt is made on the life of Santa Claus—during a parade and in front of a TV audience. But a movie executive thinks an actress may be the real target of murder, and Jeff is hired. Victor Buono; Yvonne Craig.

Jennifer

Jennifer Grey's guardian hires Jeff to go to France to check on her. It seems that accidents have claimed the lives of her rich father and her husband.

Penthouse on Skid Row

Jeff and Roscoe help some friends hang on to an old mansion. Mae Questel appears (you'll remember her as the voice of Olive Oyl on the Popeye cartoons, and also in her TV commercial role as Aunt Bluebell). Grace Lee Whitney as Mimi.

The Baker Street Caper

Stu and Roscoe finish up a case for a British client, so naturally they go to the races. They are hired to track down some stolen paintings.

The Steerer

Murder during a poker game sends a Texan running with thousands of dollars right through the hotel room of a beauty contest winner who wants to get into movies.

The Pet Shop Caper

Stu gets involved in a case six years old when a suspect in a $2 million robbery is killed. The murder bears the signs of a man deported to Spain a couple of years before.

The Long Shot Caper

Roscoe is maneuvered into being the set-up man for a hood who wants someone gunned down. The hired gunman muffs the job.

Violence for Your Furs

Roscoe figures in another case: He is planted in a diner to listen in on the activities of a group of 20th century highwaymen. But Roscoe is taken with the waitress. Mala Powers appears.

The Disappearance

A national leader is grabbed right off the golf course; Stu is pitted against a scientist with a plan for getting a million dollars in ransom money. John Dehner as Dr. Burke; Victor Buono appears.

Flight from Escondido

Faith Merrick runs away to Latin America, but Jeff Spencer finds her. But getting her back home isn't all that simple — their plane is hijacked. Susan Seaforth is Faith.

The Gemmologist Caper

Stu is handling security during the sale of some jewels — he and his male companions are baffled when an expert arrives and says fakes have been submitted — in front of all.

Framework for a Badge

The bunch at 77 Sunset Strip goes to the aid of Lt. Gilmore after he encounters a dying man and is tricked into clobbering his prime suspect.

Upbeat

Stu sent a spy to jail years ago — now, the spy wants revenge. Dorothy Provine; Andrew Duggan as Cal Calhoun.

Nightmare

A psychiatrist hires Jeff to look into the case of a patient who keeps dreaming about murdering a beautiful girl. Peter Breck appears.

The Gang's All Here

A policeman asks the crew on Sunset Strip to help with his son who has taken up with a pool hall sharpie. Sammy Davis, Jr. as Kid Pepper, Sammy Davis, Sr. and Peter Breck appear.

Pattern for a Bomb

A lunchroom and a tailer shop are bombed. The detectives team up with Gilmore to look for the motive.

FIFTH SEASON:

The Reluctant Spy

Bailey is involved with spies in Vienna.

Leap, My Lovely

A hypnotist is leading a double life—he's also an extortionist. Jeff investigates. Diane McBain and Neil Hamilton appear.

Terror in a Small Town

Kookson and Spencer play a trick on J.R. Soon after, Kookie must make a trip to small town Bromley. En route, he picks up a lookalike hitchhiker who steals Kookson's clothes and car. The young man has just raped a woman in Bromley, and Kookie is accused of being the rapist. He is thrown in jail, and when he calls J.R., he thinks Kookie

is continuing the practical joke. The townsfolk get a lynch party together and Kookson barely escapes. They string him up at the end, and he's seconds from death when it's learned that the real criminal has been caught.

The Raiders

Stu gets in with a crime syndicate.

The Floating Man

Jeff must protect a judge who's in danger. Henry Daniell as Gideon.

The Catspaw Caper

Stu is hired to hunt for a missing refugee pursued by Communist agents. J.R. helps crack the case.

Wolf! Called the Blonde

An actress' life is in danger; Spencer takes on the job of protecting her. Peter Breck, Peter Brown and Jo Morrow appear.

The Dark Wood

Stu helps an old girlfriend find the murderer of her husband. Diane Brewster appears.

Shadow on Your Shoulder

Stu goes to Paris to investigate an international jewel theft ring. Cloris Leachman as Eve.

Adventure in San Dede

Back to San Dede as Jeff and J.R. are involved in another Latin American revolution.

The Odds on Odette

Jeff helps an astrologist who's been getting threatening phone calls. Merry Anders appears.

The Snow Job Caper

Jeff trails an ex-convict who he hopes will lead him to loot hidden from the robbery of an armored car. Ruta Lee appears.

Falling Stars

The life of a TV comic is threatened. Stu gets the task of protecting him. Grace Lee Whitney and Jerry Paris appear.

Tarnished Idol

Suzanne becomes romantically involved with a dangerous swindler. Van Williams as Wade.

Scream Softly Dear

Was an automobile accident really murder? Kookson thinks so. Peter Marshall as Charles.

Crashout

Jeff Spencer poses as a convict in order to find a half million dollars that's missing. Michael Parks appears.

The Night Was Six Years Long

Stu Bailey's former secretary has been missing for six years, a victim of amnesia. But now, she's back. Myrna Fahey appears.

Six Feet Under

Jeff suspects a jewel thief—thought dead—of committing a series of robberies.

Escape to Freedom

Bailey is back in international adventure as he tries to rescue a prisoner of the East Germans.

Dial S for Spencer

Jeff protects a skid row bum who's inherited a large sum of money.

Nine to Five

Bailey protects an old friend whose wife is up to no good. Richard Long in a non-Rex Randolph role. Diane McBaine appears.

Stranger from the Sea

Kookson aids a friend in recovering some stolen family money. Robert J. Wilke as Vern.

The Man Who Wasn't There

Jeff is hired to prove a man isn't having hallucinations.

Target Island

Jeff and J.R. are trapped on an island scheduled for destruction by the Navy.

Reunion at Balboa

Jeff's girlfriend is run over by a teenage hit-and-run driver.

Walk Among Tigers

Bailey investigates the death of a respected industrialist—and the trail leads to sabotage. Warren Stevens appears.

The Left Field Caper

Jeff helps a young boy cope with his father—who's just been released from prison.

The Heartbeat Caper

A series of college murders—and Stu Bailey investigates. Andrew Duggan appears.

To Catch a Mink

An old flame of Stu's shows up with some folks at Dino's—but it's all a plot to rob those present. J.R. suspects what's going on, but fails to convince anyone—so he does some private eye work of his own. Most of the episode takes place inside Dino's. Mike Henry appears.

Lady in the Sun

A realtor hires Stu to find his missing secretary. Yvonne Craig appears.

Our Man in Switzerland

The million dollars in negotiable securities that Kookie was guarding is stolen.

Your Fortune for a Penny

A millionaire hires Stu Bailey to break up a romance between his daughter and a suspected swindler. Robert Vaughn; Susan Oliver.

The Checkmate Caper

Stu Bailey is a robbery suspect. William Windom appears.

Never to Have Loved

Kookie falls in love with the movie star he was hired to protect.

Terror in Silence

Stu Bailey helps a deaf librarian who's involved in a murder plot.

SIXTH SEASON:

5—Part 1

The sixth season episodes featured Stu Bailey working solo from a new office in downtown L.A. Jack Webb replaced Bill Orr as executive producer for the final season with William Conrad as producer and sometimes director. In the first part of "5" Bailey is summoned from his office to New York by a wealthy art collector who wants the hit-run killing of his brother solved, and runs into the opposition of Lt. Butter who doesn't like private eyes. He also discovers that the dead man had a wife and a lot of enemies. The long list of guest stars this episode: Richard Conte, Wally Cox, Peter Lorre, Herbert Marshall, Diane McBain, Burgess Meredith, William (Capt. Kirk) Shatner, Ed Wynn and Keenan Wynn.

5—Part 2

Stu finds a mysterious blonde and a missing painting after consulting a zany art teacher, a poet, and a fancy dancer. But a camera, a key and a body in the morgue make his assignment of finding a murderer more difficult than ever. Guest stars: Victor Buono, George Jessel, Leonid Kinskey, Gene Nelson, and Clint Walker.

5—Part 3

Two attempts are made on Stu's life after he broadens his search for one killer into a hunt for two. An Army colonel provides clues to still another crime which sends Bailey flying off to Italy. Guests: Luther Adler, Lloyd Nolan, Patricia Rainier, and Walter Slezak.

5—Part 4

The chase that brought Bailey to the Big Apple takes him to Italy, Holland and France, where a stolen key and two murders lead him into a deadly ambush on the banks of the Seine. Guests: Tony Bennett, Jacques Bergerac, Marisa Pavan, Cesar Romero, and Telly Savalas.

5—Part 5

Stu ends the long search which started with murder and a strange assignment to buy a man's way into heaven and which took him to Paris, Rome, Amsterdam, Tel Aviv and back to New York. There, a startling sequence of events ends the international hunt for men and treasure. Guests: Brian Keith, Carmelo Manto. Many of the guest stars appeared in more than one segment of "5."

By His Own Verdict

Famous trial lawyer Arnold Buhler enlists the aid of old friend Stu Bailey to help unravel the twisted background of a young hood, Max Dent, whom he had successfully defended on a murder charge, and who, after the trial, confessed his guilt to him. Joseph Cotton as Buhler; Nick Adams as Dent; Barbara Bain as Rachel Dent.

88 Bars

Sometimes called the "Star Trek" episode because it features two cast members of that series: When a wealthy heiress retains Stu to track down a would-be assassin, he finds himself involved with the police, a gambler, a nervous piano player, and an exotic dancer. Grace Lee Whitney is Natasha; DeForest Kelley as Phil Wingate; Cloris Leachman also appears.

The Toy Jungle

Bailey is hired by a distraught husband to check on his wife's double life. The trail leads to an old flame and a narc ring. Pat Crowley.

Lovers' Lane

Stu is called upon by big time politician "Boss" Gates to clear his son who's in death row on charges of murder and rape. Yvonne Craig, Hampton Fancher, Preston Foster and Charles McGraw.

Deposit with Caution

Stu is summoned to New York by a police lieutenant accused of accepting a $20,000 bribe and discovers that although the lieutenant needs help, he also hates private eyes.

Alimony League

When much-married, eccentric millionaire Jerry Kenzie summons three of his former brides ... and Stu Bailey ... to discuss alimony cutbacks, a far more lethal subject is injected. Lloyd Corrigan is Jerry.

Dead As in Dude

Just widowed Gloria Townsend doubts the coroner's report that her dead husband is a suicide. Bailey investigates. Diane Brewster and Robert Colbert.

Don't Wait for Me

Bailey proves a youth from the wrong side of town is not guilty of murder.

White Lie

Stu is retained by Sam Weldon, an Oklahoma wildcatter, to trace the ownership of a parcel of land and secure oil rights. Bailey turns up the Jacksons, an impoverished Negro family in California, which leads to Charlotte Delavalle who owns the title. She has "passed" and lives in Connecticut under the nom de plume, and is reluctant to reveal her true identity. Through her love for her sister's crippled child, Bailey convinces her that her heritage is worth more than deception. Elizabeth Montgomery, Gene Evans, and Juanita Moore.

Paper Chase

Bailey is hired by a paper manufacturer to discover why his top chemist is in desperate need of an advance. His findings: blackmail.

Bonus Baby

Stu is involved with paternity, bulldozers, and big league baseball when he's engaged to unearth info in a paternity case. Simon Oakland and Michael Constantine.

The Fumble

Stu's engaged by an old flame to monitor her husband Charlie's actions in order to save his life and his future in business. Richard Long is Charlie. Also, Gail Kobe, and Sue Anne Langdon appear.

Not Such a Simple Knot

When Stu's hired to baby-sit in Las Vegas, he never dreams "baby" holds the key to breaking the gaming tables wide open. Dan Tobin and Ruta Lee.

Queen of the Cats

Stu is retained by Marion Armstrong—only daughter and sole heir to a wealthy Philadelphia family—to locate her mother from whom she's been separated since infancy. Bailey opens up a plot designed to ruin the young heiress.

The Target

A distraught wife hires Bailey to protect her author-husband from the violence that his exposé of crime will bring down on him. The violence is there all right, but from what source? Lyle Talbot, Les Tremayne, Lawrence Dobkin, James Lydon, Tony Barrett, William Conrad, Keith Andes, and Jeanne Cooper.

BOURBON STREET BEAT

HISTORICAL OLD

Absinthe House

BOURBON ST.

7
This Is the Blues

ABC (1 hour) — debuted October 5, 1959
Format: Stories center around a detective firm whose office adjoins the
        Old Absinthe House on Bourbon Street
Cast: Richard Long . . . . Rex Randolph
      Andrew Duggan . . . . Cal Calhoun
      Arlene Howell . . . . Melody Lee Mercer
      Van Williams . . . . Kenny Madison
      Eddie Cole . . . . Billy the Baron
      Nita Talbot . . . . Lusti Weather
Executive Producer: William T. Orr
Producer: Charles Hoffman
Theme Music: "Bourbon Street Beat" by Mack David and Jerry
             Livingston
Location: New Orleans and Hollywood

Not a lot has been written about *Bourbon Street Beat* — in fact the
show is probably most remembered for launching its three main stars
into *other* series that *were* successful. Richard Long kept his identity
as Rex Randolph and jumped to *77 Sunset Strip*, then left Warner
Bros. to star in *The Big Valley* and *Nanny and the Professor*. Andrew
Duggan became a star in the comedy series *Room for One More*, and
then a cowboy in 20th Century–Fox's *Lancer*. Van Williams' Ken
Madison character became a lead in *SurfSide 6*, a series that eased into
Bourbon Street Beat's Monday night slot on ABC. *Bourbon Street
Beat*, in fact, came and went all in one season.

The offices of "Randolph and Calhoun, Special Services" was
home base for the two private eyes. The firm, in fact, adjoined the Old

Absinthe House on Bourbon Street—thus the series' name, *and* its flavor. And though the principal shooting took place in Hollywood, much on-location footage was used to preserve the atmosphere of New Orleans and the French Quarter.

A colorful cast of supporting characters joined Rex and Cal in their adventures. Van Williams, fresh from a football career at Texas Christian University, was Kenny Madison, an oil-rich young Texan studying at Tulane and working for the eyes on the side. Arlene Howell, in her role as the firm's secretary, Melody Lee Mercer, helped out in the sleuthing. And then there were a couple of French Quarter friends; Nita Talbot was nightclub singer Lusti Weather, and Eddie Cole was "Billy the Baron" who fronted a jazz combo in the Old Absinthe House. Cole even put out an album featuring the *Bourbon Street* theme music.

As for our heroes themselves ... Rex Randolph's background was impeccable. He was from a fine old New Orleans family, and an Ivy League man. Cal Calhoun's folks were share-croppers in the Bayou country where Cal was once a village policeman.

The origin and the very existence of *Bourbon Street Beat* seemed to be tied to other WB shows. The series developed from a 1957 episode of *Conflict* called "The Money" which featured Duggan as private eye Michael Austin. Austin roamed the French Quarter just like Calhoun would do later, but there *was* a difference. Just as Kookie made his debut as a crook, so did Duggan, and in the end it was Austin who had strangled Miss Lila Prescott (Peggie Castle) for her money. That *Conflict* episode not only featured Duggan and Castle, but also David Janssen (*Richard Diamond; The Fugitive*), Kathy Nolan (*The Real McCoys*), and John Smith (*Laramie*).

Duggan later got a chance to redeem himself for the crime he had committed earlier as Mike Austin. *Bourbon Street Beat* did a re-make of "The Money" called "Twice Betrayed." This time, Duggan didn't strangle Lila for a suitcase full of dollars—instead, he caught the person who did.

Beat not only evolved from earlier private eye series like *77 Sunset Strip*, it also inherited something from them called "shtick." Shtick can be described as "bits and pieces," "a gimmick," or maybe a hoped-for fad. Kookie's comb (the idea coming from Hugh Benson) was shtick. So it came to pass that Warners announced some shtick for *Beat*.

Richard Long would have what was called a *cooking shtick*. Duggan would have an *untidy desk shtick*. Something called "sole to sole" was to be an overall shtick in the series. That was the way they greeted each other by rubbing the soles of their shoes together.

We mentioned that one episode of *Bourbon Street* was a rewrite of a *Conflict* episode, but there were other scripts remade that weren't quite so obvious. It happened during the infamous writers' strike that always seems to come up when you talk to people who worked at Warners. Grace Lee Whitney (best remembered as Yeoman Rand on *Star Trek*) was a contract player for WB, and she remembers the strike well:

"They would take a script for *Sunset Strip* and they would move it to *Hawaiian Eye* and just change the character names. And then they would move it on to *The Roaring 20's*—and change the character names."

Could they turn a private eye show like *Bourbon Street Beat* into a Western or vice versa? Yes—according to story editor Carl Stucke:

"The strike went on and we had some 123 episodes that we still had to deliver come hell or high water. We had writers that would come and say they didn't believe in the strike and were willing to work. But there were a lot of times where we had to take [for example] a *Lawman* and make something else out of it. We changed drama to comedy. You know, people would recognize it if we kept it the same, and yet that was the only way we could keep things going."

And Hugh Benson, when asked where scripts came from during the strike, replied: "There was a writer by the name of W. Hermanos who supplied scripts to us."

Now, if you consider that "hermanos" is the Spanish word for "brothers," it's not hard to figure out what the "W" stood for.

ANDREW DUGGAN

"I'm not too good, not too bad," Duggan once said of his work. But he was referring to his *painting* and not his acting. "I used to be very representational, making good likenesses. I guess that's the best that can be said." Fortunately for television, Duggan never realized his early aspirations of becoming a painter, although painting remained a long-time hobby.

Instead, he became an actor—an occupation foreshadowed by his high school days in Houston. Born December 28 somewhere around 1924 in Franklin, Indiana, he moved with his family to Texas when

The cast of *Bourbon Street Beat*: Andrew Duggan, Arlene Howell, Van Williams, and Richard Long.

his dad accepted a job as head football coach at Houston Lamar High. (Given *that* background, a birthplace so close to Notre Dame, and his 205 pound, six-foot-five frame, it's amazing that Andy didn't shoot for a football career.)

But it was dramatics that interested Andy at Lamar, and through his drama classes he won many awards including a scholarship to Indiana University—just 50 miles from his hometown. He majored in speech and ran into a professor in the department that steered him toward acting. That professor, Dr. Lee Norvelle, then president of the National Theatre Conference, got Duggan an audition for a leading role in the Maxwell Anderson play *The Eve of St. Mark*.

Next came the draft and three years of World War II service in which Andy was eventually shipped to Calcutta with a company that became known as "The Entertainment Production Unit." For the next couple of years he was touring throughout the China-Burma-India theatre of war, entertaining GI's anywhere they could find an audience.

"We had our own Chautauqua Company of eight GI's, but

before I start sounding like Bob Hope or a hero, let me remind you the war was almost over." Duggan explained (in a press release) there were no women in the troupe, but the troops never complained.

After his release, he secured a small role in the Chicago company of *Dream Girl*, and later he got a leading role in the same production when it went on the road with Lucille Ball starring. After that, it was back to Broadway. During the run of *Paint Your Wagon*, he married the show's lead dancer, Betty Logue. That was September 20, 1953.

Back in Los Angeles, Andy played a lawyer in a pilot called *Briefcase*, and then did a pilot film about a frontier doctor. Neither sold, but then came that fateful *Conflict* episode, "The Money."

There was a party after the show was filmed, and Bill Orr had mentioned that "The Money" might become a series. It was April of 1959 before the whole idea ended up in script form, and Orr started looking for Duggan to play a lead role. It was Hugh Benson who finally found Andrew back in New York. When he got the call from Benson, Andy thought the whole offer was a phony. Not so. Soon after, Duggan was being introduced to his partner-to-be, Richard Long, and more scripts were being written for *Bourbon Street*.

A typical episode featuring Cal Calhoun might have a friend, such as Lusti Weather accused of murder ("If a Body") or perhaps threatened or beaten (as Lusti and the Baron were in "The Ten-Percent Blues").

Cal Calhoun also mingled with other private eyes in other series such as the "Upbeat" episode of *77 Sunset Strip*. In a pre-*Bourbon Street Beat* episode of that series, he was pitted against Stu Bailey as the religious fanatic "Mr. Paradise." He also turned up from time to time in the WB westerns.

Duggan guested on many other TV shows including *12 O'Clock High*, *Cimarron Strip*, and *The Defenders*. His feature credits include *The Incredible Mr. Limpet*, *In Like Flint*, and *The Secret War of Harry Frigg*.

Today Duggan is still in front of the spotlight, doing such films as *M Station: Hawaii*, a CBS movie and series pilot produced by Jack Lord, and an episode of *Lou Grant*.

RICHARD LONG

The late Richard Long was discovered by casting director Jack Murton. According to the story, Murton was passing by Hollywood

Rex and Cal on the beat (note the upturned rearview mirror which might reveal cameraman).

High School during a rainstorm. He saw two girls who had missed their bus, and being a Good Samaritan, he stopped to give them a ride. In passing, Murton asked the youngsters if there was anything interesting on the Hollywood High drama schedule. They told him about the school's production of "Louisiana Susie" and how they were in love with the play's lead, Dick Long.

To make a "long" story short, Murton gave them his card, they gave it to Long, Long called Murton at Universal, he was cast in *Tomorrow Is Forever* with Orson Welles, and a seven year contract resulted. And somewhere in there he had to find the time to finish high school.

The way Dick explained it, it really *was* an accident: "I had no intention of becoming an actor. I took the senior drama class because it was a snap course, and I needed the credit for my English requirement."

Richard Long was one of six children born in Chicago to

commercial artist Stephen D. Long and wife Dale. One studio release puts his birthday on December 17, leaves out the year (1927), and gives a terse description of his eyes: *two*. (We have it on good authority that they were blue.)

The Long family moved from Chicago to Hollywood in 1944, which is how Dick happened to attend Hollywood High.

After being discovered, he appeared in several features before serving Uncle Sam in the Korean War. The army stint didn't last too long, so Dick returned to Universal where he appeared with Barbara Stanwyck in *All I Desire*.

In 1954 he married Susan Ball, an actress whose leg had been amputated after years of treatment following a hunting accident. The next year she died of cancer, and Dick spent a lot of time feeling sorry for himself.

Dick had already appeared in a movie with Mara Corday, the woman he would marry in January of 1957. But strangely enough the two never met on the set of *Playgirl*, in which Richard played a scoundrel.

In between the two marriages, Dick became involved in television, and he learned quickly that the small screen lacked the more leisurely pace of feature-making. "It was a whole new world and my education in acting really began," he said. "My professional jubilee had finished." Up to that point Dick had considered life to be a perpetual holiday because he never identified acting with work.

His video debut was in *Climax* with Mary Astor. Then came *Reader's Digest*, *Lux Video Theatre*, *Schlitz Playhouse*, and *The Millionaire*.

In March of 1958 Long was signed to a contract at Warner Bros. where he was considered for a variety of projects such as an early attempt of *Room for One More*. That didn't work out, so he became a regular guest star on other WB shows including *Maverick* and *77 Sunset Strip*. He scored well as a deranged killer in an early episode of *Strip* called "One False Step" in which he conceived a plan involving "murder swapping." He was back soon in another episode called "The Fifth Stair," and those roles led to a $100,000 offer from a rival studio.

The situation with Dick's contract may have caused the studio to make an announcement that he would star in a series. But the early announcement that he would be in *The Alaskans* was changed when Bill Orr told him he would join Duggan on *Bourbon Street* instead.

This time the announcement stuck, and as of late 1959, Long had his first starring role as a regular in a TV show. His assignments for

"Randolph and Calhoun" took him (as one press release put it) "from the shadowed side streets of the fabled French Quarter to the eerie, mist-shrouded bayous, to the banks of the sullen, surging Mississippi, and out into the storm-lashed Gulf of Mexico." Sometimes, even farther than that. In one episode, "Last Exit," Rex was hired by a man whose son had been killed to travel all the way to South America to trap the murderer.

Following the too-short run of *Beat*, Rex Randolph lived on for another year on *Strip*. Then a bit later his old movie role with Barbara Stanwyck helped land him a part in *The Big Valley* which continued for five years. He was able to direct himself in a few episodes of that popular series. Still later he assumed a starring role in the CBS sit-com, *Nanny and the Professor*. (Ironic, since his brother *was* a professor at Southern Methodist University.)

Other TV credits included *Stump the Stars* (he was a regular), *Twilight Zone, Thriller, The Outlaws*, and *Alfred Hitchcock Presents*. His many feature credits included three Ma and Pa Kettle films. In 1961 he did *Under the Yum Yum Tree* on stage on the West Coast while doing TV roles during the day.

Dick always said he had two big loves in life. One was acting; the other was golf. Dick had played golf since he was 13 and became known as "Long on the drive" for the great distance he got off his tee shots.

During the filming of *Nanny and the Professor* Long wrote, "There was a time when I logged almost as many miles as the pros, following the Professional Golfers Association circuit to play in the pro-amateur contests. But I stopped the PGA about five years ago."

He added that the way a man plays golf can be a clue to his character. "If you cheat on a golf course, you usually cheat in life by taking the easy and devious short cuts, never squarely facing a situation."

Dick himself cheated on the course. Only once, but it gave him a great deal of pleasure:

"My partner and I were on the green of a par three hole as an unseasonable fog crept in and about us. A ball sailed from nowhere and hit me softly on the leg after it had taken a bounce. I quickly picked up the ball, dropped it in the hole, then I began to scream, 'Ole!' When the man who had hit the ball emerged from a fog bank, I patted him on the back. To this day he still believes that he made a hole-in-one. I think it cost him nearly $200 before he could leave the country club bar that night."

Richard Long died of a heart ailment on December 22, 1974 in Los Angeles.

Bourbon Street Beat — Series Index

The Taste of Ashes

Investigating the mysterious death of his partner, Rex is told it's suicide. But he doesn't believe it — and neither does police Lt. Cal Calhoun. After the case is solved, Randolph and Calhoun team up.

The Mourning Cloak

Rex investigates the sinister plot to gain control of a plantation on a rich oil site. Sherman "Scat Man" Crothers appears.

Torch Song for Trumpet

Cal tries to straighten out embittered trumpet player Kip Kiley — who's headed for more trouble after getting out of prison. Kip is framed for murder. Richard Rust is Kip.

Woman in the River

Rex, Cal, Melody and Kenny go into action when a shy college boy reports his wife is missing. Denver Pyle appears.

Girl in Trouble

Accused of murdering "benefactor" Howard Hamilton, Susan Wood is in bad trouble until Calhoun proves syndicate killer Frankie Mato murdered him by mistake. Faith Domergue is Susan.

The Tiger Moth

When a friend of Rex's is murdered, Rex is told that the dead man's girl friend is the sister of a recluse. Rex suspects the girl's father is the killer. But he finds that the girl has a problem — a multiple personality.

Secret of Hyacinth Bayou

Cal, helping an old friend, learns he killed a man accidentally twenty years ago and brought up the man's daughter as his own. A youth has found out and is blackmailing. Robert Colbert appears.

Invitation to a Murder

Randolph is hired to find out who sent formal invitations to the murder of New Orleans politico Jonathan Deckbar. But the man's campaign manager gets nailed instead. Kathleen Crowley appears.

Mrs. Viner Vanishes

A hotel guest becomes infuriated when employees of the hotel disclaim any knowledge of his having checked in with his wife. Lusti gets Cal to look for the missing woman.

Light Touch of Terror

After his friend Jack is killed at a campus party, Kenny proves the killer is a former student who's a homicidal maniac out to kill those he blames for his many failures. Sue Anne Langdon appears.

The Golden Beetle

Old letters from Jean Lafitte are found telling where to find pirate treasure. (The letters are in code.) The man who found the letters is murdered for them, and when Rex and Cal find the crooks, Rex is forced to decipher the code. Mala Powers appears.

The Black Magnolia

Cal Calhoun helps attractive Laura Montgomery to recover $75,000 hidden by her grandfather on a Mississippi riverboat many years ago.

Portrait of Lenore

Rex learns a painting of the dead Lenore—painted by her husband—has been stolen during Mardi Gras. A veiled woman-in-black exchanges the painting for $10,000. Rex reveals that the woman-in-black is Lenore, facially disfigured from an air crash. Madlyn Rhue is Lenore.

Kill with Kindness

Cal takes a handy man job with eccentric, generous Maude St. John, whom attractive Lydia (her nurse) suspects is being poisoned. There are plenty of suspects for Rex and Cal.

Inside Man

When his brother-in-law is killed by Luke Ballard, a psychotic gang leader, Rex joins Luke in jail to obtain evidence. Luke engineers an escape, and Rex comes along though Luke is suspicious of him.

Find My Face

Rex and Cal, with the aid of Lusti, Melody and Kenny, are involved in the mystery of a band drummer. It seems that the drummer's wife has conspired with an insurance man to have a non-licensed plastic surgeon make the drummer look like the insurance man. They plan to kill the drummer to make the crooked insurance agent declared legally dead.

Knock on Any Tombstone

Rex is hired to find out who's sending voodoo threats to an elderly ballet teacher who's finally murdered. His granddaughter is the next intended victim.

Key to the City

Cal and Kenny seek Timothy Talbot, a man they've never seen, who's carrying dynamite documents to New Orleans to wreck the careers of crooked politicians there.

The 10% Blues

By Hugh Benson and Dick Nelson: Cal and Rex tangle with a talent agency which uses gangster tactics to acquire clients. Tris Coffin and Sandy Koufax are in the cast.

Melody in Diamonds

Melody is thrilled when Hungarian shop owner Magda loans her fabulous jewels to wear at a costume ball at Mardi Gras. But the jewels turn out to be fake, and it's a plot to collect insurance money. Rex apprehends Magda.

The House of Ledezan

A millionaire leaves $50,000 for Rex Randolph to discover if his death was natural. But Rex is offered $100,000 not to investigate. Neil Hamilton; Ted Knight as Capt. Brent Dawson.

Target of Hate

Dale Wellington plans to assassinate his dead father's political enemy Kroeger from Rex and Cal's office as Kroeger emerges from Absinthe House. Richard Chamberlain is Wellington; James Coburn as Buzz Griffin.

The Missing Queen

Donna Lou, a beauty contest entrant, is blackmailed by her ex-husband; then he is murdered. Another contestant, Ginny, aids Cal and Rex in solving the case. Diane McBaine is Ginny.

Neon Nightmare

To help his foster brother, Jeff Tolliver, win an election, Calhoun goes to Midas County to get the goods on Jeff's corrupt rival. Richard Deacon appears.

Wall of Silence

Rex learns that a group of European refugees are being blackmailed for protecting an orphan refugee boy whom they smuggled into the U.S. illegally. Two murders occur before Rex exposes the blackmailer. James Drury and Diane McBaine appear.

Twice Betrayed

A remake of "The Money" episode of *Conflict*: Sgt. Bogart, a good cop

gone crooked, dupes Cal into helping him rob crooked Ferguson. Lila, for whom Bogart stole the money, runs out on him with the dough. Cal finds out the truth and helps Bogart track down Lila, but not before Ferguson has found and killed her. Robert Colbert; Judson Pratt.

Swampfire

Rex investigates weird goings-on in Bayou Swamp. Cajun workers for an oil company quit work, fearing an evil "entity" formed of marsh fire.

If a Body

Triggered by the murder of a nightclub singer, which puts Lusti Weather under suspicion, Calhoun uncovers a diamond smuggling ring.

Six Hours to Midnight

Unable to get another reprieve for his client who's to be executed in six hours, a lawyer turns to Cal Calhoun.

Last Exit

Also seen as "Escape to Tampico" on *Maverick*: Rex Randolph is hired by a crippled jewelry designer to find the murderer of his son.

Deadly Persuasion

Written but never produced for *Conflict*: Cal unintentionally plays a major part in the frustration of an attempt by 16 year-old Billy Norton to break out of a reformatory.

Suitable for Framing

Produced as "The Well-Selected Frame" on *77 Sunset Strip*: Framed for the murder of millionaire Lucian St. Claire by his wife Hilary and her presumed-dead first husband Mark Evans, Rex goes to trial, is freed, then tricks Hilary into admitting her guilt to police. Barbara Lord is Hilary.

False Identity

The half-mad part-owner of a trucking firm fakes his own murder; then returns to demand money from his partner. Cal suspects the man is still alive. Robert Colbert.

Green Hell

Masquerading as a newspaper reporter, Randolph joins Major Hernandez's party in retrieving the body and papers of a dictator from a plane crash in the jungle. The papers are plans for an atomic bomb.

Ferry to Algiers

Cal and Rex are off fishing, so Kenny is hired to guard an elderly store keeper in Algiers, a town near New Orleans. Diane McBain appears.

Wagon Show

Story by Hugh Benson: Cal is hired to find an escaped killer chimpanzee but goes into the circus ring disguised as a clown and traps circus owner who committed the murder disguised as an ape.

Interrupted Wedding

Fortyish twins Henry and Norman Lombard have held a 30 year grudge against John Crane, who caused their parents' deaths in a car accident. Rex and lady dick Betty Jane Robinson trace a bomb planted at Crane's daughter's wedding to Norman. Whit Bissell has the double role. Randy Stuart as Betty Jane.

Reunion

Sixteen-year-old Ellen runs away from a boarding school and places an ad in the paper for her dad to contact her. Cal is hired to find the girl. Ellen's dad is an underworld boss.

Teresa

A playboy, in love with the owner of a gambling casino, visits her on her delta island home and is captured by bank robbers. Rex is asked to enter the case, and he finds the crooks, but Hurricane Teresa forces them to stick together for survival.

8
The Soft Island Breeze

ABC (1 hour)—debuted October 7, 1959
Format: Adventure-drama of private investigators operating out of
Hawaii
Cast: Anthony Eisley .... Tracy Steele
Robert Conrad .... Tom Lopaka
Connie Stevens .... Cricket Blake
Grant Williams .... Greg MacKenzie
Poncie Ponce .... Kim
Troy Donahue .... Phil Barton
Tina Cole .... Sunny Day
Mel Prestidge .... Lt. Danny Quon
Doug Mossman .... Moke
Executive Producer: William T. Orr
Producers: Stanley Niss; Charles Hoffman
Theme Music: "Hawaiian Eye" by Mack David and Jerry Livingston
Location: Filmed in Hawaii and Hollywood

"We are accused of copying ourselves all the time," says William
T. Orr. But there was good reason for it, and Orr enjoys explaining
that it's simply a big success story.

Dick Pinkham of the Bates Agency, the company that sold commercials on *77 Sunset Strip*, had informed Warners in New York that
if another show of that type could be had, there were advertisers
waiting in line to buy it. It didn't take long for New York to get word
to the executive producer for television.

"It was Easter and I was down in Palm Springs. New York called
and gave me the story." The Warners man in the Big Apple wanted

a detective show set in the Caribbean. But Orr couldn't quite see that.

"I had been to the Caribbean. I had been to Jamaica, Nassau, and the Bahamas and all that and I said, 'I don't like the Caribbean.' First off, it's more English than American and it's got a great many natives and you don't get the polyglot of people that would come to Hawaii. I thought Hawaii would be a great place to put the show."

Orr promised to send in an outline of a proposed show the following Monday once he had returned to Hollywood. He hung up the phone, called off a tennis match, pulled out a pad and started writing down all he knew about what goes on in Hawaii.

And if you don't like that explanation of the show's creation ... there's an alternate version. Warners story editor Jack Emanuel claimed *he* got the job of outlining the new series (to be called *The Islander*) while on a combination business and pleasure trip to what would soon be the 50th state. Emanuel says *he* changed the locale from the Caribbean to Hawaii.

Well, anyway, the idea of *The Islander* as described to Emanuel bored him stiff—he just couldn't get interested in the project. But upon his arrival on island soil, things began to happen.

First of all, Emanuel was taken with the cabbie who drove him from the airport to the hotel. The tanned Polynesian kept suggesting his sister-in-law to do his laundry instead of the hotel. (She'd do it for half-price ... and even iron around the buttons.)

That's the *first* thing that happened. The second was just as important.

Emanuel got in touch with the daughter of a friend from Hollywood. And what a girl! She was a beachcomber ... she would sketch your picture on the beach ... she sold reducing equipment ... her name was Cricket. *Cricket?*

So gradually, Jack Emanuel was becoming more and more intrigued with Hawaii, and less interested in the Caribbean. And with the mixture of Polynesians, Japanese, Caucasians, and you-name-it on the Islands, he was ready to tell Warners that Hawaii was the place for the story possibilities the studio wanted.

When he arrived back in Hollywood a couple of weeks later, he had a 16 page outline for *The Islander*. The leading characters were to be house detectives who did free-lance private-eye work from their plush offices in a resort hotel. They would be aided by two colorful supporting characters—a tanned Polynesian cab driver with *almost* as many relatives as the driver Emanuel had known *and* a pretty nightclub singer with the unlikely name of Cricket.

Everyone does agree, however, that there was a meeting in Bill Orr's office after all had returned from vacation. Orr says, "We got the guys together—Hugh [Benson], our story editor [Emanuel], and a couple of other fellows. We knew we were going to have house detectives. So we came up with the idea of putting them in a hotel. Our story editor had just returned from a vacation in Hawaii. Jack came up with the idea of the cab driver...."

So the package was explained to ABC honchos and representatives of some sponsors and it sold without having a cast or script or even a pilot.

The name *The Islander* was dropped (the name would be picked up later as James Philbrook and William Reynolds starred in *The Islanders*, with an "s" on ABC—a show that would last only a few months), and another name, *Diamond Head* was considered and rejected. Orr says the title wasn't decided on until a few days after the meeting when Dick Pinkham dropped by.

"We told him the idea of the show. He loved it and said, 'What's the title?' We said we didn't have one. In the course of conversing about how we'd do it and how the show would work, we decided to go to lunch. On the way, he and I were walking together and I said, 'We should have Hawaii in there. It's a private eye show—*Hawaiian Eye*.' He said, 'Isn't that a little corny?' I said, 'Possibly. But I think it's good. It lends itself to the music.'" At this point in the interview, Bill paused to sing a few bars of the theme song.

"So, around Monday or Tuesday, we had a 40 out of 52 weeks sale. We had no cast; we just sold the show. And we got Bobby Conrad who worked for us in several things; we liked him and were waiting to find something for him." Orr had been hoping to build a series around Conrad. "We do that; we'd spot people and either put them under contract if we could use them in the other shows or keep an eye on them and hopefully grab them when we got something."

Jack Emanuel wasn't quite as happy with the casting. After the show hit the air, he complained that the two leads, Tracy Steele (Anthony Eisley) and Tom Lopaka (Conrad), were nothing like he had in mind. Lopaka, in fact, was supposed to have been half Polynesian. Emanuel left Warners about the time the series debuted and went to NBC where he said he tried to forget about the whole thing.

Meanwhile, *Eye* got off to a precarious start. Pitted against *Perry Como* (who had the advantage of being in color), *Eye* was losing in a big way. The reviews were not kind either; *Variety* complained that the show's mysteries were "snail's paced." *Como* was in no danger.

By the end of the first season things were beginning to turn around. *Eye* somehow caught up with *Como* and got itself renewed for a second season. Ratings were no problem after that, and the series lasted through 1963.

You'll recall that *Bourbon Street Beat* bit the dust considerably earlier. Since both shows were supposed to be *Sunset Strip* clones in different locations, what could the difference have been?

It probably *wasn't* the leading men. While *Strip* flourished with Bailey and Spencer, *Eye* provided Lopaka and Steele, and *Beat* featured Randolph and Calhoun. All six men were very capable actors, likeable in their roles, and extremely macho. To be sure, Bob Conrad and Tony Eisley were a big factor in the Wednesday night tune-in for *Eye*, but that's not to say that Duggan and Long caused a tune-out for their show. It *must* have been something else.

Many folks directly involved with the show were quick to point out the vacation-like atmosphere of the sets. With all the beautiful scenery of the Islands and the leis and the ocean, how could a little thing like murder or blackmail spoil the mood? Director Mark Sand-rich, Jr. once commented that even the villains in the show seemed to be on vacation.

Producer Stanley Niss agreed. He gave *Eye* the edge over *Bourbon Street Beat* because of the Island scenery as opposed to the dark alleyways and gloomy backgrounds of the Crescent City. But Niss also mentioned Connie Stevens and Poncie Ponce as big factors in the ratings.

It'd be hard to disagree with that.

In another show full of the patented Warner Bros. "shtick," much of it was provided by those two—in fact Miss Stevens was often called a female Kookie. Part of her shtick was the nightclub act—the light, bouncy numbers she would sing each week.

Connie recognized the "upbeat" rhythm of the series, and she worked hard to make her part fit. She envisioned Cricket as a girl in love with life; naive, but not stupid, and ambitious. She loved Steele and Lopaka, but only in a "chummy" sort of way; a heavy romance would have detracted from the image she was trying to maintain. Besides, how could she show favoritism for one of the Eyes over the other? (She was saving herself for Troy Donahue, perhaps?) She liked Kim (Poncie Ponce) because she found him interesting and because he too was caught up in the glamour of private investigating.

If Cricket was *Eye*'s answer to Kookie, then Kim could be com-pared to Roscoe. He didn't play the nags, but with relatives by the dozens and hundreds of other connections, the ubiquitous cabbie often came up with the same type of information. His schticks? Relatives, jokes, a ukulele, and his pupule (crazy hat).

Like *77 Sunset Strip*, *Hawaiian Eye* went through some changes during its long run. With the third season came a new member of the firm in the person of Grant Williams. Williams, as Greg MacKenzie, had been brought in a few times for special investigations in the previous season. Now he was part of the rotation of leading men.

That was the only season with three full-time eyes. The next year Anthony Eisley dropped out of the cast, leaving Conrad and Williams to share primary duties. They *did* have some help, though.

With *SurfSide 6* off the air by that time, teen idol Troy Donahue was added to the cast. He left his character of Sandy Winfield II on the shelf and assumed a new role—that of Phil Barton, director of special events at the hotel where *everything* seemed to happen in Honolulu.

Says Bill Orr, "I think the network suggested we'd strengthen *Hawaiian Eye* if we put Troy in it and added him to the cast. I don't recall whether it strengthened it or didn't, but it was a network suggestion."

Finally Connie Stevens, as Cricket, had a romantic interest. As the studio explained it, Troy and Connie would be sweethearts, but the situation would be complicated when Troy would run into beautiful girls (is there any other kind in Hawaii) who would hire him to direct their tours and social events.

Lest we forget, Phil Barton occasionally helped MacKenzie and Lopaka crack a case. No sense letting all that experience gained in Miami go to waste!

Not long after Donahue was added to the cast, Connie Stevens left the show to be replaced by equally beautiful Tina Cole in the role of Sunny Day. (Didn't *anybody* have an ordinary name?)

Warner Bros. cameras kept returning to Honolulu and Waikiki Beach to keep the flavor of the Islands in each episode of *Eye*, which was actually shot in Hollywood. (If Bill Orr had had his way, all that tropical scenery would have been shot on color film stock so that the series could have been sold to syndication in color. He failed to convince higher-ups.) Even in black and white, the lure of Hawaii inevitably came up in reviews of the show. And noting the locale, Cricket, and the high number of well-endowed girls in the series, a *TV Guide* reviewer in 1960 proclaimed it "almost as good" as *77 Sunset Strip*.

ROBERT CONRAD

One day in the late 50's, an actress asked Bob Conrad to help her with an audition for William T. Orr. He did and soon wound up with a contract and later a starring role as Tom Lopaka in *Hawaiian Eye*. That was the first role to be cast for the show, and it was the first major role for Conrad on his way to becoming a superstar of television.

Bob had been interested in performing for most of his life. He was born March 1, 1935, the son of publicist Jacqueline Hubbard, and by the time he reached high school he was on stage. About that time he came up with the name "Robert Conrad" by switching his first and middle names and dropping his last name, "Falk."

Soon he was making the rounds of Chicago's major hotels with bandleaders Johnny Gilbert, Jim Redd, and a jazz trio. He also worked some of the *less* impressive places on the outskirts of the city. And not *all* of the work he was doing was on stage.

Before he got fed up with his situation and headed for Hollywood, Bob was married (to Joan Kenlay since 1952) and was supporting two daughters by working as a delivery boy for a dairy, by serving as a dock hand for consolidated shipping, and by putting in some hours in a Skokie candy factory. In his *spare* time he sang and kept an eye on TV.

In fact, Bob says he decided to try television acting after watching other guys do things that he thought he could do better.

Another thing that helped him along was a chance meeting with *The Rebel*, Nick Adams. Adams thought Conrad might be a good actor, so he helped him obtain a Screen Actors Guild card, an agent, and finally, after 9 months of no work, a few small parts.

Some of those parts came when agent Henry Rackin became a casting director at Ziv Studios. Conrad got work in *Sea Hunt, Bat Masterson*, and *Highway Patrol*. Then came the break with Warner Bros. which was kind of ironic since Bob had always wanted to sign with that studio. (His idols were John Garfield, Humphrey Bogart, and James Cagney.)

Bob says his small stature actually paid off for a change; his 5'7" height was perfect for a screen test with a small actress named Jennie Maxwell. (Remember the infamous story of giant Clint Walker's screen kiss with an actress who had to stand tip-toed on a box?)

So Conrad got a contract and made appearances on several Warners shows — *Lawman, Maverick*, and *77 Sunset Strip* — before

Robert Conrad as detective Tom Lopaka.

getting the featured role in *Hawaiian Eye*. Even star billing didn't solve Bob's financial difficulties, though. He drew $250 a week the first season, and then when the show caught on he was raised to $315 (and they let him park on the lot, he says).

He was never too happy with his deal.

When *Eye* finally left the air, Conrad's star-studded TV career continued; he was soon playing agent James West in the cult-favorite *The Wild Wild West* (1965) on CBS. In and around series he did some less-than-critically-acclaimed films like *Hotel Madrid, Palm Springs Week-end,* and *Young Dillinger*. Later he did a couple of TV movies from the Jack Webb factory called *The D.A.: Murder One* and *The D.A.: Conspiracy to Kill*. An attempt at doing a series from the movies didn't make it. He also had a series called *Assignment: Vienna*.

Then came a couple of TV jobs that will be remembered: *Black Sheep Squadron* and the mini-series *Centennial*.

The saga of *Black Sheep Squadron* is a story in itself. You'll recall it began in September, 1976 as *Baa Baa Black Sheep* opposite *Happy*

Days and *Laverne and Shirley*. With those two shows rated one and two in the national Nielsens, you can imagine how well *Black Sheep* did.

But the show had two things going for it. First of all, it sported some spectacular aerial combat footage from the Defense Department's World War II archives, and secondly Bob Conrad *liked* playing the role of fighter pilot Gregory (Pappy) Boyington. Calling on his best fighting instincts, he went to bat for the show and managed to do alone what it took hundreds of thousands of *Star Trek* fans to do: he talked NBC into keeping the show alive.

The fight began after *Black Sheep* was cancelled after the initial season, even though it had managed to hold a respectable audience against ABC's top comedy shows. Conrad and the shows executive producer attended an NBC affiliates' meeting in Los Angeles where they solicited the sympathy of quite a few station managers who then threw *their* support behind the series. All that impressed NBC's Irwin Segelstein, who ordered more shows and had the name changed to *Black Sheep Squadron* so people would know it wasn't a children's show.

The show was cancelled again, brought back, moved to a time slot opposite *Charlie's Angels*, crept up in the ratings, and moved to still another time slot before NBC cancelled it and made the decision stick.

Centennial came next for Bob Conrad—a show he considers some of his finest work. But he almost didn't get the part. Universal first wanted Robert Blake for the role of French trapper "Pasquinel." When Blake couldn't do it, Charles Bronson was offered the job. That didn't work either, and at the last minute Conrad got the role.

There were times when the producers almost regretted having chosen Bob. His famed assertiveness caused problems at times; contract stipulations gave him twelve hours between work calls; his false beard bugged him on the set. Still, it all worked and *Centennial* was acclaimed by the critics.

ANTHONY EISLEY

Hawaiian Eye was a first for Anthony Eisley—the name, not the actor. Up until Bill Orr signed him for *Eye*, he had gone by his real name, Fred Eisley.

"It was something of a compromise," Fred/Anthony said. "I

agreed that 'Fred' doesn't have much rhythm to it, and Mr. Orr came up with 'Anthony' and agreed my last name had become something of a fixture in the theatre."

So it was *Anthony* Eisley who signed the long-term contract, grew a moustache, and joined Bob Conrad on a trip to Hawaii to film background scenes.

It was *Fred* Eisley, though, who was born in Philadelphia on January 19, 1925, the son of a division manager for the Scott Paper Company. Although Frederick Senior had no connection with the theatre, he and his wife were sympathetic to their son's ambitions.

Fred Jr. left home for three years of naval training at Franklin and Marshall College, Pennsylvania, and in 1947 he got a B.A. degree from the University of Miami. Later that year he made his professional stage debut in *A Slight Case of Murder* with James Dunn, playing in Redding, Pennsylvania.

Two years later he made his big time debut as Wiley in the Chicago company of *Mr. Roberts* which starred John Forsythe and Jackie Cooper. The troupe ended up touring the whole country and got a boost in January, 1951 when Henry Fonda joined the cast. That also led to a big break for Eisley.

On March 1st, while playing St. Louis, Fonda suffered a bad case of laryngitis. As Fonda's understudy, Fred was called on to handle the starring role. By the way, it was that same day that Fred married Judith Tubbs, whom he had met a few months earlier while in Chicago.

Later came a role as Alan Seymour in the Broadway show *Picnic*; then the part of Chuck Wright (which belonged to Gig Young in the film) in the New York production of *The Desperate Hours*.

In addition to the stage, Fred appeared in more than 200 live or filmed TV shows before getting the *Eye* role. In New York he was Barbara Britton's leading man in the soaper *Date with Life*, and he made the credits of *Philco TV Playhouse*, *Goodyear TV Playhouse*, *Robert Montgomery Presents*, and *Armstrong Circle Theatre*.

In 1958 Fred moved his wife and two children out to Hollywood where he appeared in the ABC presentations of *Navy Log* and *Walter Winchell File*. In addition, he secured parts in *Climax*, *Studio One*, and *Playhouse 90*. For Warner Bros. he appeared as Carter Henry, a suitor to Barbara Rush in *The Young Philadelphians*.

Just before being tapped for the Tracy Steele role, Eisley was starring in *Who Was That Lady I Saw You With?* at night while putting in days as Kansas City cop John Cassiano in the series *Pete Kelly's Blues*.

All that under the name of "Fred." You can understand why his family had trouble hearing the head of the household called "Tony."

Eisley, by the way, did some screen writing and even produced some scripts for *Hawaiian Eye*.

GRANT WILLIAMS

Grant Williams prefers to be remembered for what may be the smallest role in the history of films — *The Incredible Shrinking Man*. That 1957 science-fiction thriller from Universal-International got excellent reviews and developed a cult following while propelling Williams to star status.

That was four years before Williams became a regular on *Eye* in the role of investigator Greg MacKenzie. As we mentioned earlier, MacKenzie had done so-called "special assignments" for the Hawaiian Eye firm before. That was to test him in the role while he was still tied up with Warner Bros. feature films. During his off-and-on shots on *Eye*, Williams was appearing in *Susan Slade* (with Connie Stevens) and *The Couch*, a psychological drama.

Up until his starring role in *Eye*, Williams had done 14 features, 49 stage plays, and over 70 TV shows. Of those, his favorites included *The Incredible Shrinking Man* and Walt Disney's *The Peter Tschaikovsky Story* on ABC-TV, in which he played the title role.

John Grant Williams was born in New York City on August 18, 1931, the son of Thomas Ian Williams, an insurance man for Metropolitan Life. (Mr. Williams, originally from Glasgow, Scotland once won the Victoria Cross, Britain's highest decoration for valor.)

Grant spent a couple of years in Glasgow attending school but came back to New York to graduate from Andrew Jackson High in Queens. In 1948 he continued his education at Queens College, but he soon dropped out to serve in the Air Force. After tours of duty at B-29 bases in Okinawa, Japan, and Korea, he finished up college at Columbia University and secured a Bachelor of Arts degree.

Like so many others, Grant got into acting by accident. At age 12 he attended a summer camp near Garrison, New York, and won a role in a theatre there in *Ah, Wilderness*. During his military stint he produced, directed, and acted in shows in Illinois and in Tokyo, and he appeared in USO shows.

By the time he was out of the service, he was hooked on the profession, and so he decided to study at the Carnegie Hall Dramatic

Grant Williams portrays Greg MacKenzie in action.

Studios. After that, it was a string of acting jobs that led up to his movie and TV roles.

In 1953 he entered the annual auditions of the Barter Theatre in Abingdon, Virginia; he won, naturally, over four hundred other contestants. The prize was a series of leads in Barter stage productions.

Next came more dramatic training with Lee Strasberg, summer stock, and a few Broadway plays. Grant also got into television on the East Coast, appearing in *Alcoa Theatre* productions and other shows.

His first Hollywood picture was *Red Sundown*; he played a killer. He also did *Away All Boats* and *Four Girls in Town* at U-I. Other major roles came in *Written on the Wind* (1956), a sci-fi thriller called *The Monolith Monsters* (1957), *PT 109* (1963), and *Doomsday* (1972).

Grant's interests include concert piano and religion.

CONNIE STEVENS

An ABC press release dated September 11, 1959 read: *If this be type casting, make the most of it.* And did they ever! Young sexy, lively, bouncy Connie Stevens not only played the part of Chryseis "Cricket" Blake on *Hawaiian Eye*, she also was a major motion picture star for Warners. Later she became the first artist signed by the company's new recording division. But let's start at the beginning.

Concetta Ann Ingolia was born in Brooklyn, August 8, 1938, to Peter and Eleanor Ingolia. Her father, known professionally as Teddy Stevens, was a professional nightclub entertainer.

Concetta Ann attended Brooklyn schools (and a few in New Jersey) and holds the distinction of being the first girl ever to be impeached from a study body office at her high school. She was president of the freshman class, see, and she managed to convince the faculty that it would be a "neat" idea to tune in the final game of the world series for the whole student body to hear. Well, as it turned out, the student body was more rabid over baseball than the average class of today might be expected to be. As the game got more and more exciting, Connie's classmates got more excited. Bedlam broke out! The faculty decided the freshmen needed another President. Connie *still* managed to snag "most popular" and "most likely to succeed."

Connie's freshman class must have been psychic. She was already on the road to that success by age 15 when she and her father moved to Los Angeles. She enrolled at Sacred Professional School. Soon she became a singer with a theatre group and got a small part in the Hollywood Repertory Theatre's production of *Finian's Rainbow*.

Connie's first big break came when Jerry Lewis signed her for his leading lady in his York production, *Rock-a-bye Baby*.

In 1957 she did a TV commercial for a bakery because her agent, Byron Griffith, said that would be a good way to break into movies. Griffith could easily have been a member of the psychic freshman class because soon after he had Connie working in small roles in *Eighteen and Anxious* and *Young and Dangerous*.

From those roles came leads in TV's *Matinee Theatre* and the movie *Drag Strip Riot*, then a part in *Sugarfoot*. (Hey, that's a Warner Bros. show!) So Warners had Connie. She was signed to do two features a year for seven years, TV roles (the part of Cricket assigned *before* a script for the first episode had been written), and records.

Connie, as we said, helped kick off Warner Bros. Records with a string of hits. One of the first was called "Kookie, Kookie Lend Me

**Anthony Eisley as Tracy Steele and Connie Stevens as Cricket Blake
stumble upon ... what?**

Your Comb" which she did with Edd Byrnes. Another song, "Sixteen
Reasons" made it to the top of the charts.

In the movies Connie made love to Troy Donahue—a romance
that would click well enough to be transferred to *Eye* during the later
seasons. First, they co-starred in *Parrish*, then in *Susan Slade*, two 1961
Warner films. In a press release, Connie talked about her role as "Lucy"
in *Parrish*: "I actually learned how to plant tobacco, but it's not really
something every girl should necessarily know. What really fascinated

me was working with Claudette Colbert, Karl Malden, Dean Jagger and, of course, Troy Donahue who is my love in the picture."

But outside of press releases, Connie was not all that fascinated with Troy—*Parrish* the thought! She tolerated him, as he did her. Each found no time for the other during off work hours. When asked about each other, Connie and Troy somehow managed to come up with a compliment that really wasn't. Connie might say, "Troy is ... well ... friendly." Troy might say, "Connie is spirited."

Neither went out of his/her way to compliment the other's acting ability. They *did* agree on some things, though. Both felt that TV had gotten into a pattern made hard to break by its very success. Both felt TV was done too "hurry hurry" with too many business decisions mixed in. Both felt they were unduly snubbed by the critics who joked about their good looks and called them "America's Darlings." Both wanted stardom, and got it; more often than not, their names saw print together in fan magazines. Dozens of articles were published touting their on-and-off-screen romance. Later when Connie and Troy were no longer a hot item, Connie was making headlines on her own.

At 24 she married actor James Stacey. Newspapers all over the country went into great detail about the "biggest Hollywood wedding in recent years." Connie and the 27-year-old Stacey were wed in a Catholic Church in Sherman Oaks in the San Fernando Valley—seven hundred people attended the ceremony with more than a hundred fans waiting outside. A list of those present sounds like a Hollywood Who's Who: Ozzie Nelson (with Rick and David), Gary Vinson, Dwayne Hickman, John Ashley, Deborah Walley, Marlo Thomas...

Connie's gown had a seven-foot train, and she wore it to the altar, escorted by her father. The marriage didn't last, though, and Connie's relationship with Stacey took a tragic twist years later when he lost an arm and a leg in a near-fatal motorcycle accident.

On January 31, 1967, Connie was sporting an engagement ring from Eddie Fisher. That union also ended in divorce.

More headlines: Dateline Hollywood, 1973—Connie Stevens was named to the board of sponsors for surgery involving South Vietnamese children injured in the war.

Dateline Hollywood, 1974—Controversy over Connie Stevens' portrayal of Marilyn Monroe in a TV movie on ABC. The film, *The Sex Symbol*, called "a thinly-veiled biography of Marilyn" was scheduled by the network, then yanked just a couple of weeks before its airdate. The word floating around Hollywood was that Arthur Miller (one of Monroe's husbands) had talked to the network. Other "interested parties" who thought they might be easily identified in the script also were said to be urging the net to take editing shears to the print.

The script was fiction—a conglomeration of sex symbols. But Connie said the part was unmistakably Marilyn Monroe, and *that's* the way she played it. Connie even posed nude to recreate the famous calendar scene.

The girl in *The Sex Symbol* even had a fling with a politician, and it was said that ABC heard from political forces who didn't want the gossip about Marilyn and John Kennedy to be exploited.

Connie said the two-hour film was chopped to 90 minutes, and finally made the air without the nude scenes or the Kennedy references, and with watered down versions of the Arthur Miller sequences.

Headlines continue: Dateline Reno, 1977—Thieves stole six thousand dollars worth of gowns and accessories from Ms. Stevens' wardrobe at Harrah's where she was appearing. That included a five thousand dollar gown made partly of fur.

Dateline Malibu, 1978—Connie rested at home following five days of treatment for a blood clot in her right knee. She had entered Los Angeles New Hospital after complaining of a swollen leg—she had taken a nasty fall during a dance act in Las Vegas. She responded well to treatment.

In between headlines, Connie was still making movies. Some that we haven't mentioned include *Two on a Guillotine* (1964), *Never Too Late* (1965), *Mr. Jericho* (TV-1970), *The Grissom Gang* (1971), and *Scorchy* (1976). And don't forget those Ace Hardware Store commercials.

Unlike some other Warners stars, Connie has stayed off television for the most part since the days of *Hawaiian Eye*. Of course, she has made a few TV appearances—such as an episode of *Fantasy Island* in which she shared billing with ... Troy Donahue.

PONCIE PONCE

To weld ... or to act. That was the big question of Hawaiian-born Poncie Ponce. Ponce, whose given name is Ponciano, was one of five brothers and two sisters born to Maria Tabac. *She* supported the welding career.

When Poncie completed high school in Honokaa, Hawaii, he attended Hawaii Vocational School to learn the trade. His future in welding was put on a back burner when the mail came one day, and in addition to a trade school diploma, it contained a "greeting from the President." In 1953, Private Ponce was on his way to Germany for two years of duty.

While overseas, Ponce practiced singing, playing his ukulele, and worked up an impressive repertoire of impersonations. He put the practice to use in Munich night spots.

After his discharge, it was back to welding, but that didn't stop him from entering a talent contest on a Honolulu TV station. He won, of course, and that led to a string of appearances on other Hawaiian radio and TV stations.

With his mom *still* hoping for that welding career, Poncie headed for Hollywood, determined to be a professional warbler. The only job offer he got was from the Standard Engineering Corporation. As a welder.

He worked there for two years, singing wherever he could on the side. Then he landed a series of appearances in a Los Angeles TV show called *Rocket to Stardom*. That resulted in an audition at Ben Blue's night spot in Santa Monica, and that led to a contract with Warners.

Cheyenne producer Artie Silver was the one who found Ponce, and he was quick to tell Bill Orr about the discovery. Orr says, "He came in and said, 'Hey, I know you're looking for a kid for this Hawaiian show. What kind of guy are you looking for?' I said, 'We're looking for this cab driver part. He should be very personable — the Kookie of this show in a sense.' He said, 'Have I got a guy for you. I was dining in a restaurant the other night, and they had a singing waiter — he's marvelous.' We'd already tested about five guys for the part. That day we sent him down on the set — just said, 'Here's the script. You don't have to remember the lines; just do some things and we'll interview you.' And we did that, and he didn't really study the part — it was just his personality which was very cute. He was perfect. So he got signed."

TINA COLE

When Connie Stevens left Hawaiian Eye, a 19 year old named Tina Cole seemed made to step into the leading-lady role. She was in all the right places at all the right times.

She was born in Hollywood. Her father was Buddy Cole, who arranged music for people like Bing Crosby and Rosemary Clooney. Her mother was Yvonne King of the singing King Sisters. Her uncle was Jim Conkling, president of Warner Bros. Records. And she just happened to drop by the Warners studio when the powers-that-be were scratching their heads over what to do about Miss Stevens' defection.

Bill Orr's assistant Jim Phillips spotted her first; executive assistant Hugh Benson spotted her next; and together, they took her to see Mr. Orr himself. After all that, it turned out that Tina wasn't all that anxious for an acting job. She headed back to her job in an optometrist's office and left the Warners officials still scurrying to find a replacement for Connie.

Two weeks later, Warners called, and talked her into a screen test. The test involved some dancing, some singing, and a scene with Troy Donahue. She passed with flying colors and signed a seven-year contract.

A week later she was flying to Hawaii to join the cast in her new role as Sunny Day.

Hawaiian Eye — Series Index

FIRST SEASON:

Malihini Holiday

An artist, suspected of attempts on his wife's life, is watched by Tracy Steele. Efrem Zimbalist, Jr. appears as Stu Bailey.

Waikiki Widow

The mystery-shrouded death of a Chinese skin diver involves Tracy and Tom in murder and intrigue, all caused by a million dollar string of black pearls. But are they real or legend? Robert McQueeney appears.

Second Day of Infamy

An ex-Japanese spy who's been an amnesia patient since the attack on Pearl Harbor, escapes, recalling only that he had a mission to perform. Tracy takes the job of bringing him in.

All Expenses Paid

A Chicago gangster facing a grand jury investigation sends his girlfriend to the Islands so she can't testify; he also sends someone to kill her. Tom saves her and gets her to testify.

Dangerous Eden

The assistant director of a movie company has been blackmailing the star after seeing her flee the scene after killing a man with a car. Tracy exposes the racket.

Cloud Over Koala

Tracy and Tom are hired by a slick real estate operator to locate a released swindler whom he needs to complete a land deal.

Beach Boy

Peter, a beach boy, claims to be the son of wealthy Donna Lane. Her son is believed to have drowned nine years ago while swimming in the ocean with his step-father ... who now tries to kill Peter. Steele proves Peter *is* Donna's son — and that the step-father tried to kill him 9 years ago. Peter is Troy Donahue in a pre-Phil Barton appearance.

Three Tickets to Lani

A search for a missing embezzler involves Tracy and Tom with two crooks, who use a pretty, naive girl in a scheme to defraud and kill wealthy men.

The Quick Return

Steele is concerned with the disappearance of old friend Jerry Jackson's notebook — because it contains damaging information on a ruthless tycoon. Soon, the tycoon is murdered. Adam (Batman) West appears.

Secret of the Second Door

Desk clerk Paul Cummins runs off with $200,000 paid to a hood by an importer for a packet of hot jewelry. The hood thinks the importer took the money, and combs the Islands for him. Sexy Connie Cummins hires Lopaka to find the money after Paul's death in a car crash.

Shipment from Kihei

Story by Stanley Niss (*Hawaiian Eye* producer): Hired to check the loss of cattle in Bart Harrison's ranch shipments, Steele discovers that Harrison himself is behind the thefts. Gerald Mohr is Bart.

A Dime a Dozen

Tracy establishes the innocence of Army Lt. David Blair (Donald May), accused of rifling the Officers' Club safe, by tracing David's cast-off girl, Lynn, who inadvertently gave the safe combination to a tattoo artist.

The Koa Man

As Steele and Lopaka try to locate attractive Nancy Campbell, they are heckled by Harry Gulliver who had once "frozen" as a machine gunner in Tracy's plane during the Korean War. When Gulliver tries to kill Nancy, Steele vividly recalls the air flight, and Gulliver is unable to shoot.

Stamped for Danger

"Princess Aysha," an American girl recently divorced by a Near East Prince, has managed to leave the country with four extremely valuable stamps. An emissary of the Prince wants them back; at the same time, a crook is trying to steal them. Tracy protects the girl. Ruta Lee appears.

The Kamehameha Cloak

After removing a feathery cloak from an ancient royal tomb, Ames Caldwell, plantation owner, falls seriously ill — presumably by the death-prayer incantation of native Hawaiian Lanakila. Lopaka, alerted by Caldwell's wife, May, shows Lanakila to be in league with seedy Dr. Good to poison Caldwell. Kathleen Crowley is May; Tris Coffin as Ames; also Robert Colbert appears.

The Kikiki Kid

Lopaka becomes involved when a second rate singer romances a guest at the hotel who is a columnist and a TV personality. The singer murders his wife when she refuses to divorce him.

Then There Were Three

Tracy and Tom investigate when Dennis MacIntosh, one of three legatees of an island plantation estate, is killed by a whisky-induced diabetic coma.

Sword of the Samurai

Tom finds Japanese immigrant Noboru for young client Hiroshi — then learns Hiroshi plans to kill Noboru to avenge family honor. George Takei (Lt. Sulu of *Star Trek*) is Hiroshi.

Hong Kong Passage

Returning from Hong Kong to Honolulu, Tracy is a passenger on a plane which is seized by heavies who want to return passenger Lisa Barton to Red China. Merry Anders is Lisa.

Cut of Ice

Tracy and Kim close in on debonair John Miles who tricks Tracy at the airport and grabs English courier, George Crews, who's carrying a valuable gem for Paul Charring, who's also in on the plot. Kim seems implicated at first, and Lt. Danny Quon (Mel Prestidge) pressures Tracy and Tom into turning him over. But photos taken by Cricket come into play.

Fatal Cruise

Young Ginger Martin (Shirley Knight) asks Lopaka to find her husband Johnny. Tom locates Johnny, who is the reluctant lover and employee of wealthy Verna Collins, trying to accumulate a nest-egg for himself and Ginger. But when Verna is murdered, Johnny goes to jail. Tom finds the real killer.

Danger on Credit

By Hugh Benson and Jim Barnett: A racketeer named Sandor hires a killer to murder newlyweds Lois and Victor ... because Lois jilted him. But Island visitor Somerset Jones gets ahold of Victor's credit cards, causing the killer to mistake him and Cricket for the intended victims. He nearly kills the two before Lopaka steps in. Gary Vinson is Jones.

Bequest of Arthur Goodwin

The widow of Arthur Goodwin finds that she is at the mercy of "the other woman" who controls the stock in Goodwin's company. She hires Steele to stop this woman from destroying the inheritance. Fay Wray as Amelia Goodwin.

Birthday Boy

Unscrupulous Gordon McLaren uses luscious Honey Shaw (Fay Spain) as a lure to deprive his nephew, Jim, of a family inheritance. Jim is framed in a traffic death, but Lopaka exposes Gordon's plot. Troy Donahue as Jim.

Second Fiddle

Story by Stanley Niss: The murder of a violinist is plotted by his ex-wife and the former boyfriend of his present wife. They shock him into a heart attack, take his pills and leave him to die. Steele gets him to a hospital, and later catches the conspirators trying to disconnect a hose to his oxygen tent.

Kim Quixote

A man is slain in Kim's cab by a gambler who steals the dead man's money-filled suitcase. Tom is asked to find the murderer. Asked to identify him in a police line-up, Kim refuses — since a girl he's fallen for is being held hostage. Mala Powers appears.

The Lady's Not for Traveling

Red agents try to smuggle Grace Stanley (a beautiful atomic scientist) into Red China. Secretly working with National Security, Tracy Steele prevents this, and helps apprehend the Reds.

Murder, Anyone?

Businessman David Crane is murdered and Lopaka suspects Barry Logan, a tennis bum who loves Crane's wife Sarah. But Cricket, who's known Barry for years, convinces Tom that he's innocent. Tom then uses a tennis tournament to catch the real killer.

Typhoon

Surfing on a private island, Tracy, Tom and Cricket take shelter with ex-Army Col. Conway, and estranged daughter Susan. During a typhoon, a boat with four escaping bank robbers crashes on the beach, and the robbers take over the Conway home before falling out among themselves. Robert Colbert and Mary Tyler Moore appear; story by William T. Orr.

Shadow of the Blade

Also produced as "The Naked Gallows" on *Maverick*: Handsome but weak Bill Corbett awaits execution by guillotine on a French-owned island near Tahiti on a murder charge. Bill escapes, and sends a note to Tracy Steele. Steele has mixed feelings about Bill, who was the Army's biggest foul-up, but who was also the guy who saved Tracy's life in Korea.

Dead Ringer

By Roy Huggins; produced as "The Jeweled Gun" for *Maverick*: Lola has hired Tom to impersonate her husband Michael, who's now in Macao engaged in a secret transaction. But Lola has really murdered Michael, and her lover plans to get rid of Tom, thereby establishing a legal death for Michael. Warren Stevens; Dianne Foster.

Little Blalah

By Stanley Niss from a 1951 episode of the radio drama *Charlie Wild,*

Private Detective: Disappointed when millionaire John Kramer chooses his prospective son-in-law, Gavin McCleod, as his successor, longtime employee Sam Perkins stages a payroll robbery and plants evidence to show that Gavin stole the money. Tracy exposes the scheme. Mike Road as Gavin.

Assignment: Manila

To catch the Manila head of operation smuggling U.S. funds to Red China, Lopaka masquerades as the kid brother of dead nightclub owner Wally Martin.

SECOND SEASON:

I Wed Three Wives

In Honolulu, movie star Mark Hamilton's three ex-wives kidnap him to force back payment of alimony. In the meantime, Hamilton kills his business manager who knows about his income tax evasion. Efrem Zimbalist, Jr. and Roger Smith appear as Bailey and Spencer; Ray Danton is Hamilton.

Princess from Manhattan

By Stanley Niss: Lopaka succumbs to the pleas of a former flame, now wed to Prince Abdur Rahman, that he help her escape from her feared husband.

With This Ring

Patty Seldon, 7, who considers herself engaged to Stevie Hughes, 8, puts Tracy on the track of Stevie's burglar-killer Uncle Peter, because the ring the boy gives the girl comes from a recent crime. Patty is captured by Peter ... but Tracy and Lt. Danny Quon close in. Ruta Lee and Phyllis (Lois Lane on *Superman*) Coates appear.

Sea Fire

Lopaka breaks up a narcotics smuggling ring.

Jade Song

Unknown to Steele, one of the Chinese refugee musicians he is guarding is Yen Fu, a Tibetan Lama who's escaping from the Reds.

The Blue Goddess

Harmon Kane falls in love with Sharon Dunlap (daughter of seemingly rich Martin Dunlap) not knowing that she's really Martin's hired accomplice in a plan to steal the Blue Goddess, a $275,000 necklace. Martin buys the necklace with a fake check on a Dallas bank, but Tom tracks him down and recovers the valuable jewelry.

White Pigeon Ticket

Lopaka takes on pursuit of an ex-con who lams when accused of the theft of some tuna from a cannery where he's employed. He's also suspected of murder. Story by Stanley Niss.

Vanessa Vanishes

Wealthy Ray Kinard hires Tracy to find his daughter Vanessa who's believed to be a kidnap victim.

The Kahuna Curtain

Blaming herself for her father's accidental death, an heiress falls victim to two conmen out to fleece her with a fake seance. Lopaka enters the case.

Girl on a String

Sandra—Michel's assistant in a puppet show—is killed right after her look-alike doll is found crushed. When Mona (Sandra's replacement) finds her doll strangled, Steele is called in.

Kakua Woman

Pursuing escaped killer Ed Grimes to Hilo, Lopaka has a hard time locating him because he's sheltered by his loyal wife Dora. But when he takes off with a girlfriend ... she tells all to Tom.

The Contenders

The Hawaiian Eyes are in charge of security for the fight between local favorite Duke Gallipo and Joey Steck. Tom, who dates Joey's cute sister Laura, exposes an attempt to fix the bout.

Swan Song for a Hero

Abner Dexter (head of the Pacific Foundation) asks Steele to investigate Otto von Helgren, an egotistical but charming gentleman who (in his own words) can do and has done anything. But Otto is a *bogus* hero. The only real clue points to California, so Tracy calls in Rex Randolph at 77 Sunset Strip for some help.

The Money Blossom

In an effort to gain possession of a valuable orchid specimen, the wife of the orchid's grower conspires with Lover #1 to kill the grower and frame Lover #2. Tom figures out the plot.

Services Rendered

By Stanley Niss: Lopaka hires his old pal Greg MacKenzie (soon to be a full time member of the HE firm) to fly over from the U.S. to put the finger on a con man who's been blackmailing a company executive. Greg is taken with the Islands and agrees to join the firm.

Baker's Half Dozen

When six sailors discover they're engaged to Dody Baker, they hire Tom to find her and get back the "bills" money they gave her.

Made in Japan

MacKenzie helps an ex-counterfeiter who is nabbed by old criminal buddies who want him to make some $50 plates for them. He refuses and is cleared after the crooks are captured.

A Touch of Velvet

An artist is murdered and a blind girl serves as bait to help Tracy catch the killer.

Talk and You're Dead

To combat a loan shark racket on the waterfront, Tom takes a job as a longshoreman and seeks a loan.

Robinson Koyoto

Tracy takes reporter Gloria Matthews to Oko Island where a Jap holdout, heir to an industrial fortune, must be convinced the war is over.

The Manabi Figurine

An archeologist and his friends fake the discovery of the valuable Manabi

Figurine, and then take bids on it. When the figurine is stolen, and a murder is committed, Greg, Tom and Lt. Quon must track down the killer.

Caves of Pele

Arranging a marriage between his sister Maria and Harvey Cross, Mal Proctor is murdered by Harvey who then frames Carl, the boy Maria loves. Tracy solves the puzzle.

Man in a Rage

Mike Laszlos wants revenge after Steele traps him stealing ... so he vandalizes the HE offices, then attempts to bomb his sister in law. He dies trying to dispose of the bomb.

The Stanhope Brand

A reporter friend of Greg's, Mark Ellis, fails to return from an island interview with a wealthy rancher. An island drunk leads Greg to Mark's grave.

The Trouble with Murder

Professional killer Ken Grimes falls in love with would-be victim Laura, who rejects him when he kills her husband. Greg rescues her.

The Man from Manila

By Leo Gordon and Paul Leslie Peil: When a witness (who'd perjured himself to clear a murder suspect) is secretly brought back from Manila to tell the truth, a chiseler named Artie tries to make a fast buck by warning the suspect. After two murders, he's nabbed by Lopaka.

Her Father's House

Greg helps a beautiful Eurasian named Lily Shung, in Honolulu illegally, prove her right to American citizenship.

The Humuhumunukunukuapuaa Kid

Tracy tries to help unsophisticated young heiress Jenny Drake, who's the chief suspect in the murder of her selfish mother. The mother was going to disinherit Jenny for her defiant marriage to fortune hunter David Stone, who winds up as the guilty party. The title of this episode refers to a sportsman who doesn't throw even the "little fish" back in.

Don't Kiss Me Goodbye

Kitty is acquitted of murdering her husband, but still must hire Steele and Lopaka to protect her from neighbors who think she's guilty. The Eyes uncover a blackmail scheme.

Dragon Road

Learning his daughter, Men Yang, lives in Hong Kong, Po Yang hires Tracy to find her. Men, thinking her father is dead, is working for Woon Sing, unknowing that he is using the business as a front for dope smuggling.

It Ain't Cricket

The rich parents of 18-year-old Tina Robertson — trying to bust up her romance with no-good Johnny — hire the Eyes to keep the two apart. But when plans are made to kidnap Tina, Cricket is taken by mistake.

The Comics

The blackmail scheme which singer Iris and her boyfriend Chris try to pull on comic Bunny White goes awry. Iris is found strangled, and Bunny is suspected until Steele proves Chris is guilty.

Father, Dear Father

Seedy Harry learns that Beulah Mae, his daughter, is now an oil heiress ... and she's in Hawaii! He tells two con men, one of whom kills him. Then, the two mount a scheme with one of them posing as her long lost father. Lopaka penetrates the scheme.

The Manchu Formula

Hired by a publicity man to guard a secret youth-preserving formula and its beautiful Chinese owner, Tracy outwits kidnappers out to get the formula by force.

The Pretty People

When a movie company comes to Hawaii, Tom is assigned to protect Derek, an egotistical actor. Cricket falls for him; Tom protests; Derek is murdered; she is suspected; Tom solves the case and pins down the real killer.

The Big Dealer

Steele works hard to get a case against couturier Hilary Kane, head of a ring selling strategic stolen goods to the Reds. Tom goes to Hong Kong to follow a lead ... leaving Tracy and Lt. Quon to investigate at home.

Maid in America

Sam Cheong has Lan-Chih, his proxy bride from Hong Kong, smuggle in some valuable vases. A man is murdered, the vases turn out to be fake, Greg nabs Uncle Sheng who smuggled dope in the vases.

A Taste for Money

(Written by Anthony Eisley and also known as "Strangler In Paradise.") Investigating a hit-and-run accident that puts Kim in the hospital, Tom and Tracy uncover the murder of a playboy's wife.

THIRD SEASON:

Satan City

Exposé writer Hilda hires Greg when the manuscript of her second novel is swiped. It seems that two "subjects" of her novels are conspiring to do her in.

The Kupua of Coconut Bay

Lopaka uncovers a bizarre plot when he goes to the assistance of an old Polynesian woman who is being frightened by a "sea-monster" into selling her island property to land speculators.

The Moon of Mindanao

Steele is hired to buy a valuable pearl for a wealthy client from a Chinese in Manila who is murdered before the transaction can take place.

The Doctor's Lady

MacKenzie uncovers a strange gambling game and finds his own life in danger when he's hired to investigate the murder of a doctor's pretty nurse.

Thomas Jefferson Chu

When Lopaka is sent by the government as an undercover agent to Formosa to help trap hijackers who are stealing top-secret equipment, he learns he's marked for death, along with a pint-sized, self-styled "agent" named Chu. George Takei (*Star Trek*) is Chu.

Pill in the Box

As a member of a murder trial jury, Cricket discovers one of the jurors is forced to vote for acquittal because his wife has been kidnapped and threatened with death. Steele goes to Cricket's aid.

Kill a Grey Fox

MacKenzie finds his life in danger when he uncovers an unsuspected killer while investigating the murder of a beautiful girl for a famous defense lawyer. David White and Jo Morrow appear. Robert Colbert as Reed.

Point Zero

Cricket is kidnapped in downtown Honolulu by a gang, which, for some unknown reason, makes it possible for Lopaka to find its hiding place. Chad Everett; Victor Buono.

The Queen from Kern County

Tom is involved in the troubles of a 17-year-old beauty contestant, who is first drugged in a blackmail scheme, then is accused of murder.

The Final Score

Steele is ordered killed when he discovers that the rumor a volcano will erupt is a hoax and part of a land grab scheme.

Two for the Money

When millionaire Lucien Hammond learns his estranged wife has died, he hires MacKenzie to find his daughter, whom he hasn't seen in more than 15 years. The girl is found, but another girl claims to be the real daughter, despite her lack of proof. Greg doesn't know who to believe until Jeff Spencer of *77 Sunset Strip* helps uncover a fraud and murder plot. Mary Tyler Moore and Richard Deacon appear.

Tusitala

Lopaka is hired to purchase an original Robert Louis Stevenson manuscript owned by a beautiful Samoan girl. A murderer steals the document. Lawrence Dobkin as Ronald Windsor and The Exotic Sounds of Arthur Lyman.

The Classic Cab

Kim buys an old limousine for a second cab, and finds gangsters are also interested in the car—to the point of murder. The motive: $300,000 in cash. Tris Coffin, Kathleen Crowley, and John Day appear.

Concert in Hawaii

Greg uncovers a murder plot, with the help of Cricket Blake, when hired to prevent anyone from disturbing James Harrington, a 16-year-old piano genius. Jack Cassidy appears.

The Missile Rogues

Lopaka faces surprising dangers as he exposes a sinister foreign agent who's impersonating an internationally known scientist in an effort to steal the formula of a new metal alloy used in the nosecone of a missile. Warren Stevens appears.

Little Miss Rich Witch

Tracy becomes involved with Mimi Wells, a beautiful madcap heiress, who decides to try being a jewel thief for kicks. Janet Lake is Mimi. Robert Colbert appears.

Big Fever

Greg aids a professor who faces death after winning $100,000 in a poker game.

Year of Grace

Lopaka is hired to locate a Eurasian Princess, Suvi, who disappears in Honolulu en route to her home in the Middle East. Tom uncovers a plot to seize her country. Lisa Gaye is Suvi.

My Love but Lightly

Steele falls for a lovely French songstress ... but she's arrested for the murder of an international jewel thief. John Van Dreelen as Curt Viner.

Cricket's Millionaire

Cricket is the victim of a fast-talking PR man's scheme to make it appear that a millionaire sportsman has fallen for her. But when a criminal masquerades as the sportsman, Cricket's life is in danger.

Four-Cornered Triangle

MacKenzie is hired by Victor Haswell to investigate the background of Larry Brand (Chad Everett), a young man who marries an older, wealthy woman, Julia Tyler Brand. When Haswell, who had wanted to marry her, is murdered, suspicion is pointed at the wrong person. Peggy McCay as Julia.

Total Eclipse

Tom and Tracy disagree when they become involved with a beautiful girl who everyone believes murdered her wealthy husband even though a jury says she's not guilty. Tom says guilty; Tracy says innocent. Jack Nicholson appears.

Blackmail in Satin

Greg poses as a writer and takes Cricket along as a photographer while investigating a mysterious character who's moved into the home of a wealthy woman and demands $250,000 of her. Susan Seaforth appears; Efrem Zimbalist, Jr. as Stu Bailey.

A Scent of Whales

Lopaka gets an urgent message via the cab's radio from Kim that he and a lovely passenger (Sherry Jackson) are being kidnapped. Tom's investigation uncovers a murder. John Dehner appears.

A Likely Story

Tracy is hired by lovely Arnel Wade (Dorothy Provine), a wealthy divorcee, to protect her from an unknown assailant following a series of mishaps in her Honolulu home. Tracy gets in a fight with an axe-wielding criminal.

Meeting on Molokai

MacKenzie is hired to protect the life of wealthy oilman Jed Sutton after an attempt is made to kidnap him when he arrives in Honolulu to discuss a merger. Neil Hamilton and Mala Powers appear.

Payoff

Lopaka faces danger when he helps an old friend who's a prosecuting attorney accused of accepting bribes for being lenient to criminals.

An Echo of Honor

Tracy uncovers some dangerous intrigue when he investigates a series of strange hotel jewel burglaries. The case explodes into murder.

Nightmare in Paradise

Greg is almost hit by a crashing car in which he discovers the body of a man who has apparently killed himself with a shotgun. Greg tries to assist the dead man's widow, and becomes the object of threats.

Aloha, Cricket

Cricket disguises herself as a Polynesian greeter girl to assist the Eyes in obtaining evidence against a gang of smugglers. She gets in trouble by pretending to have a romance with one of them — a psycho-killer. Peter Breck as Ray Martins.

The Last Samurai

Cricket gets tangled up with a family that's involved in Japanese rituals.

One girl is killed; Cricket is threatened.

RX Cricket

The attempted poisoning of Kathie Nelson (Sharon Hugueny) is blamed on Cricket when the cops learn that both are named heirs in the will of a wealthy woman. Chad Everett appears.

Location Shooting

In the midst of making a movie, producers hire Greg to protect the star, Norman Ayres, from frantic fans. Greg quickly discovers that flighty Sue Alden is pushing the star's jealously button, his agent has larceny in her heart, and murder is likely. Joan Staley is Sue.

Across the River Lethe

When the owner of a dance school learns that Henry Porter has pocketed $50,000 of the profits, Porter kills him and accuses a fisherman. Greg takes dance lessons to get the fisherman off the hook.

Scene of the Crime

Tom discovers a plot to kill three people (himself included) when he goes on a wild boar hunt to the Island of Kauai. He soon finds himself being hunted down in the jungles like a wild animal.

Among the Living

Steele finds himself in the middle of a plot involving double-cross, murder and swindle when a former girlfriend seeks his assistance with her ex-husband. Mike Road appears; Edd Byrnes guest stars as Kookie.

"V" For Victim

Eight tourists virtually marooned by a storm find a limerick forecasting the death of one of them. Death makes two calls before MacKenzie solves the mystery.

Koko Kate

When college-trained Chris Randall (Chad Everett) returns to Hawaii and his mom, Koko Kate (who runs a hamburger stand), they hardly know each other. Swept off his feet by Cricket, he heads for trouble as he tries to impress her with a display of wealth he's forced to obtain unwisely until Tom steps in.

Lalama Lady

Tom Lopaka prys a wealthy tourist from the grasp of beachcombers and blackmailers. Peter Brown as Teo.

FOURTH SEASON:

Day in the Sun

Troy Donahue joins the cast as Phil Barton. The robbery and shooting of the Island's favorite drive-in operator spurs Lopaka to action, but it's Barton who shows heartsick Tina Billings such a glamorous time that the culprit is found. Elizabeth MacRae is Tina.

Somewhere There's Music

Lopaka and Barton recover a stolen $20,000 Stradivarius.

There'll Be Some Changes Made

Cricket finds a baby on her doorstep. Lopaka, meanwhile, has been hired

by the child's wealthy grandfather to find both mother and grandson. His ire when he finds Cricket and Phil have been keeping a secret from him is short lived when he discovers a kidnap plot. Warren Stevens appears.

The Broken Thread

Beautiful Evelyn Mason, who married for $$$ rather than for love, dies in an auto crash, leaving Ralph Mason tormentedly searching for a suspected lover. Greg gets involved in the hunt. Andrew Duggan as Ralph Mason.

Lament for a Saturday Warrior

Tom adds an old pal, Glen Thomson, to the agency's security staff. Soon after, a jewel robbery puts them both on the spot.

The After Hours Heart

Phil Barton plays host to a cousin, who falls in love with a man with only a boat. Peggy McCay as Lucy McDowell.

The Sign-Off

Phil sets out to help clear the boyfriend of his part-time secretary Lois Corey, who's accused of slaying the errant wife of the senior member of a TV newscasting team. Phil gets help from Cricket and Greg.

A Night with Nora Stewart

Greg is hired to help ex-movie star Nora regain her confidence before she makes a comeback. She reports a night prowler in her bedroom, and Greg is startled to learn that everyone in her entourage has a reason to block the comeback. Kim provides the needed clue. Dorothy Provine is Nora.

To See, Perchance to Dream

Phil tries unsuccessfully to help Eddie Croft, a race driver seriously burned in a crash, recover his courage. Jack Hogan is Croft.

Pursuit of a Lady

Luscious Liz Downing is a pro tennis player and a girl who messes up men's minds—including those of an architect, a dapper tennis pro, a middle aged club director, and private eye Greg MacKenzie. When Liz is slain, Greg is a suspect. Diane McBain is Liz.

Shannon Malloy

Cricket, Phil, and Tom are unwittingly involved in the mystery of a half-million dollars worth of pearls, a half-caste girl who wants to be an artist, and a Hollywood star who won't let herself fall in love. Susan Silo in the title role.

Go Steady with Danger

Lopaka dogs the footsteps of Honolulu gigilo Harry Larcombe after a series of his middle-aged conquests report jewel thefts. Michael Dante is Harry.

Kupikio Kid

Young Peter Kirk (Evan McCord), who has found college studies and the company of a Chinese beauty named Poppy pleasant in Hawaii, gives up both and disappears when his parents arrive in Honolulu to bring him home. His difficulties

cause Barton and Lopaka to call a truce in their battle for the attentions of new hotel employee Sunny Day—just long enough to foil a murder-kidnap plan. Tina Cole makes her debut as a regular.

Maybe Menehunes

Greg reluctantly accepts an assignment which sandwiches him between the law on the side of ex-movie star Norma Marriot and the gods of a village. Mysterious phenomena and two attempts on Norma's life are attributed to the folk gods until Phil uncovers the hands of an electronics expert. Andrew Duggan and Dianne Foster appear.

Pretty Pigeon

When "Charley" Boggs (Diane McBain) sweeps into town ostensibly vacationing without her wealthy husband, a mother and son team sets a blackmail scheme in motion. Lopaka also has a plan.

Two Too Many

When Jeff Richardson receives a series of poison pen letters which threaten the stability of his marriage to the daughter of a building tycoon, Phil and Tom combine talents to solve the mystery.

Boar Hunt

Barton sees an idol toppled as his uncle, Miles Maitland, a famed criminal lawyer who has won a murder acquittal and fallen in love with Arlenne Abbott, seeks to prove he is more worthy of her than is her husband. George Montgomery and Lisa Gaye appear.

Go for Baroque

The death of a security guard and the theft of a priceless map at the home of a deceased explorer bring Lopaka into a case involving two beautiful sisters, the explorer's young Hawaiian ward, and an ambitious archaeologist with well-hidden personal plans.

The Long Way Home

Lopaka traps kidnappers and reunites a famous actress and her wayward daughter. Susan Seaforth as Julie Keith.

Two Million Too Much

Lopaka involuntarily tells two slick operators how to snatch a fortune; then, he nabs them. Don Munroe is played by Van Williams; Barbara Bain is his wife. Connie Stevens is back as Cricket Blake.

Blow Low, Blow Blue

When Cricket hears some soulful trumpet playing in a most unlikely place, Phil Barton helps her identify and find the musician. Then, they learn that someone out of the trumpeter's past with too much money and too little understanding is responsible for the silent horn. Sunny Day and Cricket both appear in this episode.

Gift of Love

Despite the objections of Cricket and Phil, wealthy widow Helena Ogden (Peggy McCay) moves into a faith healer's rest home. Helena sets off a chain reaction when she asks Brother Love if he is a charlatan.

The Sisters

Greg falls for Nora Cobinder when she vacations in Hawaii, and just as quickly finds himself protecting her from would-be killers because the slaying of a man who caused the disfigurement of her sister is in her past. Myrna Fahey is Nora.

Passport

Greg MacKenzie inadvertently helps an errant father perform the most manly and deadly act of his life.

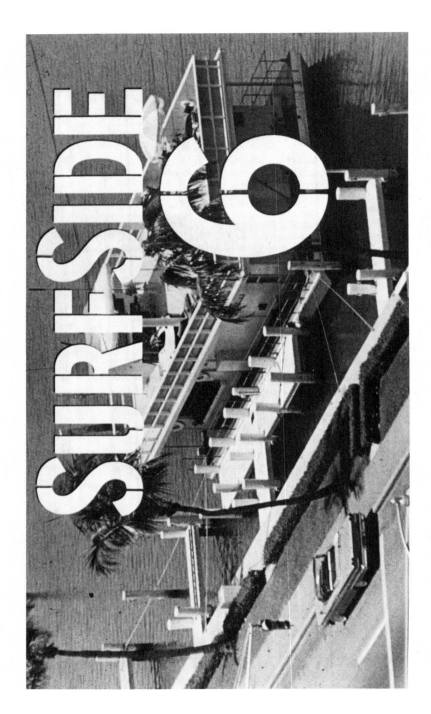

9
An Address in Miami Beach

ABC (1 hour) — debuted October 3, 1960
Format: Private investigators who work out of houseboat moored
adjacent to Miami Beach's luxury hotel, The Fountainebleau.
Cast: Van Williams............Ken Madison
      Troy Donahue ....Sandy Winfield II
      Lee Patterson ....Dave Thorne
      Diane McBain ....Daphne DeWitt Dutton
      Margarita Sierra ....Cha Cha O'Brien
      Don Barry ....Lt. Ray Snedigar
      Mousie Garner..........Mousie
      Richard Crane ....Lt. Gene Plehn
Executive Producer: William T. Orr
Producer: Jerome L. Davis
Theme Music: "SurfSide 6" by Mack David and Jerry Livingston
Location: Filmed in Hollywood and Miami Beach

You could almost hear the pitter-patter of fluttering female
hearts all over America as SurfSide 6 was pumped down the network
line every Monday evening. The cast of heart-throbs included handsome Van Williams as Ken Madison (brought over from Bourbon
Street Beat), Lee Patterson as Dave Thorne, and the man who may
have been Warner Bros. hottest property at the time, Troy Donahue,
in the role of socialite Sandy Winfield II. Just so male hearts could do
some fluttering of their own, beautiful Diane McBain was cast as
Daphne Dutton, originally described as "the girl in the yacht next
door," and Margarita Sierra as Cha Cha O'Brien, a Latin dancer in the
"Boom Boom Room" of the swank hotel on the *other* side of SurfSide 6.

185

As the fourth in the Warners line-up of private eye shows, *Surf-Side 6* had to do some searching to find its "exotic location." With Hollywood, Hawaii, and New Orleans already spoken for, the series looked to the Gold Coast off Miami Beach. Footage was occasionally shot on location to preserve the flavor.

The show's gimmick had to be the rather unique headquarters maintained by the firm. The studio press releases played it up: "In this atmosphere of swaying palms, lush hotels, swimming pools, yachts, and tennis courts, three handsome young private investigators operate from their unique headquarters—a luxurious houseboat anchored directly across Ocean Avenue from the famed and fabulous Fountainebleau Hotel. Although Miami Beach is the focal point of the series, many episodes are set on the open seas beyond, taking the investigators to the Florida Keys, the Bahamas, and the Caribbean. Their clients include people of many countries and of every social stratum."

William T. Orr says he and Hugh Benson discovered what would become the *SS6* base of operations purely by chance.

"Hugh and I went down to Florida to scout locations. The houseboat was happenstance. There was a fellow who had a houseboat moored on Indian Creek and in the background—like it had been arranged—was the Fountainebleau Hotel. So we talked to the guy who was delighted about using the boat [in the series]. He was planning to build these things—they were sort of an invention of his. So that's how they wound up having that boat as a headquarters."

Orr says a replica of the boat was built on the Warner lot, but the hotel shots were on location. He also notes that the stock footage in Florida was shot with one make of car in the scenes. Then, before the show hit the air, another car company bought time, and that footage had to be re-shot.

To put our heroes in perspective, Dave Thorne (Patterson) is a former prosecutor from New York, Ken Madison (Williams) continues his role as a lawyer (now graduated from Tulane), and Sandy Winfield II (Donahue) is a wealthy jet-setter. But instead of prosecuting, shystering and jet-setting, they'd all rather hire out their talents as private eyes—lucky for all those pounding hearts.

Naturally, the two chicks abet them in their endeavors, as do the usual supporting characters, played by Don Barry (as Lt. Snedigar) and Mousie Garner.

There may be several reasons for the creation of the SurfSide 6 Agency—not the least of which is that Warner Bros. and ABC needed a series to replace *Bourbon Street Beat*. Of the three Warners private

The cast of *SurfSide 6* (left to right): Margarita Sierra as Cha Cha, Troy Donahue as Sandy, Lee Patterson as Dave, Diane McBain as Daphne, and Van Williams as Ken.

eye shows to date, two had been huge successes (*Strip* and *Hawaiian Eye*) and *Bourbon Street* had had glimmers of hope, so Bill Orr and company decided to stick with the formula. Besides, with no detective agency operating in New Orleans anymore, the studio had to do something with Kenny Madison. Van Williams, as Kenny, had done quite well in two *Bourbon Street* episodes in which he had a starring role, and the character was simply too hot to dump.

But was *SurfSide 6* created for Williams, or for co-star Donahue? In 1961, Donahue was telling reporters that Warners approached the network about a series for Troy after he clicked in a 1959 movie, *A Summer Place*. According to Troy, ABC took the idea to the sponsors, who liked the idea, and so the show hit the air.

The studio, meantime, was telling those same reporters that Donahue got the role of Sandy Winfield simply because they needed someone to play the part, and Troy was already signed and available.

Donahue's version may be the more correct. As Bill Orr tells it, "ABC talked to our management in the East and said if we would put Troy Donahue in a series, they would sell it instantly. No problem. It became *SurfSide 6*." According to Orr, *SS6* was sort of a continuation of *Bourbon Street Beat* in a more "up" location, and with Van Williams elevated to a more prominent role. But Orr was opposed to the including of Donahue in the cast. "I was against that because I thought Troy Donahue was a valuable film property and that he could have had a longer and more productive career in films."

Does Orr think the TV series hurt Troy's career in films?

"I wouldn't say that." He pauses. "Other than *killing* it, it didn't hurt it at all."

Orr feels that the essence of what made Donahue a success was never really captured in black and white television as it was in color features.

Be that as it may, the series hit the tube (with Troy unfortunately in glorious black and white) with a premier episode called "Country Gentlemen" in which Sandy, Ken and Dave were involved in the case of an old-time aristocrat found dead. After the three detectives teamed up to solve the case, the series settled down into alternating episodes with Van Williams carrying a good deal of the load.

A frequent guest star in WB series, and particularly *SS6* was bit player Grace Lee Whitney, who still admits to being quite taken with the men from the era. "Van Williams," she sighs after completing some amorous reminiscences about Efrem Zimbalist, Jr. and Roger Smith. "There's another romantic guy. They were just good lookin'.

He had the bluest eyes I ever saw in my life." She adds, "But he had contact lenses on."

What about the typical day's schedule on the set of a show like *SurfSide 6*? Grace Lee says although it wasn't as bad as it is today, it was *hectic*.

"Up at five; be there by six. I'd walk into make-up and it would be warm. They'd always have the heaters on and they had a help-yourself breakfast bar. You'd go to the bar and there'd be fresh orange juice, fresh tomato juice, and you would make your own toast with butter and jam.

"There'd be about six or eight booths, and each booth had a make-up man waiting for whoever was coming in. On the inside there were some private booths where the big stars like Connie Stevens would be — the main leads.

"I would get into make-up ... and we'd fool around a lot. Then I'd go over on the set and start shooting at eight. And then, I'd get through and go to the commissary for lunch."

Zimbalist wouldn't be there, she says. "Efrem always ate in his dressing room. He brought a pail — a workman's pail — and if you wanted to talk to Efrem, the only place to find him was in his dressing room with this pail.

"I would go to lunch usually with Van and Roger." Then after a quick nap, it was back on the set until six. Or seven or eight. Or later if necessary.

"It was long hard hours," she puts in, "but it wasn't hard. There were frequent breaks."

VAN WILLIAMS

Van Williams was born on February 27, 1935, surrounded by cattle and eighteen thousand acres of land. And since his dad dabbled in oil, real estate, and cattle ranching, that's what Van figured *he'd* do. "Acting never entered my mind," he said. "At least not until I was almost finished with college."

So college it was for Van, and he stayed close to home, attending Texas Christian University at Fort Worth. Van's academic career lasted three years before he decided to take a year's hiatus in Honolulu.

While on the island, Williams taught skindiving at Henry Kaiser's Hawaiian Village Hotel for awhile, then became assistant manager of the hotel's aluminum dome theatre. That's where he ran into Robert Herrick, one of Kaiser's PR men, who recognized star potential and encouraged Van to try the dramatic arts.

But Van *still* wasn't thinking along those lines—at least not *yet*. He packed his bags, moved back to Fort Worth, and finished his last year at TCU.

Now he could think about acting.

Diploma in hand, he set his sights toward Hollywood, and somehow managed to get an interview with casting director Robert Walker of Revue Productions. Even though Williams had never been before a camera, Walker liked his easy-going Texas style, and decided to give him a try.

Because of Walker, Williams made his way into the cast of two segments of *General Electric Theatre*. Van said the early acting roles didn't even make him nervous.

Next came a Warner Bros. show—*Colt .45*. That developed into the Kenny Madison part on *Bourbon Street Beat* and finally a starring role in *SurfSide 6*.

Van carried more episodes of *SS6* than did his two co-stars. A typical Ken Madison episode might have him rescuing a client's daughter from a fortune hunting society bum ("The Empty House") by turning on the old romantic charm. Or representing a friend when the friend's fiancee is found dead ("Count Seven").

Meanwhile, back at the ranch, Mr. and Mrs. Bernard C. Williams were watching those *G-E Theatre* episodes. *And* the *Colt .45*. And the *Bourbon Streets*, and all the *SurfSide 6s*. They never missed anything Van was in; in fact they saw the shows in Fort Worth *before* they were on in Los Angeles, and they would telephone their son with their comments.

"They've yet not to like everything I do," he admitted.

During the filming of his two Warner Bros. series, Van and his wife Vicki lived in Pacific Palisades, California.

In 1966 Van would star for one season in a TV version of *The Green Hornet*. Co-starring with Van would be an unknown martial arts expert named Bruce Lee.

TROY DONAHUE

If Efrem Zimbalist and others in the Warner stable were clamoring to be released from their television dungeons to do feature films—how jealous they must have been of glamorous, blond, debonair Troy Donahue. He too preferred the wide screen, but the difference was that he got his wish.

So TV critics of the day were given to the practice of reporting on a "rumor" that a 24 year old by the name of Donahue was co-starring in a TV show. If *you'd* tuned in to *SS6*, you might not have believed it either. Of the first 34 episodes filmed, Troy's character, Sandy Winfield, had the lead in only ten. He never showed up at all in a few segments, and in the rest he'd make a cameo appearance, say a few words, and then leave the rest of the show to his cohorts.

That situation forced the Troy Donahue fan clubs—over 200 strong—to head for the local drive-in to see their idol. For while Efrem Zimbalist's TV commitment kept him too busy for feature films, with Troy it was just the opposite. He was starring in movies while *SS6* was being shot, and that left him little time to do much at the Agency except appear in the opening credits.

Another problem TV directors were having with Donahue was his lack of experience. While *movie* directors could work with the young star, and do a scene over if necessary, television was not given to many retakes. Working on a tight schedule made it just that much harder to use Donahue in a show. One director insisted it took at least twelve takes to get a Donahue scene right. That's why some of his appearances in *SS6* bordered on being unprofessional.

This young actor who created a sensation on the Warner Bros. lot was born Merle Johnson, Jr. to a former newsreel editor at Paramount who became a General Motors executive—ironically enough in charge of turning out the company's motion pictures. Mr. Johnson died when Merle was only 14. As the new head of the household, Merle, his mom (a former New York stage actress), and his sister decided that he should set his sights on West Point. So he made tuition at a military academy in New York by waiting on tables.

Merle's plans were changed when he became involved in some school productions, and decided he'd rather try Hollywood than West Point. He and his sister headed for the home of a family friend in Calabasas, California.

Merle's plan of attack was to hang out in a bar and hope to be discovered. It worked. By the time his mom joined him in sunny California, he was making $125 a week, signed to a contract with Universal-International. It seems that producer William Asher (who handled *The Shirley Temple Show* for NBC) figured Merle Johnson, Jr. could be a Tab Hunter type.

Margarita Sierra ("Cha Cha O'Brien") explains something to Troy Donahue ("Sandy Winfield II") with her characteristic Latin animation.

The comparison to Tab Hunter was somewhat prophetic. Johnson was introduced to the agent who thought up that name (*and* Rock Hudson's name). Henry Willson must have thought, "Merle Johnson, Jr.? No way."

So out went the "Merle" and in came "Troy," apparently taken from Helen of Troy. "Johnson, Jr." was dropped in favor of "Donahue," a name that fit well with "Troy."

The brand new moniker didn't work wonders at U-I. The studio dropped him in a money-saving move, and he made free-lance appearances on TV waiting for his big break. It finally came — from Warner Bros. — in the form of a film called *A Summer Place*. Troy had done twenty pictures — maybe a dozen TV shows — but *this* was the flick that made him a star.

Soon after came *SurfSide 6*; then Warners quickly cast him in two other features, even as *SS6* was shooting. He was the star of *Parrish*, a drama about tobacco growing, with Claudette Colbert, Karl Malden, and Dean Jagger.

With that picture still going strong, Troy did *Susan Slade*, and before *SS6* started production on its second season, he was already making plans for a trip to Rome to star in *Lovers Must Learn*.

In his "spare time" he traveled the country promoting *Parrish*. That killed off his weekends, and left about four days a week — in between movies — to film the adventures of Sandy Winfield II. *That's* why there weren't all that many adventures for Sandy.

Between the feature flicks and the "guest appearances" on his own TV show, Troy was pulling in upwards of four thousand fan letters, mostly from teenage girls. Published reports had his annual salary pegged at forty thousand dollars, and his vital statistics at 6'3" and 175 pounds.

TV and movie columnists also mentioned his glamorous wardrobe, consisting of seven suits, and fifty sweaters. They made columns out of his bachelor house in Beverly Hills, and his engagement to starlet Lili Kardell.

But the *strangest* thing they wrote about was this movie star's odd habit of showing up from time to time in a TV show. Weird as that was, Donahue would do it again when *SS6* bit the dust, changing his character and moving over to bolster *Hawaiian Eye*.

LEE PATTERSON

Lee Patterson was truly an international star. Before appearing as Dave Thorne in *SS6*, he'd made movies in Spain, Denmark, Switzerland, France, Morocco, Italy, Ireland, and Scotland.

He was, in fact, born in Vancouver, British Columbia, and was named Beverly Frank Atherly-Patterson by his father who was an actor on the London stage and screen before becoming a banker in Canada.

Patterson had several opportunities for careers other than acting. In school, he excelled at hockey and boxing, but turned down offers from pro hockey teams to pursue a career as a designer. With that in mind, he attended the Ontario College of Arts, and after graduation, he designed the famed Santa Claus Parade in Toronto.

"Travel" could have been Lee's middle name, and "jack-of-all-trades" was his game. During the time before he became an actor, he worked as a miner in Quebec, a caddie at Banff (caddying at one time for Jack Benny), a sailor on the Great Lakes, a gold prospector, a waiter, a sculptor, a painter, a cartoonist, and a lumber mill worker.

Still interested in art, and figuring Paris was the world art center, he went hoping to further his career as a designer. A few months later, he was off to London and more odd jobs — including stints as a waiter and a truck driver.

But then, he got hired as an assistant stage manager and set designer with the BBC. *That* took his mind off designing long enough to get him interested in the stage.

His first opportunity came up at the Theatre Royal in Windsor in *Death of a Salesman*. Then, he designed the sets for and starred in *Johnny Belinda*. More stage roles followed.

Lee's movie debut was *The Good Die Young*. That was quickly followed by 25 more films in Europe including *The Passing Stranger, Gulliver's Travels*, and *Jack the Ripper*. That last film led to a long term contract with Warner Bros., and *that* brought Lee Patterson an odd job he'd never tried before — that of a private eye in *SurfSide 6*.

Beginning in 1968 Lee portrayed newspaper editor Joe Riley on the soaper *One Life to Live*. When that character "died" in late 1979, Lee moved over to *Another World* in the role of Dr. Kevin Cooke.

DIANE McBAIN

Outspoken Diane McBain was never thrilled with doing television. But there she was—at age 19—helping Troy, Lee and Van solve their cases. At least she helped when she wasn't in the process of being kidnapped or something like that.

Like Donahue, Diane was signed by the studio to do a feature movie—*Ice Palace*—in 1959. Before that she had done some television on a freelance basis. In *Maverick* she played a society girl from Baltimore on her way out West, who ended up fighting Indians. She also had parts that were "simply awful" on *Lawman* and *Bourbon Street Beat*. So she decided that television wasn't for her.

But after *Ice Palace* she found herself right back on the small screen on *77 Sunset Strip*, *Maverick*, and *The Alaskans*. But then she got a part in the aforementioned feature, *Parrish*, with private-eye-to-be Troy Donahue. Diane said she could hardly wait to get on location in Connecticut where she would play one of Donahue's girl friends.

About that time the studio informed her that after the shooting of the movie, she'd be appearing opposite Troy in a new TV series.

Only a couple of years ago Diane had been a successful model while still a 17-year-old student at Glendale High. During her senior year, she raked in twelve thousand dollars doing magazine covers, ads, and TV commercials.

The modeling career began at age 15, she said, at the urging of her grandmother who paid her way through charm school. Then, back at Glendale High, a drama coach introduced her to agent Bill Barnes who would take her with him to the Warners lot after school.

Warners appeared to be interested in Diane, and after she got rid of some "baby fat," they put her in that 1959 segment of *Maverick*.

MARGARITA SIERRA

To describe Margarita Sierra is to use a string of descriptive adjectives: tiny, bouncy, bubbly, vivacious, talented, and *Latin*. *SS6*'s Cha Cha O'Brien was born in Madrid, and had sung and danced ever since she was four years old.

Margarita grew up watching rehearsals. Her father, Jose Sierra, was a stage scenery painter, and he was always taking young Margarita to the theatre. Her stage debut came when a child actress got sick, and the producer remembered Jose Sierra's young daughter. From that time on, it was nothing but acting and singing for Margarita.

At the age of eight, she headlined a juvenile music revue, and in her teen years, she became a singer and dancer in nightclubs, theatres, and Spanish pictures. After a three year tour of South and Central America, she came to the United States in 1957.

She was in the middle of an engagement at the Persian Room of New York's Plaza Hotel when she was discovered by Warner Bros. executives who sent their cards back to her dressing room. Margarita threw the cards away, never having heard of Warner Bros. What she had thrown away was the role as Cha Cha in *SS6*.

Things were finally straightened out, and Warners convinced her to drop the Persian Room in favor of the Boom Boom Room by showing her a replica of the famed Miami Beach nightspot that was to be a prop in *SurfSide*.

She was the last cast member to sign up, and because of that, it was quite a while before Cha Cha appeared in any Florida scene except those on a Hollywood soundstage.

For the first time ever, Margarita found herself singing in English. But she was doing a good job — so good, in fact, that Warner Bros. Records put out a release from the show called "The Cha Cha Twist."

Margarita bought a home in Encino during the run of *SS6* where she lived with her mom, five dogs, and her parakeet, Chicuito.

SurfSide 6 — Series Index

FIRST SEASON:

Country Gentleman

Reformed racketeer Marty Hartman tries to crash Miami society, is rebuffed, falls for an heiress and she returns his love. When her father, the Commodore, is murdered, jealous Allan Abbott hires Dave to prove Marty is the killer.

The Clown

At a birthday party for his son, Correro, an exiled dictator, is murdered. Pepe, a clown, is arrested and Lt. Snedigar is sure the clown is guilty. But Dave discovers another clown costume. Cha Cha and Mousie help, and in the end, Dave discovers that Correro's right hand man was the killer.

According to Our Files

Story by Hugh Benson: Teamed with inept insurance agent Herbert Cotler to find a freed crook and repossess $90,000 in stolen bonds, Sandy is led on a wild goose chase until Ken discovers the crook was murdered.

High Tide

The SurfSiders aid lovely dancer Jill Murray who fears she'll be killed by her ex-boyfriend, racketeer Lou Montell, before she can testify against him before a Senate committee. Lou comes out of hiding to get her.

Par-A-Kee

After an attempt is made on Daphne's horse Par-A-Kee, Dave investigates and learns a bookmaker would lose everything if Par-A-Kee won. Daphne is kidnapped to prevent the horse from running, but Dave and Ken come to the rescue.

Local Girl

Having made off with $20,000 given her by a gangster boyfriend to bribe a politician, dizzy, blonde Darcy tricks Ken into guarding her during her I'll-show-them return to a backwoods hometown.

The International Net

Threatening letters are sent to the wife of a theatrical producer, two suspects are murdered, and the husband is arrested. Ken discovers who wrote the letters ... and who the murderer is.

Deadly Male

The SurfSiders uncover a scheme in which handsome youths are hired to prey on married women, and then blackmail them. When one girl refuses to pay, she is murdered.

Power of Suggestion

A hypnotist's assistant is afraid the hypnotist has given her a post-hypnotic suggestion to murder someone. Dave, Cha Cha, and a comedian try to protect the girl ... but the hypnotist turns up murdered.

Odd Job

Madison is hired via telegram to guard a proxy fight strategy meeting from the opposition. But when he arrives, Ken Madison is already there. Ken solicits the help of Sandy and Mousie.

The Frightened Canary

Danny Rome, a celebrated but vicious comic, becomes furious at a girl singer who spurns his advances and involves him in publicity that makes him look ridiculous. Out for revenge, he tries to frame her for murder, but Sandy exposes the scheme.

Girl in the Galleon

When a professional skin-diver is murdered shortly after finding a treasure of gold coins in a sunken galleon, Sandy and Ken investigate. They discover that crooks with stolen gold have made the gold into coins, and planted them in the galleon. The crooks are captured after a savage underwater battle.

Bride and Seek

Frank Anders conspires to marry Nancy, an heiress, and extort a large sum of money from her grandmother. Frank's former girlfriend hires Dave to find him; he catches up with the pair in time to save Nancy.

Little Star Lost

Movie starlet Linda Lord and her mother Sybil arrive in Miami for the premiere of Linda's new picture, and while there, Linda discovers she's adopted. Confused, she calls her old friend Sandy and asks him to arrange a meeting with her real mom. Meanwhile, a crooked lawyer hopes to convince Linda that his girl is her real mother.

Heels Over Head

Juan Escudero, a charming thief who steals only from thieves, hides $70,000 in the SurfSide that he stole from a ruthless racketeer, Homer Garson. Ken and Dave find the cash. Kidnapped aboard Garson's boat, Dave and Cha Cha are part of the struggle going on between Juan and Garson for control of the boat—and the money.

Thieves Among Honor

Daphne falls for handsome Mark ... and gets him and his partner to head a fund drive for a hospital ... but Mark and his friend are con artists. Sandy is suspicious.

Facts on the Fire

A socialite kills her husband in the dark, thinking him to be a prowler. Her friends think the killing was on purpose, and they turn against her;

so she hires Dave to prove it was an accident. What he learns is that there was a murder plot—but *she* was the intended target.

Yesterday's Hero

Dave helps the lovely wife of a Korean War buddy locate her husband, Robbie, supposedly executed by a Caribbean island dictator. He finds that Robbie's "execution" was only a coverup for his betrayal of the rebel cause.

Black Orange Blossoms

It's carnival time in Jamaica, and Sandy is the guest of a beautiful girl at her father's estate. Before Sandy can meet neighboring plantation owner, Sir Niles Smallens, Niles is murdered by a snake bite, apparently that of a fer de lance, which is extinct in Jamaica.

License to Steal

A singer hires Dave to guard some rented jewels she wears as a gimmick in a night club act. But her insurer (in disguise) plans an elaborate armed robbery.

Ghost of a Chance

A beautiful government agent enlists Ken's aid in finding 65-year-old John Norton, a retired government engraver, who disappeared while honeymooning with his 23-year-old bride. Naturally, a counterfeiting gang wants to take advantage of Norton's expertise.

Race Against Time

Returning from New York by air, Dave is poisoned by one of the passengers. As he hovers near death in a Miami hospital, Sandy, Ken, Lt. Snedigar, and Cha Cha check out the passengers and learn that a man Dave sent to prison is the guilty party. But the suspect is killed before they find the antidote.

The Chase

Written by Roger Smith and Montgomery Pittman: Driving alone to deliver some papers to Thorne, Cha Cha recognizes a fellow traveler on a little-used swamp road as a wanted killer. The killer wants to silence her, and she becomes trapped in a swamp-surrounded ghost town. Dave traces her to the town, and finds himself also stalked by the armed killer.

The Impractical Joker

Harry's practical joke backfires when he believes he shot his partner and friend, George Papas. George later turns up alive and explains that *he* was pulling a joke. Madison goes to investigate, and is knocked out; then, George is found dead, this time for real. Ken and Dave set a trap and catch a killer.

Inside Job

Dave, posing as a bank teller, learns that a bank employee has become involved with crooks who plan to rob the bank. But the crooks become suspicious of the banker and murder him. So, Dave works *his* way into their confidence.

Invitation to a Party

To trap crooks who arrange phony drunk-driving accidents for blackmail purposes, Winfield poses as a

millionaire playboy, but is arrested for manslaughter when the victim of his "accident" turns out to be really dead — having been killed by the crooks in a quarrel.

Spring Training

Arky is the new pitching star for the Bears ... but all is not well! His girl, Robbin, is seeing a gambler named Mitch. Arky clobbers Mitch; Mitch plans to break Arky's hand; Mitch is found dead; Arky is suspected; and Ken investigates the whole mess.

Double Image

Winfield gets involved with pretty Wanda Drake, who believes her lifer Father was framed for a killing. She comes up with the crackpot notion of tricking a gambler into admitting it was all a frame.

Circumstantial Evidence

When Cha Cha's nephew Rafael is accused of killing a predatory blonde, Sunny, Dave finds a clue proving Sunny's boss killed her.

Spinout at Sebring

Sandy (a racing car trophy winner) teams up with Tony, a world champion sports car rider, at the Sebring Grand Prix. He also helps heiress Maggie, in love with Tony, thwart attempts of Harriby and Maggie's stepmother Lorraine (lovers) to kill Maggie's wealthy father. Lorraine has given him anti-coagulant pills so he'll bleed to death from a cut. Harriby crashes and dies in a seven hour race, won by Tony and Sandy. Lorraine is killed by a speeding car.

Vengeance Is Bitter

Dave is hired to find out who wrote a slanderous novel about the socially prominent Denning family.

Little Mister Kelly

The SurfSiders expose a fight-fixing ring headed by gambler Alex Boles, and enable upcoming champ, Hank Kelly, to retain custody of his young son.

The Bhoyo and the Blonde

Kevin Flanagan, an Irish writer, witnesses a murder. The killers send pretty Renee after him. Dave, hired by Kevin's wife to keep him out of trouble, loses Kevin, who keeps getting drunk. Renee tries to shoot him, but is caught by Sandy and Ken.

An Overdose of Justice

Bonnie is a greedy but foxy girl who persuades an insurance man to leave his wife to help Bonnie find an ex-boyfriend who stole $70,000. Bonnie wants the reward money. Dave reluctantly gets involved.

SECOND SEASON:

Count Seven!

Seven year old Annie unwittingly leads Madison into a double murder, stemming from a smuggling caper.

The Wedding Guest

Daphne goes to Nassau for the wedding of an heiress ... and is kidnapped. Sandy arrives, checks some clues, and rescues her. They learn that the fiance of the heiress marries women for their money.

Pattern for a Frame

A plan is carefully conceived in prison that tags Ken for the murder of an underworld king. Ken, on the run from the law, discovers that the plot was masterminded by an old enemy.

Jonathan Wembley Is Missing

Sandy is persuaded by a beautiful girl, Amy, to help a ventriloquist, Rusty Bell, and his dummy called Jonathan Wembley, get a job at the Boom Boom Room. But Sandy gets in trouble when the dummy is kidnapped. Donna Douglas is Amy.

Daphne, Girl Detective

Daphne refuses to believe that her friend Sally would take her own life. Then, she sees Sally's husband in an embrace with another woman. She frightens him into trapping himself. Bruce Dern appears.

The SurfSide Swindle

When Sandy and Ken discover a con man has duped a pizza chef into believing he's bought the SurfSide houseboat for a floating restaurant, the SurfSiders go looking for the confidence man and end up using Daphne to help track a blackmailer and murderer.

The Affairs at Hotel Delight

When Ken checks out of a small town hotel, he finds a lovely and armed young lady unconscious in the hallway. After reviving her, he finds she's on her way to pay ransom for her kidnapped boyfriend — who somehow seems to be in on the plot.

Witness for the Defense

Winfield is charged with murder when he slugs a drunken attacker who's found dead a few minutes later. Thorne tries to defend Sandy in court.

Laugh for the Lady

Thorne becomes involved in a marital triangle when he runs into an old girlfriend who's working for a famed nightclub comedienne. Dave ends up in the middle of a suicide try — or attempted murder.

The Old School Tie

When Dave attends a college reunion, he finds himself involved in a murder as a former classmate is slain and a has-been football hero is suspected.

One for the Road

Daphne Dutton falls in love with a mysterious young wanderer, Ernie Jordan, who follows the sun and calls the world his home. The SurfSide 6 trio investigates the nomad and finds his trail crosses with that of a dead man. James Best is Ernie.

Prescription for Panic

Winfield tries to find a friend's murderer and ends up in the arms of a beautiful couch doctor who's the next intended victim of the killer. Kathleen Crowley as Dr. Leslie Halliday.

A Slight Case of Chivalry

Thorn finds himself in the middle of a wild comedy of errors when a swashbuckling old friend, Dan Castle, flees to Miami Beach with a murder charge and a $5000 price on his head. John Dehner as Castle.

A Matter of Seconds

After finding his girlfriend beaten to death in her apartment, an in-and-out-of-trouble ex-fighter, Harry Lodge, is trapped at the scene by a policeman. No match for the fighter, the cop becomes his hostage. Dave is called in, and the SurfSiders have less than an hour to prove Lodge's innocence. Claude Akins as Lodge.

Pawn's Gambit

The death of a friendly old shopkeeper sends the crime-solving trio off in search of his killer. Dave's sleuthing turns up a smuggling ring.

The Empty House

A business tycoon hires Madison to separate money-seeking society leech Vince Lederer from his daughter Shirley. Ken's SurfSide pals advise him to change his method from disdainful disgust to romantic interest — which makes him a terror in search of the truth when Shirley confesses the slaying of the resort huckster who was trying to cadge $25,000 from her. Susan Seaforth is Shirley.

Separate Checks

The SurfSide crime fighters are called in when young Joe-Too loses $25,000 to a smooth confidence artist. But the conman is trapped by a marriage bid. Evan McCord as Joe-Too.

The Roust

Angered to the killing point by the sight of pompous Bernard "Chilly" Childress, whom he knows to be trafficking internationally in human misery, Dave Thorne is determined to torment Chilly until he exposes him for what he is. David White as Chilly.

The Green Beret

Recalled because of his knowledge of guerrilla tactics to train a team of special forces troops, Thorne is also pressed into service to find the enemy cell leader outside the military establishment, and the fifth columnist inside his own team.

The Neutral Corner

A bomb planted on the SurfSiders' houseboat after Ken has been hired to protect prize fighter Bongo Macklin (Chad Everett) raises the eyes' temperatures and sends Ken stalking a gangster, a sports writer, and Bongo's ex-wife. Grace Lee Whitney appears.

Find LeRoy Burdette

Plain looking Aimee Tucker — in search of the man who promised her marriage and then skipped out — gets the SurfSiders to help her look for country bumpkin LeRoy Burdette. Ken unearths clues that link the disappearance with the apparent death of a gang boss. Aimee is Susan Seaforth.

Elegy for a Bookkeeper

Dave and Ken part company after a brawl over pretty Jan Coates, and Dave ends up working for underworld boss Emergy Stark who wants a former bookkeeper eliminated before a Senate crime hearing comes up. Shirley Knight as Coates.

Anniversary Special

Egomaniacal deejay Robby Brooks sets out to use a TV show to catapult him into the White House on the strength of the votes of 60 million fans. Dave trips him up before he tries to use murder as a springboard to fame. William Windom as Brooks.

Artful Deceit

The apparent robbery-slaying of an art dealer interrupts rehearsals for a little theatre production in which Sandy and Cha Cha are to do a dance number. Sandy solves the crime when he realizes that the skill of one acting student for mimicry is not his only talent. Chad Everett appears.

Green Bay Riddle

Although acquitted of slaying his father-in-law in a small Florida society colony, the husband of Peggy Allen remains guilty in the eyes of the people. She hires Ken to dig up the truth — and he gets an assist from a pretty girl with the unlikely name of Henri. Lisa Gaye as Henri; Donald May as Richie Linden.

Irish Pride

The SurfSiders meet Cha Cha's Irish cousin and help him get off to a good start in America. When he is accused of murder, Dave investigates.

The Quarterback

An entangling web of intrigue engineered by the team of Wally Barker and his girl grips the SurfSiders' pal Lt. Gene Plehn when his young brother Tom comes to town to play in the Orange Bowl classic. But the SurfSiders help the Lt. block the football fix. (Richard Crane played the part of Lt. Plehn who replaced Lt. Snedigar in many of the last season episodes.)

Portrait of Nicole

Dave and his pals draw an assignment to find an ex-hood's girlfriend named Nicole. But how many Nicoles are there?

Many a Slip

Sandy becomes curious about what goes on behind the scenes at a lingerie fashion show. So he gets Daphne to uncover her lush figure to become an undercover agent.

Squeeze Play

A girl in love with her mom's boyfriend asks the SurfSiders to check his background because her mother has given him $10,000 to bet on a horserace. Peter Breck stars.

Who Is Sylvia?

Dave Thorne leaves a twist party to solve a murder among a bevy of bikini bathing suit models. Jack Cassidy appears.

Dead Heat

A convicted hood is in jail because of the SurfSiders; but he asks Dave to protect his wife from old pals who believe he has $100,000 missing from the syndicate's bankroll. Warren Stevens appears.

The Money Game

Sandy and Ken are hired to arrange a meeting between an American oil developer and a prince whose homeland abounds in black sand. But Hermes Doratis has his own plans for gaining control of the oil rights.

Vendetta Arms

Daphne stumbles into the retirement home of notorious gangsters. The SurfSiders are hired to track down petty thieves pilfering linen, spittoons, pictures and pool tables. Inevitably, their paths cross. Dennis Hopper appears.

A Piece of Tommy Minor

Sandy comes to the rescue of a popular nightclub singer when a gambling czar decides Tommy Minor's IOUs are worth a part of his professional future. Kenny Roberts as Tommy. The Frank Ortega Trio (from *77 Sunset Strip*) appear.

A Private Eye for Beauty

While on the assignment of maintaining security at the Miss Universe contest, the SurfSiders get an additional client when Latin government official Francisco Hernandez (John Dehner) employs them to keep his beautiful niece and her lover apart.

Love Song for a Deadly Redhead

Jeff Spencer of Baily and Spencer pops in at the houseboat while in Miami Beach to help an old client, Dooley Baker, find the source of poison pen letters. Later accused of murdering the jealous husband of former girl friend Carol McKee, it takes Kookie, all of the SurfSiders, and Daphne Dutton to change a deadly lilt to a song of freedom for Jeff. Roger Smith and Edd Byrnes appear. Grace Lee Whitney as Bernice.

Masquerade

Dave disguises himself as a clown and joins a circus in winter quarters to learn why a normally gentle horse has trampled its groom to death. He unearths a Nazi still fighting the war.

House on Boca Key

When bullets (meant for Sandy) cut down a neighborhood pal, the SurfSiders set out to learn why.

Midnight for Prince Charming

Approaching the twilight of life, Paul Wyatt is a likely prospect for con artists who bait their trap with pretty Laura Jarrett. Complications set in when Harry Noonan wants in on the cut. Noonan's death makes it possible for Ken to convince Wyatt that beauty and romance belong principally to the young. Mike Road appears. R.G. Armstrong is Wyatt.

10
There Was a Gun
That Won the West

ABC (half hour) — debuted October 18, 1957
*Format: Western drama about a United States federal agent working
        undercover as a gun salesman to rid the West of desperados*
Cast: Wayde Preston ....Christopher Colt
       Donald May............Sam Colt, Jr.
Executive Producer: William T. Orr
Producer: Cedric Francis
*Theme Music: "Colt. 45" by Bert Shefter and Paul Sawtell. Lyrics by
        Hal Hopper and Douglas Heyes.*
Location: Filmed in Hollywood

Colt .45 was, at the very least, a unique show. It was sold before
being created and contained a plethora of action — most of it not on
the screen. With all of the strange things that happened on Warners
TV shows, probably no other show was as bizarre as this one. In its
three seasons on the air, *Colt .45* was a hodgepodge of uncertain
sponsorship, a walkout, many repeat episodes, and an abrupt change
in the starring role with no explanation.

The creation of the show came after Warner Bros. received a call
from ABC's New York office. ABC announced that a national beer
company wanted to sponsor a television show, a Western. William T.
Orr responded, "Give us half an hour and we'll give you a show."

At this point Orr, Hugh Benson, and others went to work to
create a Western series for the waiting sponsor.

"We had made a film called *Colt .45* with Randy Scott," says Orr,

"and it had been a very big success. We loved the title, so from the title we came up with this idea of Chris Colt, who was part of the Colt family [firearms manufacturers], who was out West selling his wares. And naturally that led into all sorts of [adventures]."

Warners called ABC back and told them the idea for *Colt .45*. ABC instructed Warners to wire the detailed format to New York. In no time at all Warners had a deal for *Colt .45*.

On October 18, 1957, Christopher Colt debuted as a dashing, young U.S. Government undercover agent posing as a gun salesman for the Colt Firearms Company. The initial episode, "Judgment Day," had Chris demonstrating his wares to the much-impressed townsfolk—with the exception of two: Sister Helen, a young missionary who detested guns and violence, and Jim Rexford, a sadistic crook whom Colt had been sent to watch as a contact to an infamous, elusive criminal. Rexford repeatedly tried to force Chris Colt into a gunfight, but each time Colt, knowing he couldn't kill the contact, backed down. This act of cowardice disgusted the townspeople, who were bewildered at Colt's lack of fighting spirit. But Sister Helen regained her recently faltering faith at his decision to "turn the other cheek." After Colt received word that the sought-after criminal had been apprehended in another town, Chris was forced into the inevitable showdown with Rexford. Colt gunned him down with lightning speed, but Sister Helen realized the act was in self-defense.

From that episode on, Chris Colt kept moving through the West fulfilling various, dangerous assignments from his superiors.

That's what the viewers at home saw of the *Colt .45* production. But what about the off-camera happenings?

The original star of *Colt .45* was a good-looking, curly-headed actor named Wayde Preston. Preston was a rugged, former Wyoming boy with a 6'4" stature.

After 26 episodes of its first season, word got out that its sponsor and the network had dropped *Colt .45*. However, a short time later ABC announced that the series would return in the fall of 1958 but without its original sponsor.

Preston was furious. He blamed both Warners and ABC for causing the problem by a low budget and a lack of promotion. He claimed that the only way viewers knew it was on was by stumbling upon it. The actor had just returned from a cross-country promotional tour financed by ABC and the Colt Firearms Company.

Preston's reasoning for the sponsorship being dropped was that the Colt Company got a fortune in free advertising while the actual

Less Hellman, Wayde Preston, and Don Gordon in "Amnesty."

sponsor dished out the bucks. The sponsor dismissed Wayde's accusations as hogwash and claimed that the subject matter of the series had nothing to do with the cancellation. *Colt .45* did make it into the 1958–59 season, but it was not very long before the bottom fell out.

"One day the word came up to my office that there was some problem down on the set," recalls Orr. "If something got 'hairy,' then I always ended up hearing about it. He [Wayde Preston] was down on the set shooting a process shot where he had to get up on top of the coach [shooting at outlaws], and he didn't want to do it. He said it was a stunt — they should get a stunt man.

"We said, 'You can't get a stunt man. This is your close up.'"

Wayde responded, citing the danger of his precarious perch.

Orr continues, "He was making it very difficult. So now the word comes up to me that Chris Colt won't get up on top of the wagon. So I sent [producer] Cedric Francis down there." Orr became more amused retelling such a ridiculous tale.

"I always found out if I didn't go down there for a while, it got settled up some way or another; or if it really got bad, then I'd have to go down and look it over.

"But about a half hour later Cedric showed up rather ashen, and I said, 'Well, what's happening? Is he back at work — that's all straightened out?' He [Cedric] said, 'I may have said the wrong thing.' I said,

Christopher Colt demonstrates his family's hardware.

'What do you mean Cedric? What did you say?'

"He said, 'Well, we were discussing the problem and I said to Wayde, 'You know, Wayde, maybe you're not right for this business.'

"And Wayde said, 'You may be right,' and got in his car and left the lot and never came back. That was the end of Wayde Preston."

At that point the immediate future of *Colt .45* was inundated with doubt. A replacement had to be found quickly, and that came in the person of Donald May, a Warners contract player who had appeared on an earlier *Colt .45* episode as Chris's cousin, Sam Colt, Jr.

While filming switched over the Sam Colt episodes, ABC ran repeats of Chris Colt stories. The unfinished Chris Colt episode was scratched. As Hugh Benson put it, "We had to dump a lot of film."

One of the strange things about the transition was that no explanation was made in the story line as to why Cousin Sam was now the focal point of the weekly undercover work. Benson said that he did not think the public cared what happened to Chris Colt.

Apparently it bothered some viewers because Benson himself, asked if the series was more successful after the switch, admitted, "No, I think we went on a downgrade."

With increasing amusement Orr reminisced, "Those days were great. We thought that [introduction of Sam without mention of Chris' fate] was the thing to do, and we did it. The network didn't ask for stories; they didn't ask for approval — they *asked*, but they didn't get it. The advertisers had nothing to say in the sense from day to day, show to show. Nobody on the set, no representatives, nobody saw dailies. Nobody read outlines. Nobody read the scripts." More somber, he went on, "That was the way it went, and, God knows, it's very different today."

Somehow, some miraculous way, *Colt .45* survived and was awarded a third season. The "new" Colt emphasized his more rugged attire — a newly grown mustache and buckskin clothes. But Warners knew the series was dead and proceeded to kill it themselves by producing only three new episodes and rerunning ten. Donald May went on to star in the new Warner series, *The Roaring Twenties.*

Colt .45 had served a useful purpose other than filling up thirty minutes of air time each week and fattening the accounts of Warners and ABC. The show was a virtual training ground for new directors and producers.

Orr explained, "We used *Colt .45* to develop new writers, new directors, new producers. No matter what we seemed to do, we couldn't kill it for a while. That was our kind of tryout show. You couldn't do that today, of course."

The last episode of *Colt .45* aired on September 27, 1960, and brought an end to a most unusual series of unprecedented events.

WAYDE PRESTON

Portraying the role of a man in the West came natural for Wayde Preston. He grew up in Dan Troop's town — Laramie, Wyoming — as the son of a high school teacher. William (his real name) entered the University of Wyoming where he eventually received a degree in pharmacy. While attending U of W, Preston played bass fiddle and vibraharp with a jazz quartet and also began to develop his acting talent by appearing in school plays.

After a hitch in the Army and a job as an electronics technician at a guided missile plant, Preston found himself dabbling again in dramatics. He was spotted by Warner Bros. and given a test in a *Cheyenne* episode. This led to a contract with WB in July, 1957, for a reported $200 a week. The blond, curly-headed Preston, who was christened "Wayde" by the studio, soon earned a couple of $50 raises, but this was still a very low salary—even for television (which was nowhere as lucrative as movies).

Toward the end of *Colt .45*'s first season, Wayde found himself in trouble in the show and in his marriage. The latter culminated with a separation in April, 1958, from former Paramount contract player Carol Ohmart. The former was whether the show would make it another season.

Preston's agent, Harry Bernsen, suggested that Wayde's ego had been hurt by the apparent dropping of the show by ABC. Wayde had been sent on a promotional tour stretching from St. Louis to New York. The twelve-day crusade was full of appearances on local TV interview shows which Wayde regarded as some fast-talking boys who were out to make a fool out of him.

His brief experience with network television taught him to watch out for number one and to be suspicious of those marketing him as a product. Preston had no close friends in acting because he claimed he never knew when he would have to cut somebody's throat for a part. Neither was Wayde overly fond of agents. He believed that agents work more for the studios than for their clients. If an agent loses an actor, it's nowhere as disastrous as losing the working relationship with a studio.

Wayde Preston's distrust of the industry kept building until his unexpected walkout on the *Colt .45* set. After plenty of time to think in Australia, Wayde realized that his suspicions got the best of him.

If you are wondering what became of Wayde "You'll Never Get Me on That Coach" Preston, here is the latest, told by Hugh Benson:

"Ultimately he went to Australia. He was flying planes. I've seen him since. He said, 'I was foolish.' He's been trying to get back into the business. He still flies planes; he's a commercial pilot—flew bush planes in Australia, does charter work here."

The future of Wayde Preston is uncertain. Maybe he will continue to be a pilot, but then maybe he'll make it back to the tube for another shot — several years older and many years wiser.

Colt .45 — Series Index

FIRST SEASON:

Judgment Day

Chris Colt's skill with guns earns the enmity of a man Colt has been sent to watch as a possible contact for an elusive crook. Colt backs down from several showdowns and earns the respect of a young nun. When the crook is captured in another town, Colt is free for a gun duel. Andrew Duggan and Peter Brown are featured.

A Time to Die

When Indians attack Chris Colt and his prisoner, Colt gives his captive a gun and saves the prisoner's life. The prisoner then turns on Colt and escapes. Colt tracks him down, is taken alive by two of the prisoner's gang, but is released unharmed for saving the man from the Indian attack. Although Colt promises not to return to the hideout, he later tracks down his former prisoner.

The $3,000 Bullet

Chris Colt takes on the identity of an outlaw as part of a plan to capture a smuggler. He meets the smuggler in a blaze of gunfire, but the trouble of his assumed identity pits him in a dangerous situation with a local rancher.

Gallows at Granite Gap

When Colt learns that a recent jail escapee is the son of a kind, middle-aged lady who has come to town to verify the kinship, the undercover agent recaptures the killer and then poses as her would-be son to spare her much grief. Ken Osmond (Eddie Haskell on *Leave It to Beaver*) has a small role.

Small Man

A little metalsmith with a penchant for Western novels guns down the leader of a notorious gang. A gang member discovers the metalsmith's secret, a bullet-proof vest, kills the little hero, and makes off with the vest. The outlaw then boldly challenges Colt to a gunfight with the security of a protected torso.

Final Payment

Colt appoints a deputy of dubious character for collecting tax money from a vicious band of brothers. But Colt second-guesses his decision when it appears the new deputy might abscond with the money.

One Good Turn

Searching for raiders in Mexico, Chris Colt finds a dying man. Everyone in the town refuses to offer aid.

After the man dies, Colt learns that he was one of the raiders for whom he was searching. Now the town fears retaliation, but Chris has a plan.

Last Chance

A bit of detective work is necessary when Chris helps out a sheriff friend in finding the murderer of a book-keeper at the Last Chance Mine. The sleuthing results in the discovery of a surprise killer.

Young Gun

A young man buys a gun from Colt and explains that it is a gift for his father. Chris learns that the boy ac-tually intends to use the gun on his father's killer. Knowing the teenager is no match for the gunman, Colt moves to protect the youngster from his fatal mission. The gunman is played by Charles Bronson.

Rebellion

When an unreconstructed Southern judge places his reputation and his friends' money on the line, Chris comes to the rescue to preserve the judge's dignity, but not before the shooting starts.

The Gypsies

Colt has his hands full when the marshal's new son-in-law is at the mercy of a lynch mob. The groom is a gypsy and a disappointment to the marshal. The deputy, an admirer of the marshal's daughter, is insanely jealous and causes more complica-tions.

Sign in the Sand

Indian signs drawn in the sand by a dying government undercover agent enable Chris Colt to track down the killer who is posing as the dead agent. The impostor has fooled Colt and now has a secret money ship-ment in his possession.

Mirage

When a group of Mexicans are driven out from their land by a group posing as Army troopers, Colt enters the picture along with a phan-tom army to do combat.

Blood Money

An escaped convict turns himself in to Colt with the condition that the $500 reward money be given to the convict's girlfriend. She needs the money for a life-saving operation. Chris also agrees not to reveal that he is a convict. But that information becomes available when the girl's no-good ex-boyfriend appears on the scene.

Dead Reckoning

Chris Colt impersonates an in-famous gunman who has been hired to assassinate a senator. Everything goes well until the real gunman ap-pears and proceeds to carry out his mission while Colt is held prisoner.

Decoy

Chris and the daughter of a dis-graced colonel, seeking the identity of a Mexican bandit, discover the object of their search is actually the host of a hacienda where they are staying. The couple escapes but be-comes the prey of the bandit.

Rare Specimen

After suspecting that a train holdup was carried out by local residents, Chris Colt discovers an important lead while getting his coat mended from the same bullets that wounded him in the robbery.

Mantrap

When a group of brothers target Colt to be the groom for their sister, Chris has to act fast to save her from a kidnapping and himself from the bonds of marriage.

Ghost Town

On the trail of a kidnapped girl, Colt finds that she is actually not a prisoner but the voluntary companion of an outlaw to escape her overpossessive father. The runaway couple takes refuge in an old ghost town where the girl makes a startling discovery about her past from an old prospector.

The Golden Gun

A boy inherits his gunfighter-father's golden gun and decides that he also should live by the gun. But inside the gun is a map showing the location of stolen government gold. Edd Byrnes co-stars.

Circle of Fear

Chris Colt, escorting a prisoner and other passengers on a stagecoach are attacked by Apaches. After the coach overturns, the travelers escape to a mountain pass. Conflict enters the picture as it must be decided who of the seven will ride the four horses for help while the remaining three will hold off the regrouping Indians.

Split Second

A former marshal who used to never carry a gun has now turned into a dispassionate gunman after the murder of his wife by a no-good. Colt, a friend of the ex-marshal, helps him to find a purpose for living.

Point of Honor

There is a new doctor in town—but the physician is unexpectedly a "she." Her medical schooling was financed by her brother who, unbeknown to his sister, is really a thief and killer. Colt runs into trouble when he tries to convince her to cooperate with the law in the apprehension of her outlaw brother.

The Deserters

Chris Colt goes undercover as an Army deserter to discover the reason for several desertions from an Army post. He trails another deserter and ends up in a deadly racket run by a trading post owner. Angie Dickinson co-stars.

Manbuster

A former bronc buster, bitter over losing an arm, plans to join a gang of bank robbers. He later changes his mind and decides to settle down, but the rest of the gang comes looking for him.

Long Odds

An aging grandfather, who was once a famed marshal, must live up to his legend in the eyes of his eleven-year-old grandson. The former marshal is humiliated by two badmen in front of the whole town and now he faces the awesome task of regaining his prestige. Chris Colt lends a hand.

The Escape

A young, inexperienced Army corporal is sent to escort a prisoner of Chris Colt's to the federal authorities. Chris follows the two because he suspects the prisoner is more than the young corporal can handle.

Dead Aim

Chris Colt runs into a determined bounty hunter, a jailed man with amnesia, and a dead body identified as a killer for whom Colt has been searching. Things become complicated until Chris uncovers an old wedding picture.

The Magic Box

An itinerant photographer and Chris Colt team up to find the killer of a U.S. Indian Commissioner. An Indian brave has been accused of the crime, but Colt suspects the witness is lying.

The Confession

When a poor nester confesses to holding up a gold shipment, Chris Colt doubts his story and suspects that he has made the confession so that his pregnant wife can get the reward money. Dorothy Provine and Louis Quinn co-star.

The Man Who Loved Lincoln

A bit of history comes to life when Chris Colt agrees to protect the actor-brother of John Wilkes Booth from an anonymous would-be killer. The climax comes during the production of "Hamlet." Robert McQueeney co-stars as Edwin Booth.

The Sanctuary

A sheriff who shelters outlaws in his town for a $1,000 fee is providing asylum for a murderer whom Chris Colt wants. Chris is advised to get out of town, but things start to go Colt's way when the murderer makes a play for the sheriff's daughter, which causes some enmity from the not-so-straight lawman. Van Williams is featured.

The Saga of Sam Bass

Chris poses as a jailed criminal so he can initiate a friendship with infamous outlaw Sam Bass. Hoping that Sam will lead him to a heisted government payroll, Chris arranges an escape.

Amnesty

When the New Mexico governor elects to pardon Billy the Kid in hope that the Kid will abandon his wayward tendencies, Chris Colt is given the job of delivering the pardon to Billy's hideout. But Colt is being followed by tough lawman Pat Garrett who wants the Kid for his trophy. Robert Conrad is Billy the Kid.

The Pirate

The subject of Chris' search is a fugitive Confederate naval officer who relieved a U.S. ship of $100,000 in gold six months after the end of the war. Colt finds him, establishes a friendship, and agrees to testify in the ex-officer's behalf—but associates have their eyes on the loot.

Law West of the Pecos

Chris Colt is sent to retrieve an Army sergeant who is suspected of having taken an Army payroll. Chris comes to believe that the sergeant is not guilty and begins to ferret out the site of the money, allegedly stashed before an attack. Complications arise when Colt is thrown into jail by the law-bending Judge Roy Bean.

Don't Tell Joe

Following a gunman whose brother has disappeared and is wanted by the Army, Colt becomes involved in a very tense election. Chris discovers that the gunman he is tailing has been imported by a shady candidate who is out to unseat the Honorable Mayor Andrews at any cost.

Return to El Paso

A wealthy Texas rancher is forced by his outlaw brother to buy arms for Mexican rebels. Chris enters the scene and teams up with the rancher to seek out the renegade who has taken the rancher's wife hostage.

Night of Decision

On the trail of a handsome outlaw, Chris Colt becomes the prisoner of his prey and a girl and her mother. The mother saves Colt from a sure death but is faced with having to surrender her son, partner to the outlaw. Leonard Nimoy guests.

SECOND SEASON:

Queen of Dixie

Chris seeks out counterfeiters when some of the bogus bills are found on the body of a drowned gambler. Getting hired on the riverboat, Queen of Dixie, Colt discovers stolen government plates on which are printed money that is distributed through the boat's gambling facilities.

The Reckoning

When a novice outlaw is repulsed by the blood-letting actions of his leader, he tries to leave the gang. The young outlaw confesses his misdeeds to a priest, but the leader tracks him down and kills him, then seeks out the priest. Chris Colt discovers the impending peril of the priest and comes to the rescue.

The Devil's Godson

On the trail of a vicious gang of brothers, Colt meets up with Doc Holliday, who reveals that he, too, is after the brothers because they killed the father of Holliday's godson. Chris uses Doc as bait.

The Rival Gun

Chris seeks out the possessor of a stolen shipment of 1000 Colt .45's. George Kennedy and Robert Mc-Queeney co-star.

The Hothead

A young bank teller, living in the shadow of his famous father who is now deceased, rebels against his strict guardian and unknowingly becomes involved with outlaws who plan to steal Army payroll from the bank. Guest star is Troy Donahue.

A Legend of Buffalo Bill

On his way to Dodge City to investigate a series of train holdups, Chris meets up with Buffalo Bill Cody. Working together, they solve the holdups and prevent a kidnapping.

Yellow Terror

Serious problems develop when a prisoner Colt is escorting by riverboat contracts yellow fever. Other passengers become panic-stricken and demand the prisoner be thrown overboard.

Tar and Feathers

A villainous land-grabber controls the town but not his daughter. She plans to marry a visiting ambassador's son who has been writing articles exposing the misdealings of the land-grabber. Chris Colt is assigned to protect the ambassador's son from any foul play.

Alias Mr. Howard

This is the first episode with Sam Colt, Jr. in the starring role. Sam Colt, Jr. is after a mail robber who is hiding out on a farm owned by Zee and Jesse James. The Jameses are trying to mend their ways under another name, but the mail robber-former associate of Jesse's complicates their good intentions.

Calamity

Chris Colt fights off Indians as he takes a stagecoach on a perilous mission to get vaccine to a town stricken with smallpox.

Under False Pretenses

Sam Colt, Jr. faces some difficult decision-making when he discovers the girl he has fallen in love with is the sister of a stagecoach robber whom he has been sent to apprehend.

Impasse

When one member of an Army payroll holdup gang is captured by Chris Colt and other lawmen, the remaining members of the gang take refuge in the local marshal's house and hold the marshal's wife and daughter hostage. Tensions build as the outlaws demand a prisoner exchange, but the captured outlaw has died and someone has to come up with a fast plan.

Arizona Anderson

A fake kidnapping enables Sam Colt, Jr. to locate the loot taken in a federal payroll robbery twelve years before. But Sam is not the only one in the search; his competition is a couple of fast guns.

The Cause

Sam must negotiate a prisoner exchange between a band of Mexican rebels and the U.S. Army who hold respectively an escaped Army officer and the rebel leader's son.

Phantom Trail

Chris and Sam team up to discover why herds of cattle being shipped to an Indian reservation have disappeared with their crews.

Breakthrough

When several stagecoach robberies remain unsolved, the railroad decides to tunnel through a mountain so future shipments of gold can be made by rail. Chris Colt is trapped in an intentional landslide while inspecting the tunnel, and rescuers dig feverishly to save him.

Chain of Command

Rather than going through Indian country, an Indian-fearing Army colonel takes his column of soldiers and civilians through the desert. When water becomes scarce, Colt and others mutiny against the headstrong colonel but are then faced with an Indian attack.

Alibi

Chris Colt tries to help a man unjustly accused of murder and uncovers the real murderer who has threatened the entire town into lying.

Absent Without Leave

A young lieutenant, who hates the Army and would rather paint, deserts his post. Chris Colt, upon request from the deserter's colonel-father to find his son, begins the search but runs into trouble from a revenge-seeking sergeant.

Strange Encounter

While escorting two prisoners to Fort Leavenworth, Chris finds two hurt men by an overturned stagecoach. Chris puts his trust into one of his prisoners, a doctor who can give the necessary medical attention. Robert Colbert is featured.

Trial by Rope

Chris leads a posse after a man wanted for murder, but Colt is unsure of the man's guilt. When the man is captured, Chris has his hands full as the posse elects to hang the alleged killer.

The Gandy Dancers

Sam Colt, Jr. protects a young woman whose father has been murdered by men who threaten railroad workers with death if they do not forfeit half of their wages.

Martial Law

A wild town is placed under martial law, but the Army has been called away temporarily because of an Indian uprising. Sam Colt, Jr. and an Army lieutenant must keep things orderly until the troops return, but that is not an easy job.

Attack

Sam is an acting Indian agent as trouble between settlers and redskins gets intense after the apparent murder of a townsman by Indians. But the real situation is more than meets the eye as greedy white men want to stir up trouble in order to lay claim to gold-rich land owned by Indians. Robert Colbert is featured.

Bounty List

An ex-con is tracking down his former gang members and killing them for the reward money. Sam Colt shadows him in hopes of finding the stolen federal loot the gang stole years before. Ray Danton co-stars.

Appointment in Agoura

Sam Colt, Jr. has a reason for meeting a man in Agoura but must first protect him against a bunch named the Sangers, one of whom the man killed in a fight.

Showdown at Goldtown

To check out the progress of a young parolee, Sam Colt is sent to investigate. But many in the town are suspicious and distrustful of the man. More trouble develops when the parolee is caught up in an attempt to steal gold by his gunman-foster father.

The Trespasser

Trailing badmen, Sam is ambushed and captured by the daughter of one of the renegades. She falls in love with her prisoner and gets into trouble with the no-goods who want to kill Colt.

11
The Badge and the Gun

ABC (half hour) — debuted October 5, 1958
Format: Adult Western series set in Laramie, Wyoming, where Mar-
shal Dan Troop and Deputy Johnny McKay use their com-
bined skills and experience to maintain law and order in the
frontier community. Lily Merrill owns and operates the Bird-
cage Saloon.
Cast: John Russell ....Marshal Dan Troop
Peter Brown ....Deputy Johnny McKay
Peggie Castle ....Lily Merrill
Executive Producer: William T. Orr
Producer: Jules Schermer
Theme Music: "Lawman" by Jerry Livingston and Mack David
Location: Filmed in Hollywood

About the last thing that ABC and Warner Bros. needed in the
fall of 1958 was another Western. Already on the air were *Cheyenne,
Sugarfoot, Bronco, Colt .45*, and *Maverick*. But success breeds success,
and the result was another Western which was to have a good four-year
run.

Yet this Western was different from the others. One might say
that *Lawman* was *Gunsmoke, The Lone Ranger*, and *Father Knows
Best* all rolled into one.

Dan Troop, played by John Russell, was the personification of law
and order in its purest, most unadulterated form. He was tall (about
6'4"), ruggedly handsome, highly intelligent, and put dedication to
his job above all else. Troop was characterized by taciturnity and
seriousness of purpose. He was a good marshal and his confidence was

overwhelming. His historic 1870 attire, replete with string tie, emphasized the marshal's authenticity and intentionally avoided any similarity to the "Hollywood" cowboy.

"We liked John," says Bill Orr. "We tested him and kept it [his style] that way. He had no vestige of anything but dedication to duty, directness, and lacked any small talk—very monosyllabic."

His deputy was Johnny McKay, played by Peter Brown. Johnny was a young man who constantly looked to "Mr. Troop" (as Johnny always addressed him out of deep respect) for leadership and answers to tough problems because of the Marshal's talent with a gun and integrity as a man.

Contrasting Russell and Brown, Orr remembers, "Peter was a little lighter, although he wasn't funny or anything. He had a little more to do or say in the sense of a lighter character."

But Johnny was not a young man incapable of thinking and acting for himself. In the first episode, "The Deputy," Johnny had to prove to Marshal Troop that he was capable of handling the job of deputy of Laramie. After Troop had brushed off McKay several times because he was "too young" for the job, Johnny stepped in and aided the Marshal in a shootout with two very onerous brothers, one of whom had killed the previous Laramie marshal. With this deed Johnny won the respect of "Mr. Troop" and was pronounced deputy of the budding Wyoming town.

Each week there would be new threats to the peace and tranquility of Laramie, but somehow Marshal Dan and Deputy John would straighten things out.

Sounds like a neat little show, huh? Well, it was.

In fact, the show was so straight that the audience loved it as a refreshing change. In its second season (1959–60) *Lawman* ranked 16th in the A.C. Nielsen ratings, putting it above all other Warner Bros. Westerns.

"The whole idea grew out of a heavy role I did on *Cheyenne* ['The Empty Gun']," said John Russell. He played the part of a gunslinger whose hand had gone bad and, bothered by a bad conscience, wanted to set things straight with the widow of one of his victims. On the basis of Russell's strong character the wheels began to turn on creating a series with Russell on the side of law and order.

"Generally, the Western story now is treated as adult fare. It is not only a story of the great outdoors. It is a story of man versus man in a challenging and almost angry environment," commented John in a Warners press release.

Bill Orr says, "Jules Schermer produced *Lawman*—and very well. He loved sparse dialogue anyway. He was a good choice to produce it because he liked very sparse scenes. His whole career he had done pictures that were kind of that way. He'd done some good films as a producer."

Producer Schermer called *Lawman* a "thinking Western," one that allows the relationship of the characters to reach a deeper dramatic intensity. This could be done only if the cast and crew were close and could work well together without fear of jealousy or prima donnaism. Schermer declared that the chemistry of the cast and crew was responsible for *Lawman*'s success, "Ours is very good. We pull together." John Russell added, "On Laramie Street, where *Lawman* is played, prima donnas are off limits—by mutual consent of myself and my co-stars, Peggie Castle and Peter Brown."

The stories of *Lawman* were full of human conflict, creating intense situations for the people of Laramie.

"The stories we've done on *Lawman* are about people under stress," said Russell. "Men under stress do desperate things. At times the Old West was a desperate, daring, suspenseful place. We have tried to play it that way."

"We play the story off our heavies and others. This way we can use such stars as Edd Byrnes, Sammy Davis, Jr. and Ray Danton in conjunction with our running stars," explained Schermer.

With the mention of Sammy Davis, Jr. comes an interesting story. He appeared in an episode titled "Blue Boss and Willie Shay" as the Willie Shay half of the title. Blue Boss was his pet steer and best friend. Willie would treat Blue Boss just like a human.

A sadistic trail boss, Janaker, taunted Willie Shay. After saddling up Blue Boss for a joy ride, Janaker emptied his gun on the defenseless steer. The trail boss got carted off to jail, but Willie vowed to kill him when he was released, wanting to avenge the murder of his beloved pet. Upon release from jail the trail boss went looking for Willie and the two met in a blaze of gunfire. Janaker died and Willie lay seriously wounded, lacking the will to live because of his grief for Blue Boss.

But the story ended happily with Janaker's trail hands presenting Willie with a cute young steer calf which Willie named Blue Boss Two. This gift gave Willie the will to continue living and the hope of leading a herd from Texas with Blue Boss as the lead steer.

Now that's a nice story full of human emotion which, no doubt, would be a real audience-grabber. But it almost didn't get aired.

The R.J. Reynolds Tobacco Company, upon hearing that a Negro

was cast in the guest role, refused to sponsor that particular episode. That's the way Bill Orr tells it. But "Blue Boss and Willie Shay" did get aired by getting another sponsor.

Lawman was definitely a family show. The drama attracted the adults and the action kept up the kids' interest. Schermer was proud of the influence *Lawman* had on its young viewers.

"You have to think of the kids. So we've tried to set up a relationship between Troop and Johnny that will serve as an example. Johnny always shows respect for Troop. Calls him 'Sir' and 'Mr. Troop.' If something rubs off on the kids in the living room, it ought to be good. At any rate, we keep Johnny the way I would want my children to be."

The commencement of the second season saw the addition of Lily Merrill (Peggie Castle) as the owner of The Birdcage Saloon. Lily was an attractive gal who made it abundantly clear that she was going to run her business in an orderly manner and take no sass from any disorderly cowpokes.

As the season progressed we gathered the idea that she had a warm spot in her heart for Mr. Troop. The Gibraltar-like marshal was somewhat responsive, but guardedly so. After all, he couldn't let anything come between himself and the welfare of Laramie — especially a woman.

With the addition of Lily, one might see a resemblance to the giant of TV Westerns, *Gunsmoke*. When Hugh Benson was asked about the addition of a female co-star and the placing of her in the town saloon, he answered that it was not meant to copy Kitty in *Gunsmoke*: "It is only natural that the lead should have a girlfriend, and the best place to put her is in the saloon."

Even with Lily now in town, Marshal Troop showed little emotion. His granite jaw seldom moved except on one rare occasion when a mysterious stranger was to arrive in Laramie. Not knowing what to expect, the Marshal was prepared for the worst. But when the coach arrived, the stranger turned out to be a little girl. Dan Troop broke into a very uncharacteristic wide grin, something the people of Laramie and viewers at home cherished as a big event. After shooting the scene, the bosses had him taken back to the photo gallery to snap the grin for publicity purposes. As John Russell emphasized, "Troop is Man doing his job." And when a lawman is doing his job to keep his town safe, there is little occasion to smile. He has to be suspicious of everyone, never letting down his guard.

Opposite: *Lawman* cast John Russell, Peggie Castle, Peter Brown.

John Russell as Marshal Dan Troop with Peter Brown (right).

"As time went on," reflects Orr, "I said we could use a little levity in this series. It wouldn't hurt to have fun, too, with another character. So I kept urging [Schermer] to find another guy. I suggested we get a barber [or similar character]—not cornball—but a *real* character who had *some* humor.

"Julie gave me what I call the 'sponge.' He agrees with everything and never does it, which is a method I used to use myself," Orr snickered. "I'd get him in periodically, and then he'd throw something into one show—some little character."

Although *Lawman* remained a serious undertaking on-screen, sometimes some rather humorous things took place on the set. A group of Mexican people had been brought onto the *Lawman* set cast as peasants. The assistant director shouted, "Strike all the peasants!" This meant only to remove the Mexicans from the scene, but the people were not familiar with this connotation. They immediately began dispersing, fearing that they were going to be attacked.

As *Lawman* moved into its fourth (and final) season, the TV Westerns were beginning to fade due to tremendous overexposure. Producer Schermer planned no major changes in the show declaring, "We are not toying with any gimmick ideas to upset the successful formula of this series." He did announce that Johnny McKay would be given more responsibility. "It does make sense to let Johnny grow up a bit—be given more authority and a feeling of independence."

But the public had had enough of gun fights, rampaging Indians, and dance hall girls by 1962; thus Westerns began to bite the dust. The public had reached the saturation point and wanted more variety in viewing. Among the many victims of viewer backlash was *Lawman*. It was a good show to the end, but Marshal Troop learned that being good and dedicated to one's job does not make one immune to the blazing guns of Nielsen.

At least "Mr. Troop" could look back at four seasons of intense drama with an uncharacteristic grin, knowing that it was a job well done.

JOHN RUSSELL

John Russell was somewhat like the character he portrayed in *Lawman*: he was a man doing his job with extreme dedication.

"John is a very direct man," says William Orr. "Humor is not necessarily one of his great assets. I don't want to put that in a negative sense—I mean he's a very direct, sincere, straightforward fellow. He used to come in and talk about his contract with me as a businessman. He'd say, 'Bill, I've done this and that. I think now I ought to do this and that.' He'd come in and talk about it as if he were a banker."

Russell's day would begin with his rising at 4:45 A.M. and promptly tackling the task of studying his scripts. He would arrive at the Warner Bros. lot by 7:15 A.M., prepared to put in a full day as a professional. Russell made no outrageous demands about enlarging his dressing room or shortening his work days. His desire was to be professional, allowing him to make a good living for his family. John Russell was a producer's dream.

The movie, *Frame-Up*, was Russell's 1937 screen debut. He went on to star in other features: *Jesse James* (1939), *The Bluebird* (1940), *Forever Amber* (1947), *The Fat Man* (1951), and *The Sun Shines Bright* (1954). Then came his first TV series, *Soldiers of Fortune*, in 1955, playing the role of adventurer Tim Kelly.

Up until *Soldiers of Fortune* Russell played mostly heavy roles. He saw this as an opportunity to show his versatility as an actor, not just as a hero-personality. But his friends thought that he was hurting his future by being typed as a villain. They told him the public wouldn't turn around and accept him as a man on the side of law and order. Russell retorted that he had to accept a wide range of parts in order to keep steady work. He placed his family's security above being extremely picky when parts were available.

Russell's devotion to his family was another aspect of his dedication as a man. His early awakenings to study his scripts were ritual so that his evenings could be completely free to spend with his wife and three children.

"Nobody makes much of a fuss over me at home because I work in *Lawman*," explained Russell.

"One of my brood, John (age 10), told a columnist over a soda pop one day what he thought of his dad's TV career.

'Daddy is just a guy who works on TV to make money,' said John.

"At our house, the fact that father is an actor is played down to the point of routine. It is a hard, demanding job living up to the responsibilities of a TV series, like any other job. We impress the children in just that sense."

Russell explained that he would be doing his children a disservice to let them think they were unique just because their dad appeared every week on the neighbor's television set.

Even with the rigorous demands of *Lawman*, John managed to make two feature films between seasons: *Rio Bravo* and *Yellowstone Kelly*. In the latter he played the role of an Indian with two other Warners stars, Clint Walker and Edd Byrnes.

John was very much at home in Hollywood. Born January 3, 1921, in Los Angeles, he never strayed very far from the West with the only exception being a stint in the Marine Corps during World War II.

"The West has been my whole life," he commented in a *Lawman* press release. "My family helped pioneer California."

So with roots firmly implanted in the soil of the world's greatest movie lots, acting just had to rub off on him.

"I had no idea of ever getting into TV or pictures. Dramatics was taken as an easy credit — that's a laugh. If I'd known how hard I've had to work, I would have done something else."

Fortunately, for the sake of *Lawman* fans, he didn't do "something else."

As the fourth year of shooting began on the *Lawman* set, John proudly stated that the show was the most profitable, harmonious, and efficiently run series on the Warner lot. With problems cropping up within other shows, he didn't mind letting the reporters know how close the cast and crew were. Even with the addition of Peggie Castle as Lily the second season, Russell saw such a move as very beneficial and welcomed her with open arms (strictly a figure of speech; Marshal Troop would never let the idea cross his mind).

"The increased use of women in Western stories, with bigger and more definitive roles, has given the Western story dimension. The ladies played a big part in settling the West," he boasted concerning Lily's arrival on the set.

But all good things came to an end on October 2, 1962 with the final episode. John Russell turned in his marshal's star and went back to movies: *Fort Utah* (1967) and *Cannon for Cordoba* (1970) among others. It also gave him more time with his family and dabbling in two of his hobbies: collecting guns and butterflies.

John Russell could be justly proud of his disciplined professionalism. He had given his all for *Lawman* and was held in respect no less than that held by the people of Laramie for Dan Troop.

PETER BROWN

Ever since he was a young boy, Peter Brown (born Pierre de Lappe) had been exposed to the world of entertainment. His mother worked in radio and portrayed the Dragon Lady in *Terry and the Pirates*. Peter got his chance on the air waves when, at the age of seven, he appeared on children's programs as an elf or fairy.

But two years of radio was brought to an abrupt halt when his family pulled up stakes in New York City and moved to the West Coast. Peter's father had died when Peter was four years old, but the future Johnny McKay of *Lawman* got a stepfather and new name when his mother married businessman Albert Brown. In the West Peter did a lot of moving around, having attended 18 schools by the time he graduated from North Central High School in Spokane as a member of the Class of '52.

While in high school, Peter participated in dramatics but didn't really get hooked until serving with the 2nd Infantry Division in Alaska during 1954–56. During this time he appeared in 23 shows.

Upon being discharged from the Army, Peter appeared in the

Spokane Civil Theater production of *The Torch Bearers*. He then journeyed back to California landing a job as a filling station attendant by day and hopefully breaking into films at night.

His first Hollywood dramatic role was at the Horseshoe Theatre in *Desire Under the Elms* followed by an appearance in *Teach Me How to Cry* at the Gallery Theatre. During this time Brown came to the attention of producer Albert McCleery who signed him up for four NBC *Matinee Theatre* productions. These appearances led to parts in *West Point Story* (TV) and the Warners film, *Darby's Rangers* (with James Garner). After that came appearances in the Warners TV shows: *Cheyenne, Maverick, Sugarfoot*, etc.

When it came time to cast for the new series, *Lawman*, producer Jules Schermer was familiar with Brown's talent and was pleased to have him as the young deputy, Johnny McKay.

Peter displayed a professional discipline much like that of John Russell. Between scenes he could be seen practicing his fast draw or riding his horse, Houdini.

After Brown was divorced from actress Diane Jergens, he shared a Burbank residence with another Warners contract player, Bob Colbert. Houdini shared the stable out back with Colbert's horse, Shady Lady. On days off the two handsome young actors could be seen riding their mounts through Griffith Park, sometimes stopping off at the golf course for a round of 18 holes.

When not riding, Peter would spend his free time swimming, diving, or out on the courts for some tennis. His inside interests consisted of listening to classical and popular music (from his large record collection), and reading plays, history of the theatre, or psychology.

After *Lawman* became a ratings success and Brown an equally successful co-star, he didn't forget those who helped him to get where he was. He gave credit to his mother for inspiring him to adopt acting as a profession. Others to whom his thanks went included actor James Edwards, drama coach Hannes Lutz, UCLA theatre arts professor Ralph Freud, TV producer Albert McCleery, and drama coach Jeff Corey.

With the end of *Lawman* in October, 1962, Brown turned his ambitions toward being a director with a healthy enthusiasm and sense of purpose: "I don't usually fail at what I attempt."

PEGGIE CASTLE

August 11, 1973. Peggie Castle, alias Lily Merrill of the Birdcage Saloon on *Lawman* was dead. Cause of death was cirrhosis of the liver and a heart condition. The American leading lady of the 1950's second features was only 46 years old.

She was born Peggie Thomas Blair in Appalachia, Virginia. In her late teens Peggie moved to California and entered Mills College in Oakland. But after two years of academics, the entertainment world began to intrigue her.

Peggie left Mills to take part in *Today's Children*, a radio soap opera in which she was paid a handsome salary of $375 per week. From there she went on to appear on other radio shows such as the *Lux Radio Theater*.

Not to be content in front of a radio mike, Peggie worked her way into a screen test at 20th Century–Fox. She read from a scene in *Dinner at Eight* with a dashing young Fox contract player who meant little to her at the time, but who became a close professional friend years later—John Russell. Though she was in nearly thirty movies and dozens of TV shows, Peggie didn't appear with John again until over a decade later in the second season of *Lawman*.

Her film debut was in 1949 with *Mr. Belvedere Goes to Washington*. Other films of note were *The Jury* (1953), *Two Gun Lady* (1956), and *Seven Hills of Rome* (1958).

After landing a contract with Warner Bros., Peggie appeared in several Warners TV productions including *Cheyenne* and *77 Sunset Strip*. In 1959 she was given the part of Lily, Laramie businesswoman and badgethrob of Marshal Troop.

Her career began to decline after *Lawman* was canceled, and she divorced her third husband, producer William McGarry.

The on-screen, tough saloon owner from Laramie was in reality a reserved, soft-spoken lady whose life was cut far too short.

Lawman — Series Index

FIRST SEASON:

The Deputy

Dan Troop takes over in Laramie after the previous marshal is killed. His first job is to bring in the marshal's killer, and in the process he gains a fine deputy in Johnny Mc-Kay. Edd Byrnes is featured.

The Prisoner

When Troop arrests and jails a brutal, gun-quick bully for killing a man in an unfair shootout, the town will not back his prosecution because they fear reprisals from bully's companion cowhands.

The Joker

Deputy McKay's family was broken up when he was very young, and now a ruthless killer with a cruel sense of humor shows up in Laramie claiming to be Johnny's father. Ashamed, McKay turns in his badge.

The Oath

While escorting two prisoners to a Cheyenne prison, Troop comes upon a wrecked stagecoach and a woman on the verge of giving birth prematurely. One of the prisoners is a doctor. He tends to the woman, even at the cost of giving up a chance to escape.

The Outcast

The man who killed Jesse James for the reward comes to Laramie and runs into a friend of Jesse's and his trailhands who seek revenge.

The Jury

A beautiful female saloon owner gets away with several crimes because no male jury will convict her. But Troop reopens an old murder case against her with an all-woman jury, since now women have gained the right to serve on juries.

Wanted

Trouble comes to Laramie in the form of a brutal bounty hunter who is after a fugitive, a decent man who, for more than a year, has led a respectable life in the Wyoming town.

The Badge

Johnny McKay puts his badge on the line that his friend is a law-abiding man, despite being part of an outlaw family which has a certain amount of influence over him. Peter Breck is featured.

Bloodline

A man raised by his father to be a gunman is now the prey of another man — his own son.

The Intruders

Chinese laborers are being mistreated and exploited by a shakedown group. When a laborer is found beaten to death in the street, Troop looks for witnesses.

Short Straw

When Marshal Troop initiates an early curfew that closes down the saloons before their biggest business hours, he is first offered a bribe which he expectedly refuses. Now he is marked for death.

Lady in Question

When Johnny McKay's old sweetheart comes to town, she is followed by her lover who goads Johnny into a gunfight. Johnny kills him, but the man's gun is missing when Johnny returns with Dan Troop. Troop must place Johnny under arrest for murder.

The Master

Dan Troop's mentor, a legendary lawman now retired, comes to town as a trouble-shooter for a cattlemen's association concerned with ridding the land of nesters. Troop, who is bent on protecting the rights of nesters, must face a showdown with his former teacher.

The Outsider

Marshal Troop is framed for murder when he locks horns with a bitter rancher who prevents cowboys from working for a half-breed. James Drury co-stars.

The Captives

Johnny takes Doc Stewart out to look after the injured leg of an old crusty individual who lives in an isolated cabin. There they are taken captive by gunman Jack McCall. McCall holds Doc and his patient hostage while Johnny is sent into town for a fresh horse and supplies.

The Encounter

While trailing outlaws, Troop is injured by a bear, found by the sister of one of the men he is trailing, and taken to the outlaws' cabin.

The Brand Release

A man innocent, but accused, of cattle rustling is pursued by sheriff and another man who are connected with a gang that sold the herd and are now trying to steal the cattle back.

The Runaway

An inflexible Army colonel asks old friend Dan Troop to search for his son who has been missing for four days.

Warpath

Marshal Troop is caught in an Indian attack after buffalo hunters have provoked an uprising.

The Gunman

A once-notorious gunman is in Laramie just long enough to meet his fiancée on the morning stage. Even though he claims he has hung up his gun forever, Troop keeps a close eye on him. His fiancée is delayed, but he thinks she has stood him up. The gunman begins to drink and faces Troop in a showdown.

The Big Hat

When a rancher wins the heart of a dance hall girl, he earns the hatred of a jealous gunsmith. The gunsmith tries to kill the rancher but by mistake kills another man.

The Chef

Because of a previous agreement, a German chef must leave his job at the Laramie Hotel which he loves very much to work for a wealthy and dictatorial couple. But the chef takes a subtle suggestion from Dan Troop to solve his problem.

The Posse

When a girl brings a dead body into town claiming the man was shot by a man who came to foreclose the mortgage, Troop is suspicious. He organizes a posse from irate townspeople but fears they will overpower him and lynch the alleged murderer. Pernell Roberts guest stars.

The Visitor

A gunfighter's son is living in Laramie with foster parents, but his father comes to town to claim his son. Dan Troop tries to convince the gunman to leave his son where he is. Doug McClure is featured.

Battle Scar

A Civil War hero's clinging militarism alienates him from friends and wife. He has a dark secret which he fears being revealed. Robert Conrad co-stars.

The Gang

A gang of brutal gunmen are on their way to Laramie with one purpose in mind — to kill Marshal Dan Troop. A former member of the gang rides with incredible swiftness to tip off Troop of upcoming fight.

The Souvenir

A dangerous killer breaks jail while Deputy McKay is standing guard. The town council is furious and demands Johnny's resignation. When

Dan Troop tries to help, McKay misinterprets and friction develops.

The Young Toughs

Johnny McKay has his hands full while minding Laramie in Dan Troop's absence. A group of roughnecks come into town and threaten to take over. One of the toughs is played by Van Williams.

Riding Shotgun

An ex-convict comes under suspicion when the stage for which he is riding shotgun is held up by the gang to which he used to belong.

The Journey

Troop goes to a neighboring town in an effort to save an innocent man accused of murder, but the Marshal finds the job is not so simple.

The Huntress

A woman seeks the Pierce brothers who are responsible for the death of her boyfriend. She kills one and follows the other one to Laramie.

The Return

Dan Troop befriends an ex-con who is trying to go straight, but the man meets stiff resistance from a rancher, father of the girl the ex-con loves. Distraught, he decides to return to his old gang.

The Senator

A senator is to arrive in Laramie on the midnight train, and Troop has only one hour to track down three men who plot to assassinate the visiting statesman.

The Ring

A dance hall girl is murdered and later the same fate is accorded a kleptomaniac who possesses the ring of the dead girl. Troop, figuring the second murder was to remove a possible witness of the first, sets a trap for the perpetrator of the two murders.

The Bandit

A bandit holds up the Laramie bank and flees with the loot. He stops at a farmhouse where he discovers a couple who are sick with fever. Marshal Troop catches up with him, but the Marshal also contracts the fever. The bandit stays to show a bit of good-Samaritanism.

The Wayfarer

Doc Holliday is in Laramie and is forced to draw on a drunken tough. The dead man's father and brothers seek revenge, but Doc refuses to leave town.

The Conclave

A group of notorious gunmen plan a daring stagecoach robbery but are foiled when one of them gets drunk, is thrown into Dan Troop's jail, and begins to talk.

Red Ransom

Johnny is held by Indians and is to be killed at dawn if Dan Troop cannot find the murderer of the chief's son.

The Friend

After ridding Laramie of Dan Troop and his posse through trickery, a gang plans to rob the bank. But when one of their members discovers an old friend, Johnny McKay, he abandons the gang and joins McKay.

SECOND SEASON:

Lily

Peggie Castle makes her debut. Dan Troop is eager to close down a newly-opened saloon but relents when the pretty owner is the unfortunate victim of a scheming gambler.

The Hunch

A well-educated man suffering from alcoholism now occupies his time as a dirt farmer, but his life becomes more complicated when framed for murder.

Shackled

Johnny McKay chains himself to his prisoner after the ambush of a prison van and its resulting immobility.

The Exchange

Lily is blackmailed into helping her ex-convict former husband rob a bank when he holds their young son hostage.

The Last Man

Dan Troop and a Sioux chief negotiate a peace between warring factions. But the chief's half-brother is intent on destroying the parley.

Breakup

After duty demanded that Johnny kill a friend, he decides to resign and move to California.

Shadow Witness

When a nearly blind man stumbles upon a murder of a dance hall girl, Marshal Troop gambles that the killer thinks the man was a seeing witness and will try to silence him.

The Prodigal

A wandering son is reunited with his father, but the homecoming is threatened by two bank robbers who are after $5,000 given to the son by a fellow gang member.

The Press

Marshal Troop is forced to resign by an ex-con who has moved to Laramie and begun printing a newspaper.

9:05 to North Platte

Lily and a young boy are held hostage by a man and his two sons who demand that Marshal Troop get a third son off a train due in Laramie. The third son is on his way to be executed.

The Hoax

Two conmen move into Laramie and pose as clergymen who are raising money for a new church.

The Shelter

Troop and McKay are pitted against two escaped killers in a remote cabin and are aided by an Indian woman.

Last Stop

Embittered over the death of his impoverished mother, a youth goes looking for his father whom he plans to kill for abandoning her years before. With Dan Troop's help, the son learns things are not as they seem.

The Showdown

A gunman rides into town and vows to kill his former partner who has put away his guns to lead a decent life. James Coburn co-stars as the gunslinger.

The Stranger

Troop receives threatening letters after he is forced to kill a man in the Birdcage Saloon.

The Wolfer

An old wolf killer is hired by the local stockmen's association to capture a vicious wolf, but he claims he has already captured it and demands $5,000. If he doesn't get the money, he will release the wolf.

The Hardcase

An alcoholic's daughter is found unconscious and near death. A trail boss' son is thought to be responsible, but the trail boss and his men will use force if necessary to get his son back.

To Capture the West

An itinerant Western painter comes to Laramie and reveals that he is being followed by an escaped convict and his gang. The outlaw wants revenge because one of the artist's paintings was used as evidence to convict him.

The Ugly Man

Lily is threatened by an unknown who calls himself the Ugly Man.

The Kids

An outlaw's three children have been living with their uncle since their mother died. But the children have run away because they believe their uncle, a mild-mannered Quaker, is a coward and not the dashing hero they believe their father to be.

The Thimblerigger

A man proficient at the shell game comes to town to use his talent not to gamble, but rather to ferret out a man who abandoned his wife during a holdup years ago.

The Truce

A wounded outlaw being pursued by a bloodthirsty sheriff and his posse rides into Laramie and surrenders to Dan Troop. By a previous agreement Troop is to escort the outlaw to the governor to ask for a pardon, but the politically-ambitious sheriff makes the trip dangerous.

Reunion in Laramie

An incident of cowardice during the Civil War causes a confrontation between a buffalo hunter and a pianist.

Thirty Minutes

A crazed killer shoots a cowboy, wounds Deputy McKay, and holds the patrons of the Birdcage Saloon hostage. He demands a horse to make his getaway and tells his hostages that he intends to kill Marshal Troop when Troop delivers the horse.

Left Hand of the Law

An outlaw who was shot in the arm by Dan Troop and had to have it amputated returns to Laramie to settle the score. He brings with him his son who has been instructed to shoot Troop in the right arm so his dad can finish the lawman off on equal terms.

Belding's Girl

A rancher, embittered because of his wife's desertion, raises his daughter with suspicion and cruelty. She escapes to find work in Lily's saloon and falls in love with a young cowhand.

Girl from Grantsville

Johnny McKay falls in love with a new girl in town, but a young gambler who knew her previously claims that she loves him. Johnny plans to marry her, but Dan Troop and Lily are suspicious—and rightfully so.

The Surface of Truth

In a fit of rage, a white trapper kills his Indian wife. According to tribal law, he is given one day to make peace with God before his wife's brother executes him. The trapper flees to Laramie where he swears innocence to Dan Troop.

The Salvation of Owny O'Reilly

A Laramie kid troublemaker finds stolen gold and shapes up to avoid suspicion. He then learns how decent people live and makes many new friends. Wanting to keep his new life and its rewards, the former delinquent decides to turn in the gold to Troop and McKay. But that is when the robbers show up looking for their gold. Joel Grey co-stars.

The Lady Belle

The mastermind of a clever bank-robbing gang is a beautiful young lady. But her plans for the Laramie bank are not carried out with the same efficiency as with previous jobs.

The Payment

A gunman who was forced to kill his friend now meets up with his friend's son who is determined to settle the score. Troy Donahue and Robert McQueeney are featured as the son and the gunfighter.

The Judge

An outlaw known as the "Actor" ambushes and wounds Dan Troop. The Marshal is found by a girl who takes him home where she resides with her older sister and her sister's husband, an egocentric judge.

Man on a Wire

The Black Hand Society has sent an assassin to eliminate a young Sicilian tightrope walker who has recently come to Laramie with his wife and baby.

The Parting

An escaped prisoner turns himself in to Dan Troop so his reward money can be given to his fiancée for a necessary operation. She doesn't know about his outlaw past, but an ex-con drifter threatens to expose it.

The Swamper

An alcoholic swamper comes into some money—enough to send his daughter away to school, but the money comes with strings attached.

Man on a Mountain

An old friend of Dan Troop's steals some money to help his sick wife and is holed up in his mountain cabin, surrounded by a posse led by a ruthless deputy.

Fast Trip to Cheyenne

When Troop finds out an innocent man is about to be executed in Cheyenne, he tries desperately to arrive in time to save him.

THIRD SEASON:

The Town Boys

Dan Troop arrests four juvenile delinquents, but Johnny McKay wants to try to reform the boys.

The Go-Between

Deputy McKay is used as a go-between when Lily is kidnapped and held for ransom.

The Mad Bunch

A new member of the Mad Bunch Gang is repulsed when the gang guns down a man on the way to town to get a doctor for his sick wife. The member deserts the gang and takes the sick wife into Laramie where he joins forces with Troop and McKay and falls in love with the widow.

The Old War Horse

An unscrupulous snoop tries to fatten his pocketbook by taking half of an inheritance left by the estranged husband of an ex-dance hall queen. The penniless widow and the establishment of a new college stand to lose.

The Return of Owny O'Reilly

Johnny McKay convinces Dan Troop to deputize Owny O'Reilly to collect evidence against a robber.

Yawkey

A renowned quick-draw comes to Laramie and challenges Marshal Troop without any provocation. Troop, clearly no match for the lightning draw of his opponent, discovers the gunman's private torment.

Dilemma

A doctor on the run from three outlaw brothers takes on as swamper in the Birdcage Saloon. Marshal Troop becomes suspicious of Lily's new help as a possible fugitive until his real identity is revealed when he must save the life of Laramie's doctor at the risk of being discovered by the three brothers who have come to Laramie on his trail.

The Post

While returning a wanted man to New Mexico, both Troop and his prisoner are captured by an evil sheriff and his no-good deputies who hold a town in terror.

Chantay

An innocent Indian maiden confesses guilt in a murder rather than risk being killed by the real murderer.

Samson the Great

Troop must square off with a giant of a man who has come to Laramie to challenge anyone in the boxing ring but carries his barbarism beyond the ring.

The Second Son

A young man pleads guilty to a robbery-beating committed by his stepbrother in order to acquire love and understanding from his stepbrother and stepfather. But the man finds out the true colors of his stepbrother when the victim dies and the charge is now murder.

The Catcher

A huge, good-natured, simple man is a suspect in the death of a fellow sheepman and is encouraged to flee the law by the real murderer who joins the search.

Cornered

Deputy Johnny McKay is forced into a gunfight with a brutal, fast-draw killer. The killer's gun misfires, allowing Johnny to come out on top. But before he can explain how he managed to beat such an expert gunman, the townspeople proclaim him a hero. Trouble follows when the dead gunman's even faster-drawing son appears.

The Escape of Joe Killmer

An outlaw's wife turns her seriously wounded husband over to Dan Troop so he can get necessary medical attention. Once he recovers, his outlaw brother and gang plan to break him out.

Old Stefano

A wealthy, arrogant, and cruel rancher refuses to destroy a valuable horse when it breaks a leg. An old sheepherder, who loves all animals, takes it upon himself to relieve the horse of its pain by shooting it. The enraged rancher vows to kill the well-meaning sheepman.

The Robbery

Dan Troop is lured into a trap set by three outlaws—one of them an old friend of Troop's.

Firehouse Lil

Lily, Laramie's newly elected fire chief, comes to the aid of Marshal Troop when bank robbers create a diversion by setting ablaze the livery stable.

The Frame-Up

Dan Troop is removed from office when discredited by a lawyer and widow of a man hanged for murder.

The Marked Man

A gunman is hired to kill Dan Troop but refuses when he discovers his victim-to-be is an old friend. However, the gunman is forced to take action when his sister is threatened.

The Squatters

To get control of ranch and evict squatters, a trusted hired hand deliberately miscares for his elderly boss who has come down with pneumonia. But little does he know there is a witness to his foul deed.

Homecoming

A notorious gunman whom Troop sent to prison three years before has escaped from jail. The gunman swore that one day he would return to kill Troop. The Marshal is a little on edge because his gun hand is injured and is therefore no match for the gunslinger.

Hassayampa

An elderly, white-bearded reformer smashes up the Birdcage Saloon and condemns it as a den of iniquity. He is supported by the ladies of the Tuesday Club and causes the Birdcage to close down. But Troop and McKay suspect a racket.

The Promoter

Dan Troop buys half interest in the Birdcage Saloon to foil the plan of a whiskey company salesman to buy out all the saloons in Laramie.

Detweiler's Kid

Johnny McKay must face a fight— with a girl raised as a tomboy because her father always wanted a son. The deputy is saved from the precarious situation by a cowboy's love for her.

The Inheritance

A proud farmer, who is believed to be a rich man because of his wise financial counseling, is misunderstood by his son, refusing his father's help to buy a pair of boots.

Blue Boss and Willie Shay

A deliberate act of cruelty results in a gunfight between a happy-go-lucky cowpoke and a sadistic trail boss. Sammy Davis, Jr. is special guest star.

The Man from New York

A New York police detective shows up in Laramie looking for a bank thief—a man now leading a decent, respectable life under an alias. The mission changes its course when the wanted man saves the detective's life.

Mark of Cain

A man vindicated of his brother's murder returns home only to be accused of the death of his father.

Fugitive

A wounded outlaw escapes the evil influence of his partner and hopes to flee with his wife and young son to California to begin a new life.

The Persecuted

A jury acquits a vicious gunman who goaded a man into a gunfight. After the trial he picks up where he left off.

The Grubstake

A middle-aged woman with little hope for a better life invests her entire savings in a mine owned by an old prospector.

Whiphand

When a bully's wife runs away with a benign peddler, the brutish man comes gunning. Marshal Troop convinces the men to settle their score with a fist fight.

The Threat

A hired gunman kills a farmer but cannot be arrested for lack of evidence proving it was not in self-defense. But the farmer's physically weak brother decides to even the score with the gunman by using fear as a psychological weapon.

The Trial

A judge visiting Laramie is captured and put on trial with the jury composed of men he has sentenced in the past.

Blind Hate

A rancher who wants supreme control over his daughter has horse-whipped blind his foreman who desires to marry her. Troop must step in to avoid a shoot-out when the daughter runs away.

The Stake

Dan Troop is puzzled when a wanted man turns himself in to collect his own reward.

Conditional Surrender

A wounded outlaw father agrees to surrender himself and his outlaw sons under the condition that his daughter be given a proper dress and put on the eastbound stage. When the father dies, sons renege.

Cold Fear

After marriage, an ex-marshal's gun hand becomes useless because of a mental block to gunfighting. He loses his fear after his wife is kidnapped by two gunmen.

The Promise

Johnny McKay is at Fort Laramie when a murderer about to be hanged calls out to an unknown person to kill Dan Troop.

FOURTH SEASON:

The Juror

The leader of a train robbery goes on trial in Laramie after jurors in a nearby town are intimidated by the uncaptured members of the gang.

Trapped

A banker is forced to turn over all of Laramie's funds or eight persons will be put to death. To make matters worse, the town is cut off from the outside world when telegraph wires are cut down and the stage fails to show. Peter Breck is featured.

The Four

Four range riders defy Marshal Troop and threaten the peace of Laramie as they search the town for a young killer. Meanwhile, the killer has taken Lily as his hostage. Johnny Weissmuller, Jr. has a supporting role.

The Stalker

A half breed trapper is taunted by two rough trailhands and accidentally kills one of them. The trapper then flees with two men on his trail—the companion trailhand vowing revenge and Marshal Dan Troop offering a fair trial.

Porphyria's Lover

An escaped prisoner plans to carry out a death threat during a flash storm which has cut Laramie's communications.

No Contest

Johnny McKay's cousin travels from Boston to Laramie for a visit and gets initiated in the ways of the West.

Trojan Horse

A wagon with a dangerous payload passes through Laramie and sets up the possible destruction of Laramie unless the bank is allowed to be robbed with no retaliation.

The Catalog Woman

A Laramie citizen withdraws his life savings and disappears with his mail order bride, which causes Dan Troop to grow rather suspicious.

The Cold One

A beautiful young woman who testified against her husband returns to Laramie, her childhood home, knowing that her escaped husband will find her and kill her.

Owny O'Reilly, Esquire

The one and only Owny O'Reilly returns to Laramie and involves himself in an array of situations: a dog he buys which hates his horse, getting robbed, falling in love with the governor's missing daughter, and foiling a jailbreak. Joel Grey stars.

The Son

Johnny McKay finds himself trying to prevent a couple of killings when a father brings his blind son to Laramie in order to identify the voice of the man who murdered the boy's brother. Chad Everett co-stars.

The Substitute

The proper ladies of Laramie have their feathers ruffled when Lily offers a substitute for the school teacher position vacated when the previous school marm eloped.

The Lords of Darkness

Marshal Troop finds himself in a difficult situation while trailing two brothers who provoked and killed the new bartender at the Birdcage Saloon.

By the Book

Trouble comes to Laramie when a big-city marshal arrives to inspect Troop's efficiency as a lawman.

The Appointment

Johnny McKay is offered an appointment to West Point and is torn between a glamourous military career and his job as deputy of Laramie.

The Prodigal Mother

A mother who gave up her son to be raised by a Laramie couple nine years ago returns to claim him.

Get Out of Town

One of Marshal Troop's old enemies returns to Laramie to open a new saloon. The Marshal finds himself in the middle of a battle between the new arrival and a leading town citizen.

Mountain Man

When a monstrous, shaggy mountain man comes to town looking for a wife, he decides Lily will do just fine. To escape his advances, Lily tells the man she is already engaged to Dan Troop and hopes this will make him leave town. Instead, the mountain man decides to eliminate the competition.

Explosion

Dan Troop, Johnny McKay, and a frontier doctor stand alone against a mob of citizens determined to hunt down a young man who gunned down an old couple. Troop realizes the boy is not responsible because of a brain injury.

The Locket

A driverless stage arrives in Laramie with an injured, unconscious girl on board. The mystery broadens when she and Lily are taken prisoner by two gunmen. Robert Colbert is featured.

A Friend of the Family

Dan and Johnny arrest two bank robbers, and one of them turns out to be a man Johnny knew as "Uncle Joe" during his childhood and was McKay's father's best friend.

The Man Behind the News

A new newspaper editor drives Dan Troop to a showdown when the paper glorifies the outlaws of the West and criticizes Troop for not treating them as heroes.

The Vintage

Two fighting cowhands accidentally destroy the grapevines belonging to two settlers. Marshal Troop assures the settlers that they will be compensated for the damage, but one of the settlers wants more.

Tarot

An old gambling friend of Lily's comes to town but not for reminiscing—rather plotting a payroll robbery. The gambler is played by Robert McQueeney.

Heritage of Hate

After serving three years in prison for manslaughter, a young woman returns to Laramie but is the victim of a hate campaign initiated by the father of the man she killed.

The Tarnished Badge

An old-time lawman who taught the ropes to Dan Troop begins to operate outside the law. Troop and McKay are forced to track him down.

Change of Venue

Dan Troop is taking a handcuffed killer-bank robber to another town for trial. But Troop doesn't know that the stage is to be ambushed.

The Barber

One of the members of a gang poses as a barber as part of an ingenious plot to rob the Laramie bank.

Clootey Hutter

Marshal Troop is faced with something he has never come up against before—a lady gunfighter.

The Holdout

When Troop refuses to let a vigilante committee take over Laramie, he is fired by the town council and threatened with death.

The Long Gun

Troop has to stop an ambush of two young killers by a veteran marshal Troop has always admired.

The Bride

Troop cannot convince one of Laramie's richest ranchers that the beautiful girl to whom he has become engaged is trying to swindle him.

The Actor

A once well known Shakespearean actor, now an alcoholic, comes to Laramie and becomes the target of an irate woman. John Carradine stars as the actor.

Sunday

For a very unusual reason, a reformed outlaw tries to take from Troop a captured killer being held in the Laramie jail for federal authorities. The reformed outlaw is played by Andrew Duggan.

The Doctor

Marshal Troop accompanies a reluctant witness on a stagecoach ride to Laramie when the driver comes down with the plague, forcing Troop to place all the passengers under quarantine.

The Youngest

A cheating gambler who tries to shoot Marshal Troop in the back is laid low by the lawman. This enrages the Martin family, with the exception of the youngest son who has a better idea.

The Wanted Man

The wife of a wanted outlaw is seriously ill and about to give birth. The Laramie doctor tells Troop that she will die unless allowed to see her husband. Meanwhile, a bounty hunter lies in wait.

The Witness

After a woman is killed, her son gives the murderer's description to a traveling artist who sketches the described face. Marshal Troop is forced to place a good friend under arrest.

Cort

Marshal Troop stands between a man who has been hunted for revenge the past ten years and the man who is after him.

The Unmasked

Two strangers come to Laramie and claim to be seeking a cousin to share an inheritance, but Dan Troop suspects them to be gunslingers.

Jailbreak

A cute young girl sweet-talks Johnny McKay in hopes of getting her fiancé loose from the Laramie jail.

12
All Roads Lead to Rome

ABC (1 hour) — debuted October 5, 1962
Format: Dramatic series about a company of GI's fighting their way
through Italy and meeting stiff resistance from Nazis and
emotional encounters with Italian civilians — all recorded by
war correspondent Conley Wright
Cast: Robert McQueeney . . . . Conley Wright
William Reynolds . . . . Captain Jim Benedict
Robert Ridgely . . . . Lieutenant Frank Kimbro
Richard X. Slattery . . . . 1st Sgt. John McKenna
Eddie Fontaine . . . . PFC Pete D'Angelo
Roland LaStarza . . . . Private Ernie Lucavich
Robert Gothie . . . . Private Sam Hanson
Roger Davis . . . . Private Roger Gibson
Executive Producer: William T. Orr
Producer: Richard Bluel
Theme Music: composed by Howard Jackson
Location: Filmed in Hollywood

The 36th Infantry Division had an impressive record: a victorious Italian campaign against the Nazis and Italian fascists and the honor of having the most decorated soldier amongst its ranks — Audie Murphy. That was in real life.

In *The Gallant Men* our boys from the fighting Texas Division suffered a disastrous defeat — not at the hands of Hitler but the even-more-bloodthirsty Nielsen ratings and ABC. The sad part about it was that *The Gallant Men* was a great show and didn't deserve its fate any more than our GI's would have deserved a military drubbing in the Big One.

"I was very disappointed," reflects Bill Orr. "The network didn't renew it. They said it didn't do well enough. It didn't do that badly as I recall. It wasn't a flop."

Unfortunately in the war of television ratings the loss of a few battles can immediately spell one's defeat. Despite excellent stories, *The Gallant Men* bit the Italian dust after one year of *Combat* (as in Rick Jason and Vic Morrow). *Combat* debuted the same week (October 2, 1962) by hitting the beaches at Normandy and fought its way through the French countryside and across the Rhine for five years. (The series was filmed at M-G-M by Selmur Productions.)

Says Hugh Benson, "We started before *Combat*." He was referring to the WWII series idea rather than the actual premiere date. *The Gallant Men* debuted October 5, 1962.

"We had great facilities to do a war show," Orr explains. "They [ABC] said they thought it would be good, and they thought they'd pencil it in for the next year's schedule. We didn't have a firm commitment, but we had an understanding that we were going to go ahead and get together, thinking about the cast and so forth. Then we went to work and they gave us a commitment to do the pilot."

After filming the pilot and sending it to ABC in New York, Orr picked up a trade paper which stated the network had bought *Combat*. He picked up the phone and placed a call to ABC's New York office.

"What the heck is that? You've got our show and you haven't said it's definitely in, and I see you've just bought *Combat*. We've spent all this time doing this for you, and we spent more on the pilot than you gave us. Now we want a commitment," Orr demanded. And with a sense of satisfaction he recalls, "We got the commitment."

Now ABC had two World War II dramas and the competition was on to see which would do better in the ratings and be awarded another season. The chance that both would survive was not an impossibility, but a reasonable improbability. Therefore, somewhat of a rivalry developed between the two shows. Warners began its publicity campaign by announcing that the cast of *The Gallant Men* would undergo basic training on its back lot. This, as press releases claimed, would get the cast in a military frame of mind (and body) to realistically portray their characters. *Combat* counterattacked by announcing that its cast would take part in military training with real troops at Fort Ord, California. So before production ever began for either series, their stars were getting accustomed to firing machine guns, going through obstacle courses, and saluting their superiors.

In the beginning *The Gallant Men* was not the title of the series but merely the title of the first episode. Warners preferred the name *Battlezone*. William Orr claimed no credit for the title change: "I never liked the title *Gallant Men*. It was innocuous to me. The network came up with that name."

Orr explained that the plan was to start the series in North Africa and carry through the war. "We would follow the course and flow of the Allies' invasions through the invasion of Normandy. If the show went on up to Berlin, depending upon how well the show was doing, we'd slow down so we wouldn't run out of material."

Warners had a wealth of battle footage for splicing into the series. The Warners librarian had worked in the Air Corps motion picture unit during the war and had a large collection of battle footage which *The Gallant Men* used to add authenticity to its stories. The pilot episode began with the arrival of war correspondent Conley Wright on the shores of Salerno, Italy, under heavy German fire. Salerno and then Naples were captured.

Wright was assigned to a unit commanded by a young Captain Benedict, who was uncertain of his ability to command under fire. Benedict relied on the judgment of one particular private, Jake. Wright recognized Jake as a major he had known in Casablanca.

Jake had cracked under the strain of his command and took on the identity of a private who had been killed. He was desperately trying to redeem himself for the cowardice in action. Conley agreed not to reveal Jake's true identity.

When tanks became unsuccessful in ridding the small, strategic San Pietro of German occupation, Jake suggested letting the infantry take it. At Jake's suggestion Captain Benedict gave the order to attack. The assault was costly but victorious. Jake died from wounds sustained in heroic combat, but not before he begged Conley Wright not to write the story of his heroism. "The captain has won his spurs. Let him keep them," spoke a dying Jake.

The taking of San Peitro gave the young Captain Benedict the courage and self-confidence necessary to lead his men onward to Rome. Each week thereafter the viewers got to know the men of Benedict's unit: Lt. Kimbro, Sgt. McKenna, and Privates D'Angelo, Lucavich, Hanson, and Gibson. The growing personal revelations of the soldiers came from the intense situations encountered with Italian civilians, enemy troops, and fellow Allied soldiers. One episode might revolve around a love affair between one of the men and an Army nurse or Italian damsel, followed the next week by the fear of a Ger-

William Reynolds (left) and Robert McQueeney.

man infiltrator within the unit. Conley Wright recorded the experiences and lent a helping hand in various ways like his fluency in Italian for easy communication with civilians.

It seemed that *The Gallant Men* had all of the essentials for a successful series, but ABC refused to renew it for another season. No cause for its lack of success was ever found. It could have been the time slot, lack of network promotion, or any number of other things.

Hugh Benson summed up what Nielsen had: "It apparently

didn't catch on with the audience." Searching for a more subtle rationale, Orr speculated, "I think their show [*Combat*] was more excitingly cast. Maybe because we were doing the Italian campaign."

Whatever the reasons, *The Gallant Men* faded into video history. Orr, figuring ABC had decided to keep whichever proved to be better, reflected, "They [ABC] stayed with *Combat* and let us go."

Perhaps if *The Gallant Men* had been awarded another season, it would have caught on with the viewers. But now this excellent show is but a memory to those who saw it and relived some of those exciting and trying experiences of the famed 36th Division.

ROBERT McQUEENEY

Robert McQueeney seemed to prefer performing "live" to audiences rather than displaying his talents on film. After being discharged from the Army at the end of World War II, he appeared in several off-Broadway shows before making his Broadway stage debut in *Billy Budd*. After that came parts in *Dial M for Murder*, *Affairs of State*, and *Fragile Fox*. Not limiting himself to Broadway alone, McQueeney appeared in many Shakespearean plays including the Helen Hayes production of *Macbeth* and toured with *Rain*, *The Second Man*, *The Tender Trap*, and *The Barretts of Wimpole Street*. He won considerable attention for his award-winning performance in *The Warrior's Return*, an off-Broadway production in which he played a crippled war veteran.

With all of his theatrical experience Robert headed for the budding fields of television. The "live" shows to his credit include *Robert Montgomery Presents*, *Philco TV Playhouse*, *Kraft Theatre*, *Studio One*, *Omnibus*, and *Playwrights '56*. These appearances proved to be stepping stones for him to enter the lucrative area of daytime soap operas. He landed roles in both *Love of Life* and *The Guiding Light*.

McQueeney was born in Bridgeport, Connecticut, where his father, Dr. Andrew McQueeney, was a renowned surgeon and his mother, a school teacher, gained prominence in local and national politics. He attended grammar school in Bridgeport and secondary school at Taft School in Watertown. In high school, McQueeney got his first professional job with a summer theatre group at Jennerstown, Pennsylvania. Robert majored in drama at Bard College in New York and spent his summers participating in plays.

Upon graduation he joined the Army as a combat engineer,

serving as a lieutenant in New Guinea, Moro Tai, Dutch East Indies, and the Philippine Islands.

McQueeney lived on the East Coast during his stage play and early television days. But after a tour with Chico Marx in *The Fifth Season* he was invited to appear on television in Hollywood. For a while he commuted from East to West coasts but soon the wide, open spaces of California enticed him to pack up his bags and move to Palmdale, a town about 50 miles from Los Angeles in the Antelope Valley. It was in Hollywood that McQueeney came to the attention of Warner Bros. and became a contract player, appearing in the running Warners TV shows. Finally Robert McQueeney had abandoned performing "live" for acting before the film crews.

During this time he separated from his wife, Patricia Noonan, with whom he had three children in their three years of marriage.

In 1962 Robert was given the role of Conley Wright in the new Warners effort at creating a WWII dramatic series. McQueeney's starring role in *The Gallant Men* was a gallant, but fruitless, effort.

WILLIAM REYNOLDS

"I'm an actor, pure and simple. I make my living at it and consider myself a pro ... in the same sense that some athletes are pros and some are amateurs."

That's a pretty confident statement, but then it came from a pretty confident individual, Bill Reynolds. When discussing his career, Bill was very fluent, if not downright eloquent. Perhaps that came from his father who had been an associate professor of economics at the University of Chattanooga.

Bill had worked his way up through the ranks of one of the more demanding professions and was rightly proud of his achievements. But then, Bill Reynolds learned to fend for himself at an early age.

His mother, Gladys Reynolds, had been a noted sportswoman and aviatrix until she was killed in an air crash. Bill was only four at the time. He was sent to Redwood City, California, to be raised by his uncle and aunt, Dr. Thomas and Florence Magee.

While no one in his family had ever entered show business, Bill vowed to be the first after getting a taste of dramatics his senior year at Sequoia High School in Redwood City. He also became fascinated with radio and frequently visited a small station in San Mateo. Bill even convinced the management to let him do some acting bits and handle an announcing chore now and then.

Upon graduation from high school he returned to the city of his birth, Los Angeles, to enter Pasadena City College as a radio and drama major. For practical experience Bill joined the Century Theater Group in Hollywood. During his freshman year at Pasadena, Reynolds was signed by Paramount Studios and made his film debut as the son of Laurence Olivier in *Sister Carrie*. This was followed by *Dear Brat*.

But all of his studies and film career was interrupted when Uncle Sam beckoned Bill Reynolds to spend two years in the Army. With the end of the Korean conflict came his return to Hollywood in 1954.

Bill had no trouble picking up where he had left off (remember, he's a pretty confident individual). Universal-International signed him to a contract and cast him in four pictures: *All That Heaven Allows*, *There's Always Tomorrow*, *Mister Cory*, and *Away All Boats*.

Next he turned his career toward television and signed with Warner Bros. Bill began with appearances on *Cheyenne* and *Maverick* and earned his first starring TV role as a Roaring Twenties trumpet player who got involved in murder, missing persons, and other non-musical happenings in *Pete Kelly's Blues*. The series debuted on April 5, 1959, and was produced by Jack Webb, who had played the part of Pete Kelly on radio and in the 1955 movie. Although Bill Reynolds was a 1920's enthusiast and former high school trumpet player in real life, the show did not enthuse many in the viewing audience. Pete blew his horn for a last, lamentable tune on September 4, 1959.

The ever-confident Reynolds landed another starring role just a few months later as a pilot flying his own one-plane airline based in the Spice Islands of the East Indies and bumping weekly into smugglers, beautiful women, and escaped convicts. The series, *The Islanders*, lasted no longer than did *Pete Kelly's Blues*.

About a year later came Bill's third series, *The Gallant Men*, but for him it was no charm. Even though it lasted longer than his previous two shows put together, *The Gallant Men* could only muster one season on the tube.

By this time Bill could have thrown in the towel, but he didn't. Television was now a challenge to him and he was determined to meet it head-on.

But radio was his first love. In 1959 he commented, "For the beginning young actor, radio provides the greatest area for development. There is little time for this in TV. The pressure is too great. But there is no doubt that TV is the 'starmaker' of today."

While waiting for the chance to conquer television, Bill returned to the big screen in the Warners film, *A Distant Trumpet*, and Disney's *Follow Me Boys*. He also made appearances in the TV series, *Dragnet* and *The FBI*.

In 1967 he finally beat the one-season stigma and became a co-star in *The FBI*, going into its third season. As Special Agent Tom Colby, Reynolds spent six glorious years in the much-respected series which won the commendation of FBI Director J. Edgar Hoover.

Finally with a successful series to his credit, Bill Reynolds could now relax just a little and enjoy some life beyond the studio lots.

Being a golf enthusiast, Reynolds became a member of the Hollywood Hackers, a group of actors who played in golf tournaments to raise funds for charities. His other interest outside acting was his two real estate offices in the San Fernando Valley.

He married actress-model Molly Sinclair and moved to Northridge, California, where they raised their two children, Carrie and Eric. Bill and Molly had met at Paramount Studios, but after marriage she abandoned her acting career for family life.

Bill Reynolds made it in all categories, but it took a lot of confidence.

The Gallant Men—Series Index

The Gallant Men

Conley Wright, a renowned American war correspondent, joins Allied forces at Salerno, Italy, under heavy enemy fire and is assigned to an Army unit under the command of Captain Benedict. The Captain is unsure of his capability to lead in battle but overcomes his fears through the courage of a private with a secret past. William Windom guest stars.

Robertino

Private Lucavich saves the life of an indigent Italian boy. After wrongly accused of stealing by the private, the boy runs away into Nazi territory where he makes a discovery which aids the Americans and helps him to avenge the death of his parents.

The Ninety-Eight Cent Man

After being wounded by a grenade saving the life of Lieutenant Kimbro, Private D'Angelo is captured and faces brutal interrogation which endangers the lives of his platoon and friendly Italian guerrillas.

A Place to Die

Captain Benedict must make a crucial decision when a wounded soldier takes refuge in a convent.

Retreat to Concord

War Correspondent Conley Wright helps a combat-fatigued GI through quotations from Thoreau, and a small, war-ravaged village sees a renaissance. Peter Breck is featured.

And Cain Cried Out

Complications on the battlefield and romantic repercussions back home enter Captain Benedict's life when his brother is transferred to the Captain's unit. Robert Conrad guest stars as the brother.

One Moderately Peaceful Sunday

Private Gibson is the only survivor after he and two other soldiers are caught in an enemy ambush. Gibson has valuable information that he must get back to his unit — if he can. John Dehner is featured.

The Dogs of War

An American infantry unit is threatened by German infiltrators but the Nazis are thwarted by Privates Hanson and Lucavich, a beautiful Countess, and a shaggy dog.

Fury in a Quiet Village

Arriving in an unusually tranquil village, Captain Benedict and his men soon learn that all of the town's children are being held hostage. The Germans remain behind to guard a dying, aged general. Captain Benedict has ten minutes in which to decide whether to mount an attack.

Lesson for a Lover

Lieutenant Kimbro, a victim of psychosomatic blindness in combat, is hospitalized. While undergoing treatment, he shows a troubled lady a bit of chivalry.

Signals for an End Run

Sergeant McKenna finds romance with an Italian girl, but the remaining part of the triangle imperils the couple and McKenna's men.

And the End of Evil Things

Lieutenant Kimbro wants to go to the aid of a dying soldier, but Captain Benedict adamantly refuses to grant permission because it would endanger the entire outfit. Later the Lieutenant finds himself in the difficult decision-making role when Benedict gets into danger, and Kimbro sees the responsibility of leadership.

Some Tears Fall Dry

Conley Wright feuds with a female correspondent in the battle area but makes amends when the two retreat for a stay in Naples. The romance ends when she gives her life to save two Italian children from enemy bombs.

Boast Not of Tomorrow

Captain Benedict, on leave in Naples, is puzzled when a nurse seems unaffected at the news of her fiancé's being listed as missing in action on the eve of their marriage.

The Bridge

Two demolition experts join Benedict's unit on a mission to destroy a bridge, the enemy's only escape route. The mission is guided by the man who erected the bridge, and he is suspected to be hindering efforts more than helping them. Peter Brown guest stars as one of the demolition experts.

To Hold Up a Mirror

With a German major and nurse as prisoners, Captain Benedict and some of his men hide out in an Italian farmhouse and prepare to do battle with an approaching enemy patrol.

Advance and Be Recognized

Private D'Angelo, taking some time out of war in an Italian town with some of his buddies, falls foolishly in love. When a pal kids him about it, D'Angelo loses his senses and the result is shooting, shouting, and sadness — and the exposure of a group of battle area racketeers.

The Leathernecks

When Conley Wright learns his brother is missing in action fighting the Japanese, he leaves the Italian campaign for the Pacific theater. While in the Pacific, Wright observes a tough, battlewise Marine breaking in a new commanding officer. Phillip Carey and Van Williams guest star.

Operation Secret

Conley Wright does a bit of detective work after discovering the grave and dog tags of an American officer whose death predated the Allied invasion of Italy. Information is furnished by a beautiful contessa, Italian partisans, a talkative puppet,

and outraged German POWs. As he pieces the stories together, Conley learns of a startling espionage mission. Ray Danton is featured.

Next of Kin

Private D'Angelo is reunited with a beloved uncle and girl cousin in the native village of D'Angelo's mother. But the private discovers how the pressures of poverty and war can drastically change people.

The Warriors

As Conley Wright, Private D'Angelo, and Private Gibson seek furlough time in Naples, a bombardment halts them on their way. They hole up with some other men who are separated from their units, including two British soldiers. When the Germans close in for the kill, Conley discovers what real heroes are made of.

One Puka Puka

Sergeant McKenna and his men seek refuge in an inn which is manned by a rather unmilitary group of soldiers. This informal band is led by a pint-sized (but warwise) lieutenant. McKenna is amazed that this mischievous bunch ever got as far as they did but is convinced when they meet the enemy like a well-oiled fighting unit. Poncie Ponce stars as the little lieutenant.

Ol' Buddy

After an altercation over a swap, Privates Hanson and Lucavich bury their friendship. But Lucavich relents when Hanson does not return from a mission. Lucavich risks his life to find his friend, and, after doing so, joins his buddy in tackling some Germans.

The Crucible

Captain Benedict needs valuable intelligence information from a wounded German soldier, but someone stands in the captain's way: a major who was blackballed from the captain's fraternity in their college days. The major's vindictiveness causes a tense situation.

A Taste of Peace

While recuperating from a wound and battle fatigue, Captain Bene- dict meets an attractive nurse who exposes him to the scars of war and tempts him not to return to the killing.

Tommy

A USO act arrives to entertain the GIs, and Captain Benedict recognizes the blonde attraction as a former girlfriend. She has a strange weakness for wounded soldiers — and one in particular whose wounds are largely psychosomatic. Benedict devises a cure for her weakness. Dorothy Provine stars as the ex-girlfriend.

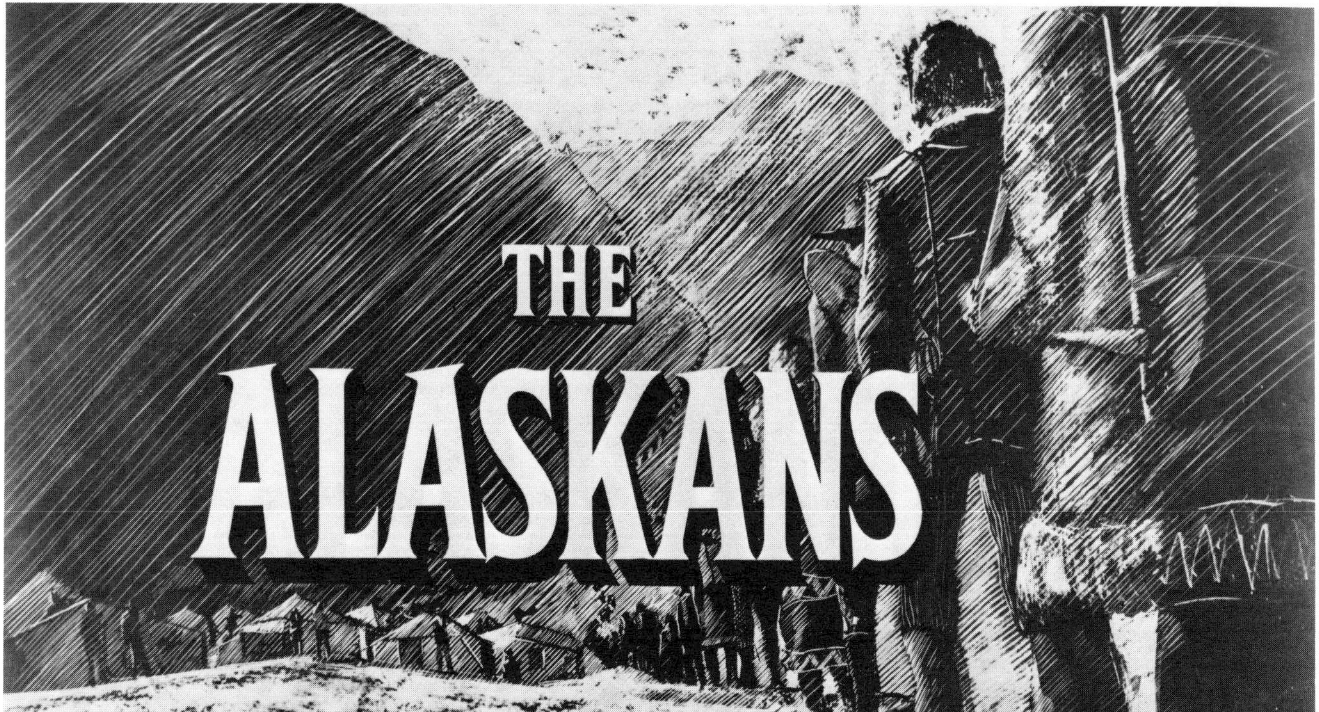
THE
ALASKANS

13
Come You Dreamers

ABC (1 hour) — debuted October 4, 1959
Format: The adventures of three people who seek to get rich quick in
*   the Klondike and Yukon regions of 1898*
Cast: Roger Moore .... *Silky Harris*
*   Dorothy Provine* .... *Rocky Shaw*
*   Jeff York* .... *Reno McKee*
*   Ray Danton* .... *Nifty Cronin*
*   John Dehner* .... *Soapy Smith*
Executive Producer: William T. Orr
Producer: Harry Tatelman; Boris Ingster
Theme Music: "Gold Fever" by Mack David and Jerry Livingston
Location: Filmed in Hollywood

The Alaskans could have just as easily been called the *Canadians* — there was just about as much action on that side of the border as on the Alaskan side. The show was set in the year 1898, the time of the last great gold rush, a very exciting and dangerous time. It was a period when people from all over the world flocked to the Yukon and Klondike regions to hunt for golden fortunes; some in the rivers and streams or in the hills, others at the gambling tables or along the trail by bushwhacking and robbery, and still others by scheming to make the easy buck. There were many fortunes won and lost and sometimes won again. Many lost more than just their gold — they lost their lives. All this is the story of *The Alaskans.*

The Alaskans introduced us to three people, each different but with a common objective: to get rich quick. The three protagonists were Silky Harris, Reno McKee, and the beautiful Rocky Shaw.

The cast of *The Alaskans*: Reno, Rocky, and Silky.

Silky Harris (played by Roger Moore) was a smooth talking confidence man who lived by his wits. He could talk himself into and out of trouble with equal skill. Silky's philosophy was "why dig for the gold if there was a better way to get it?" and Silky always had a better way to get it. There were occasions when Silky was out working a claim, but that was really the exception rather than the rule. Silky was, however, one of the good guys as evidenced by the time he saved the small village from avalanche by planting dynamite charges to release the snow under controlled conditions. He nearly got killed in the process because of a man bent on revenge who wanted the town to suffer the avalanche. Or, as in "Cheating Cheaters," where he and Reno saved the miners' gold from the hands of Nifty Cronin.

Reno McKee, played by Jeff York, was a huge, towering hulk. He was an extremely powerful man who in one episode ("Gold Sled") whipped Silky's bear and put an end to that particular scam. Reno was an honest, aboveboard man but, like Silky, figured there was a better way to get rich than to work the claims. For this reason he often followed Silky's elaborate schemes even when he wasn't really sure where they would end up. Matched with Silky's brains, Reno's physical prowess made them a perfect team to fight both the Alaskan wilderness and the hordes of evildoers lured to the territory by the chance of wealth.

Dorothy Provine was cast as Rocky Shaw. She was the woman every sourdough dreamed of while he was off working his claim or fell for when he made it to town for supplies or to assay his diggings. Rocky was the object of more than one gift of a lost mine or hidden fortune. Naturally she needed Silky and Reno to help her recover these gifts, some of which were real, some imagined. There were times when they were lucky to get away with their lives. Meanwhile Rocky spent her time singing and dancing in the dance halls of Skagway, Dawson, Nome, and any other town the group happened to be in for a particular episode.

Another character that popped up from time to time was Ray Danton as Nifty Cronin—a real rat. Nifty was as slick as Silky, but his shrewdness was used mostly to help himself at the expense of others, such as when he scuttled a boat that should have contained all the gold that the miners had brought in for shipment to Seattle. The gold was actually in Nifty's safe, but for Nifty crime didn't pay and he was caught.

Another scoundrel to show his face a few times was Soapy Smith, played by John Dehner. A shrewd and unethical wheeler dealer, he once tried to lead a group of Skagway volunteers over the border to attack the city of Dawson under pretense of being under the orders from the government in Washington D.C. Actually, the federal government had turned down Soapy's request to form and take charge of a militia.

At first, each episode had all three of the main stars playing a role in the story, but since the show wasn't gathering the ratings, the format was changed so that only one or two of the stars would show up each week. Jeff York left the show after the first 23 episodes when his contract ran out. The ratings for the show climbed as the season progressed but not enough to save the series. In November, 1959, the ratings were below 20 with only a 28 share of the audience, but in January of 1960, they were up to a 24 rating with a 32.5 percent share. Despite all the obstacles, the show was pulling viewers. However, with the loss of Jeff York, Roger Moore moving over to do *Maverick*, and Dorothy Provine going to her new series, *The Roaring 20's*, there were really no *Alaskans* left. The show died a quiet death.

Hugh Benson says *The Alaskans* simply had too much going against it: "*The Alaskans* was really expensive to do. We built a stage on one of the stages with snow and huts and so forth; and then, on the back lot, we built a whole street. It was a very expensive show. We never should have done it; it just didn't catch on."

But Bill Orr still has fond remembrances of the show's origins.

"Life and death is the biggest dramatic element there is; the love story is the second most dramatic. What you have is life and death and sex in a sense. So, with that in mind, we always tried to keep our shows simple. Getting in early like that in the TV business, we could make simple shows. Later on, people tried to do shows that were different. The problem with being different is that you get rid of a lot of the basic dramatic elements that make it possible to do strong dramatic shows. Suddenly, the hero doesn't shoot anybody in a western; he doesn't wear a gun; he's a former parson; he does it by intellect or this or that. That's very hard to do. It sounds good in the format, and you sell it, and then you sit around saying, 'how do we get this guy out of this situation?'

"So we were looking for an area to do a western, but not in fact in the West. So we came up with *The Alaskans*—the battle for rights and the mining. They were pioneers—people who went up there weren't CPA's with a good job in Boston.

"The rationale as to why the show didn't last over the season was that it was too cold. People wore too many clothes and somehow the people didn't identify."

And Carl Stucke remembers: "*The Alaskans* was *Maverick* on ice."

ROGER MOORE

London-born Roger Moore is better known for his roles as Simon Templar, *The Saint* of the series by that name, and James Bond, Agent 007—not to mention his days as Beau Maverick.

Moore started in acting as a student at the Royal Academy of Dramatic Arts in London. His early professional experience came from plays like *Circle of Chalk* and *The Italian Strawhat* with the London Arts Theatre. Roger might never have gotten into acting if some friends working as extras on a film hadn't dragged him along one day after he had been fired from his job as an animator. Acting struck him, so he decided to go to the Royal Academy. With a ratio of four girls to each boy in class, he said he'd learned a great deal, but not much about acting.

Soon after, Moore went into the British Army with which he served as an officer in the Guards Armored Division. He spent time in Austria and Italy and was discharged in 1948.

Moore then joined a repertory group and toured with the play, *Miss Mabel*. This led to his first role in a film, a bit part in *Trottie True*. After he played roles in the shows *The Little Hut, Mr. Roberts*, and others, Roger began some work in British television and radio.In 1953 he decided to make a move to the United States and was rewarded for his effort by a supporting role in *Robert Montgomery Presents*, just four days after his arrival.

In 1954 Roger went to Hollywood where he spent the next couple of years making pictures. Like most actors this was what Moore really wanted to do. He was in *The Last Time I Saw Paris* (MGM), *Interrupted Melody, Diane, The King's Thief*, and two Warners films, *The Miracle* and *Rachel Cade*. Then in 1957 and 1958 Roger returned to England to do the *Ivanhoe* series for Screen Gems. Moore said that everyone stumbled about feeling rather like boy scouts in suits of armor. In all, 39 episodes of *Ivanhoe* were filmed. Roger also managed to put in an appearance in the *Maverick* episode of "The Rivals" during this time. Warners was trying to put him under contract, but Roger held out. He was asked to join the cast of the then-projected series *The Alaskans*; Moore wanted no part of it. His decision changed after he made an *Alfred Hitchcock Presents*. When Roger saw the episode, "The Avon Emeralds," he felt the show was so bad that he should move under the protection of the studio. A seven year contract was signed, and Roger became Silky Harris for *The Alaskans*.

Alas, Moore was not extremely happy with his role in *The Alaskans*, feeling that the shows gave him scarcely more challenge than the juvenile parts he had had in repertory theatre. He did feel that the latter episodes of the series were much improved over the earlier ones (but by then the show had already died on the network and would not be renewed).

With *The Alaskans* canceled, Warners decided to place their young star in the *Maverick* series as Cousin Beau. This role, like the Silky Harris character, lasted only the one season. The show was declining and apparently the cousin wasn't the one to salvage it.

Also during this time, Roger made *The Gold of the Seven Saints* for the studio with Clint Walker. This was the only western picture

Moore ever made, and though he said that he didn't really like westerns, he had enjoyed making the movie.

For the next year or two, Roger played guest shots on other Warners shows, such as the "Tiger by the Tail" episode of 77 *Sunset Strip* and the "Right Off the Boat" episode of the *Roaring 20's* — the only two-part episode of 44 films for that show.

In 1963, Moore took on a role that would keep him working steadily for the next seven years. The series was *The Saint*: the character was Simon Templar. The series was by far Roger's most successful outing in television. Though American audiences were only treated to this program for three of its seven years (1963, 1968, 1969 — NBC), most people, when they think of Roger Moore as a TV actor, will remember this role first. It was extremely popular in England and was sold to 80 countries.

Simon Templar was something of a crook in *The Saint* series — a modern-day Robin Hood who would go to bat for those who had been swindled or taken advantage of. Police of six continents knew him well, but often didn't know what to think of him. After all, he *was* on the side of justice, but some of the means he used to accomplish his goals were not exactly within the realm of legality. Templar's trademark was a stick figure with a halo — *The Saint*.

The next series that Moore did was *The Persuaders* with Tony Curtis. It would seem that with such a heavyweight set of co-stars the show would have been a smashing success. But big stars or not, the series never made it. Roger played the part of Lord Brett Sinclair. Lord Sinclair was an Englishman born to the purple; an aristocrat whose family was extremely wealthy, giving him the freedom and opportunity to live life as he wished. Curtis played the part of Danny Wilde, a self-made man who gathered his millions through hard work and lots of sweat as befits the American ideal. An unlikely pair of crime fighters, they met in the initial episode (titled "Overture"), discovered they complemented each other well, and formed a team to fight injustice. Their adventures took them across Europe, placing them often in perilous situations, but in the end, like Batman and Robin, they always overcame the odds — and like the Lone Ranger, they rode off into the sunset (except they drove sports cars).

The next year a bit of film history was made. Moore became the successor of Sean Connery in the ultra-successful James Bond movie series. Connery had made seven Bond films which in return had given Sean super-star status, and he felt it was time to get into new projects. George Lazenby took the character for one picture, *On Her Majesty's*

Secret Service, but did not continue in the role. Roger's first outing as Agent 007 came in *Live and Let Die*. He brought to the role of James Bond a character nearer to Ian Fleming's written Bond. Connery had molded the character to suit his own style of personal magnetism. Moore made the conscious effort to not allow any of his past roles to creep into his new characterization or to allow Sean's portrayal to affect his own. He went into the role as though it had never been played before. Before he began his new role, Roger lost 15 pounds and began an exercise program to put himself in shape for the rigors of filming the action spy series. The director for the film, Guy Hamilton, sent Roger back to the hairdresser three times before he was satisfied that Roger's hair was short enough to pass for James Bond's. Roger chose conservative clothing for his wardrobe because he felt Bond to be slightly square, and anything flashy would detract from Bond's ability to slip about unnoticed.

Roger greatly enjoyed making the film because there was lots of action and less dialogue than in most of his past hour-long television shows. In fact, for the first two weeks of shooting, dialogue was practically nonexistent. When dialogue was present there was more humor with the "new" Bond. Moore did much of his own stunt work for the film, including a scene where he waded through a snake-filled marsh. They told Roger not to jump if a snake bit him because doing so would cause the reptile's teeth to break off in his flesh. Roger later mentioned that if the alligators in another scene that had been left unfed for a couple of months to make them more active came out for a bite, he would be on the move. Moore suffered three holes burned in his backside from another stunt.

The next Bond movie for Moore was *The Man with the Golden Gun* in 1974. Again he saved the world from impending doom, defeating Christopher Lee in a gunfight and escaping just before Lee's island stronghold blew up.

Three years later *The Spy Who Loved Me* was released. As with his past 007 pictures, Moore made the rounds of interviews and banquets to publicize the release. By then the menus for the banquets were made up of James Bond's food and drink from the shows.

Roger's fourth Bond movie was *Moonraker* in 1979. He, as before, performed much of his own stunt work, occasionally suffering from injuries such as a cut hand from landing on a glass during a fight scene. *Moonraker*, like all other Bond movies, was full of action, explosions, and fantasy.

Moore likes the Bond movies because they fill a need people have

Rocky (Dorothy Provine) belts out another saloon song.

to escape the work-a-day world, experience fantasy and be entertained.

Between Bond pictures, Roger did make other films such as *Shout at the Devil*, an African adventure flick that involved sixteen weeks of on-location shooting on the coast of South Africa. He and fellow stars Lee Marvin and Barbara Parkins were flown in in small single engine planes, swam in shark-infested waters, and lived a fairly rugged existence during the completion of the shooting.

DOROTHY PROVINE

Dorothy Provine was born in Deadwood, South Dakota, while her parents were visiting her mother's family, but her first memories are of San Francisco where they lived until Dorothy was in high school. She finished high school in Seattle at Lincoln High.

She began acting in grammar school plays and continued with musicals in high school where her work won her a four year scholarship to the University of Washington. Dorothy starred in 35 shows in her four years at the university and proved herself to be the most promising student in the department. She was receiving some good television exposure at the same time because of a daily local show in which she starred. Dorothy worked in the Seattle Equity Musical Theatre during the summers, starring in productions like *Damn Yankees, South Pacific,* and *The King and I.*

Right after graduating from the university in 1957, Dorothy headed for Hollywood, but there was no waiting on tables for this young actress. Two days after her arrival, she had a good agent — and work. She starred in *The Bonnie Parker Story* (in the title role), in *The Secret Bride of Candy Mountain* with Lou Costello, and in some others that she said she'd just as soon not be reminded.

Dorothy had co-starred in 31 television shows by the time she had spent her first 15 months in town. She was seen in *The Millionaire, Lawman, The Real McCoys, Alfred Hitchcock Presents, Sugarfoot, The Texan, Colt .45, Cheyenne,* and others. Warners decided they wanted Dorothy for their *Alaskans* series, but Dorothy turned them down because she didn't want to do a weekly series. But when the studio upped its offer, Dorothy's interest was captured — especially when she was told the series would be a clone of *Maverick* with all the comedy of that series. When the filming started, Dorothy felt that the show was more of a melodrama than a comedy. She wasn't happy. She felt that Rocky Shaw had nothing more to do than wander around. She also felt that the show they were doing wasn't the same one that had been described to her in the beginning. She thought that there had been some improvement over the life of the series, but that it happened too gradually.

With the death of *The Alaskans,* Dorothy moved on to another series, *The Roaring 20's.* As with *The Alaskans,* she was the only female lead, and her part was also very similar. It seemed that names, places, and co-stars were changed with the series change — but her character remained the same.

After her stint with *The Roaring 20's* was finished, Dorothy went back to guest starring in other shows. She also got back into the business of making movies. She appeared in other Warners shows such as *Hawaiian Eye* and *The Gallant Men;* she played in *The Man from U.N.C.L.E., Dr. Kildare, The Danny Thomas Show, Love American Style,* and a movie made for television, *The Sound of Anger.*

Provine made two movies in 1963 — *Wall of Noise* and *It's a Mad Mad Mad Mad World*. The next year, it was *Good Neighbor Sam* and *That Darned Cat*. All but the first were comedies, for which Dorothy seemed to have a natural flair. Her next picture was another comedy, *The Great Race*, followed by *One Spy Too Many*, *Kiss the Girls and Make Them Cry*, *Who's Minding the Mint*, and *Never a Dull Moment*.

JEFF YORK

Jeff York, the 6'4" mountain of an actor, was perfect for the role of Reno McKee in *The Alaskans*. How many others would be believed to actually win a fight with a bear?

Jeff was best known for his role as Mike Fink in the Walt Disney series, *Davy Crockett*. The Fink character was the captain of a boat hauling cargo up and down a river, who had occasional run-ins with Crockett and who usually came out second in a contest with Davy.

When it came to *The Alaskans*, York thought the show did the state a great injustice. He felt that to represent the state as snow and ice and nothing else was a real shame since there was so much beautiful green wilderness to be seen during the summers. He wanted the writers to make the show come across with more accuracy, (for example, to leave Kodiak bears on Kodiak Island and out of Skagway), and about the time his contract ran out, Jeff *did* feel that there had been some improvement.

York could speak with some authority on the state since *he* at least had been there.

The Alaskans — Series Index

Gold Sled

Formerly "Trail North": Rocky, looking for a buried gold-laden sled, joins Reno and Silky on the difficult trek to the Yukon. An avalanche carries away their guides and the gold, leaving the three without their fortune but happy to be alive.

Cheating Cheaters

Formerly "Trick for Treat": Robbed of gold and almost murdered by a thief whom Silky kills, Reno and Silky find that their gold (and that of other miners) supposedly sank in a ship owned by Nifty. But they make Nifty admit that he hid the gold then had the ship scuttled. Louis Quinn appears.

The Devil Made Five

Reno, conned by Silky out of funds intended to go toward buying a restaurant, contracts to deliver some dynamite to Nome by sled. But he's pressured into taking along three outcasts. John Dehner as Cornish.

Petticoat Crew

Trying to get some dancing girls to Dawson by a certain time, Harris buys an old paddlewheel boat. But Cronin, who wants the chicks for another saloon, tries to sabotage the voyage.

Starvation Stampede

A storekeeper, who's been selling food to snowbound miners at excessive prices, secretly hijacks a supply boat and puts the stolen food up for auction. Reno McKee turns up proof of the hijacking.

Big Deal

Formerly "Gold Deed": Reno and Silky find a long lost title deed to a hotel in Pelly Flats and manage to return it and the hotel to the rightful owner. To do it, they must defeat Soapy Smith and Diamond Jack Collins. Tol Avery is Diamond Jack.

Contest at Gold Bottom

To meet a mine option payment (held by Nifty Cronin), Reno and

Silky create a baby fund, using an abandoned infant. The miners contribute 10% of their take for the honor of naming the baby and being its godfather. But the scheme, engineered by Silky, backfires when the miners get the idea that the winner also gets Rocky's hand in marriage.

Winter Song

An opera star loses her voice in mid-concert, and her manager takes off with a $5000 advance paid by the miners. Another miner, in love with the singer, is robbed, and his gold is poured into glass jars above the Palace bar—all supposed to contain fool's gold. Reno bets on the jars.

The Golden Fleece

Story by Jack Emanuel and Joel Rogosin: Silky and Nifty go with four men to an abandoned gold mine where one of the men plans to recover gold by use of a chemical process. But the four men are smugglers—chemically reducing French government ingots into saleable gold dust.

Doc Booker

When typhoid strikes several prospectors, "Doc" Jason Booker breaks down and admits he isn't a true medic. The townspeople turn on Doc. But Reno, finding the source of the polluted water and a mule which drank from it, injects himself with a serum, gets the disease, but recovers, proving the mule is the carrier. The town changes its attitude toward Doc. Simon Oakland is Doc.

The Abominable Snowman

An Alaskan town is terrorized by a monster until Silky kills the beast.

Then the monster reappears, but Silky proves his crooked partner is behind the revival. Ruta Lee appears.

Remember the Maine

Soapy Smith plans to capitalize on the new Spanish-American War by forming a group called the Skagway Guards and by attacking the town of Dawson. He plans to loot the town during the clash. But Silky and Reno join the group and learn that Soapy has no official authorization for what he's doing.

The Million Dollar Kid

Kat, an Indian youth, sells shares in a gold strike to businessmen for goods to accompany his dead prospector friend to Heaven. The businessmen think they've been duped, but the mine turns out to have real value.

The Trial of Reno McKee

Formerly "The Trial": Drunk and drugged by adventuress Ellen Chambers, who forces him to shoot her accomplice, McKee is tried for murder. Silky sobers up derelict John Conrad, once a famed Boston lawyer, to defend Reno. Efrem Zimbalist, Jr. as Conrad.

Gold Fever

The story is by producer Harry Tatelman: When Reno's kid brother Danny learns the truth about his new wife, he leaves her and starts gambling away his new gold strike.

The Challenge

On the face of a snow covered peak, Silky fights off murderer "Grant"

who's trying to stop him from setting dynamite charges that will save his village from destruction by an avalanche. Don Dubbins is Grant. Robert Colbert appears.

The Long Pursuit

This one was produced by songwriter Mack David: Hate-ridden Ed Bundy, posing as a Chicago detective, urges McKee to help him find a murderess. But Amy Landon gunned her sadistic husband down in self-defense. Ruta Lee is Amy, Mike Road as the Marshal. (The same story was the basis for "The Bounty Killers" on *Cheyenne*.) This episode is also known as "The Safe and the Hunted."

Spring Fever

A sourdough named Happy puts his new gold strike in Rocky's name. But two heavies kill Happy, and one of them tries to get Rocky to marry him. Silky learns of the scheme. Rex Reason appears.

Black Sand

By Hugh Benson; produced by Mack David: Reno, a cardiac invalid, his worthless wife, and two heavies team up to work an isolated mine.

The Seal-Skin Game

Silky, Reno, and Rocky break up a States-bound trip when Reno falls for Jacqueline St. Clair, a lady fur buyer, who peddles a tale of a great, new market for seals. Using all their money, the boys buy up all of Cronin's seals, hoping to zoom profits with a new crop of pups. Jacqueline Beer appears.

Peril at Caribou Crossing

Outlaws have killed an Indian girl, and Harris, a prospector, and his wife are in jeopardy because they supposedly helped the murderers escape. Jerry Paris and Fay Spain appear.

Behind the Moon

Ambitious Tom Kirk marries an Indian girl to gain access to valuable copper deposits in the Indian village. But Kirk has a change of heart. Lee Patterson is Kirk; Diane McBain and Michael Forest appear.

Partners

Ashamed to face his boy due in Dawson, drunken Jim Hendricks fakes suicide. Rocky white-lies a hero's death for the boy's dad. But the boy learns of the trick, stows aboard a boat, and is held for ransom. After the boy is saved, the father quits drinking. Warren Stevens as Jim.

Disaster at Gold Hill

Silky, working in a gold mine, is pursued by a crippled giant who feels his young wife has compromised him. An explosion is set off, trapping the two men. Rex Reason appears.

The Last Bullet

Also produced as "Hideout" on *Sugarfoot*: Riding a dog-sled through a forest, Silky rescues a middle-aged man from a pack of wolves. The two are joined by an arrogant, gun-brandishing teenager who wants to join an outlaw gang. Gary Vinson guest stars.

A Barrel of Gold

A promoter sells canned meat to a prospector not knowing it's contaminated.

The Bride Wore Black

Also produced as "Man Wanted" on *Sugarfoot*: Silky gets in an awkward position when his friend Cass sends Silky's picture off to the states for a mail order bride. If that's not bad enough—the bride is already married. She and her hubby are working a scheme to bilk would-be grooms. Fay Spain appears.

Odd Man Hangs

Also seen as "High Card Hangs" on *Maverick*: At Last Mile, a remote gold camp, Harris and two miners are accused of murder. Silky plans to "admit" the crime to flush out the guilty party, but the plot backfires.

Counterblow

Also seen as "Decision at Gunsight" on *Cheyenne*: Silky acquires a newspaper in a town that's been taken over by hoodlums who extort protection money from citizens. Silky starts a rival protection racket. Robert McQueeney appears.

Heart of Gold

Rocky is given a bad time by a crook posing as a lay-preacher while executing an elaborate plan to steal gold. Murder and kidnapping enter in. Troy Donahue, Michael Forest, and Gary Vinson appear.

Kangaroo Court

Seen as "The Spanish Dancer" on *Maverick*: Harris, and his partner

Harry Seattle, stage a mock fight and "murder" to trick John Ryan (Robert Lowery) into digging out a dynamited mine shaft to find Harry's body and pin the crime on Silky. The trick works, but Ryan again buries the shaft. This time, the explosion exposes a rich gold vein. Larry Penell as Harry.

The Silent Land

A Mountie named Watts finds a mercy killer, Dr. Jim Manning, hiding in an Eskimo village and is impressed with the humanitarian work he's doing. After Jim admits his identity to save Watts' life, the Mountie promises a new trial. Michael Forest as Pierre; Claude Akins and Arthur Franz appear.

Calico

This episode appeared as "Silent Witness" on *Cheyenne*: Silky wins half interest in a gold mine but is framed for his partner's murder and is nearly lynched. Myrna Fahey, Rex Reason, Tris Coffin, and Leo Gordon appear.

Sign of the Kodiak

In Alaska to forget a broken marriage to wealthy Ruth Coleman, Jeff

Warren (Lee Patterson) gets rich but loses a leg to a Kodiak bear. Bitter, he relentlessly hunts the bear. Michael Forest appears as Pierre.

Phantom Pursuit

Also called "White Vengeance," and produced as "Ring of Sand" on *Sugarfoot*: Silky and a sourdough swear vengeance on a giant Russian who has robbed and killed the sourdough's son. The Russian forces the two men to act as guides en route to Skagway. He is finally outwitted, weakened by hunger, and falls off a cliff. Robert Colbert appears.

Northern Lights

Also called "The Ballad of Whitehorse": Silky Harris aids in promoting the marriage of saloon gal Yukon Kate and dying poet Bob Howard—then after Bob has written the epic that later makes Kate famous, he turns out to have a chance to live. She returns to her old lover Joe Holland to get money to send him south for his health. In the end, Bob dies at Holland's hand, and Holland dies at Silky's. James Coburn as Bob. Rex Reason as Joe.

14
Prohibition and Bathtub Gin

ABC (1 hour) — debuted October 15, 1960
Format: A girl nightclub owner and three newspaper reporters fight
politicians and gangsters of the prohibition era
Cast: Donald May . . . . .Pat Garrison
      Rex Reason . . . . Scott Norris
      Gary Vinson . . . . .Chris Higbee
      Dorothy Provine . . . . .Pinky Pinkham
      Mike Road . . . . .Lt. Joe Switolski
      John Dehner . . . . .Jim Duke Williams
Executive Producer: William T. Orr
Producer: Boris Ingster
Theme Music: "The Roaring 20's" by Mack David and Jerry Livingston
Location: Filmed in Hollywood

The Roaring 20's debuted on ABC one year to the day after another series set in the same era, *The Untouchables*. And in all likelihood, *20's* was influenced by its predecessor. *The Untouchables* was one of the more violent series ever to make its way to the home screen, and to be sure, *The Roaring 20's* had its share of the same. But the shows had their differences.

While *The Untouchables* followed the machine-gun of Treasury agent Eliot Ness (Robert Stack) through the bullet-riddled streets of Chicago, *20's* was seen from the point of view of two reporters for the *New York Record* and their friend on the force, Lt. Joe Switolski. The reporters, Pat Garrison and Scott Norris, liked to dig up their scoops while playing detective in order to put crooks and racketeers in jail as well as on the front page. Oh yes, *20's* had something else to separate

Donald May (left), Dorothy Provine and Rex Reason.

it from Eliot Ness' gang: the beautiful Pinky Pinkham who owned the Charleston Club, and who starred in her own show.

Pinky's club was a popular night spot in the Big Apple of the prohibition era. You could always count on finding a big shot crime boss somewhere in the audience enjoying the show with his cronies.

Not to forget the Jimmy Olsen type on the paper: Chris Higbee was the bumbling office boy on the paper, and as you might expect, he often managed to work his way into the adventures.

During the second season reporter Scott Norris was gone, and a new reporter, Duke Williams, appeared. Duke worked for a rival paper and sometimes stirred up trouble. Lt. Switolski got a beefier role, as did Chris Higbee, who was promoted to cub reporter. Pinky (real name: Delaware) and Pat continued as usual the final year.

When you think of the Twenties and who was breaking the law in those days, you naturally conjure up images of bootleggers, racketeers, and crooked politicians. And naturally those are the types of evildoers our heroes fought each week. Most of them had a life expectancy of one hour—that is, at the end of the show they were sent to that booze warehouse in the sky. In "Burnett's Woman," the title heavy dies in a fall from a building after being shot during a rooftop chase by Lt. Switolski. In another episode, "Vendetta on Bleecker Street," Steve Zorich, a prison escapee, dies in a storm of bullets.

Another memorable episode came near the end of the series' run. "Asparagus Tipps" was based on a newspaper comic strip by that name that appeared in the Twenties. The man who created the strip, Will Gould, also helped write the episode.

Warners always tried to lend authenticity to its series by filming on location, as it did occasionally with *Hawaiian Eye*, *Bourbon Street Beat*, and *SurfSide 6*. In a way, the studio sometimes went "on location" with *The Roaring 20's*. That was accomplished by splicing in old newsreel footage from the Twenties and also using those scenes as background through rear screen projection. The prop department also furnished some old cars of the era to help with the illusion.

Today Carl Stucke feels it may have been the leading characters' profession that made the show difficult to pull off: "Our problem with *The Roaring 20's* was that it was so difficult to get your leading character, who was a reporter, involved in the story personally. The same thing is true of any newspaper series because there's a whole story going on while all the reporter can do is be in the periphery and can't really motivate anything as a rule."

Bill Orr says the series did not work because of a mixup in the time

Dorothy Provine as Pinky, Donald May (seated left) as Pat, Rex Reason (seated right) as Scott, and Gary Vinson (rear) as Chris.

slot. "We had prepared it as a late night show, doing more mature themes, and going a little further with relationships and violence of the era. Other shows had action and adventure, fun and games, but this was to be a bit different — we hoped to do it more maturely.

"So we put it together for that format, bought stories, and the next thing you know, Ollie Treyz [the man Leonard Goldenson picked to head up the network during this time] has put it on at 7:30 or 8:00. I said, 'Ollie, I don't know what you've done to us. We had big discussions on how our themes could be more mature, and now you've put us [at an early hour]. We've got machine guns flying all over the place and I don't like the kids seeing it.'

"I was overruled because there's nothing in the contract which says I can go in at that hour. They buy you, and you fight for that hour—but it's finally their decision. So we lost the battle, and I always thought that hurt *The Roaring 20's*. It was just at the wrong place."

Orr says his natural instincts were to "mute" the show because of its early time slot. He says he didn't want his own kids to see it.

Hugh Benson's memories are a little more upbeat: "We felt we should do a show about that era, and we did—with singing and dancing, and nightclubs. It was happiness time with a line of eight girls and Dorothy Provine—just fun time."

DONALD MAY

Before going on *The Roaring 20's* to the role of Pat Garrison, Donald May had established himself as an actor with some credentials, having appeared in over 250 plays on and off Broadway. In 1956 he had appeared as host of *The West Point Story* (as Cadet Charles C. Thompson) on CBS—a series that dramatized actual events from West Point. Donald had also appeared in a great number of live TV shows out of New York, and, of course, had been cast by Warner Bros. as Sam Colt, Jr. in *Colt .45*. During this tenure at WB he was a frequent guest star in other series, often playing the heavy.

Of his role as Pat Garrison, columnist for *The Record*, Donald said he looked at each week's episode as though it was an entity unto itself, and not as a continuation of last week's character. One of his greatest concerns was to keep the character from becoming boring, so he maintained a flexibility to bend with the demands of each script.

Donald May was born on Washington's birthday (Feb. 22, 1929) and moved with his family to Houston when he was eight. There May spent most of his school years, but the family moved again and Donald ended up graduating from high school in Cleveland in 1944.

The next stop-off for Donald was Oklahoma City where he attended the University of Oklahoma, graduating with a B.A. in 1949. Then it was off to Yale to study drama, a season of summer stock in New York City, and finally a real job in a play—*Yellow Jack* in Albany, New York.

May's acting career was interrupted for a time as he served with the U.S. Navy as a gunnery officer on a destroyer in the Korean theatre. That was in late 1951. He was released in 1955, retaining his commission in the reserve.

After the Navy stint, May returned to New York to resume his acting career; then, in mid-1959, he decided to try Hollywood. Early guest shots for Warners were in *Hawaiian Eye* and *Sugarfoot*, and before long, Donald had a contract with the studio.

REX REASON

Science fiction fans remember Rex Reason (Scott Norris) chiefly for two films — *This Island Earth*, and the third in the "Creature" series, *The Creature Walks Among Us*. *This Island Earth* (1955) featured a group of scientists more or less kidnapped to the planet Metaluna. Rex played one of the aliens — complete with a four-inch, egg-shaped bald extension on his head. The film was a very impressive, full-of-effects film that stands up well today, even when compared to big budget pictures like *Star Wars*. *The Creature Walks Among Us* was made the next year; both films also featured Jeff Morrow and came from Universal-International.

But science fiction wasn't the only type of film Reason appeared in prior to his career at Warner Bros. He had been signed by Universal in July of 1953 and was immediately cast in a 3-D film called *Son of Cochise* in which he "menaced" Rock Hudson and Barbara Rush. He also appeared with Dana Andrews and Piper Laurie in *Smoke Signal*.

Before his Universal contract, Rex had appeared in *Storm Over Tibet* (winning a role over scores of other unknowns who were tested), in *Salome* with Rita Hayworth, and in *Mission Over Korea*.

Reason was born on November 20, 1928 in Berlin, Germany, while his family was in the country on a business trip. But Rex always considered himself a native of Glendale, California since he attended high school there and since his grandfather, Spencer Robinson, was the first mayor of the town.

During his early years in Glendale, Rex worked as a carrier for *The Hollywood Citizen News*, a gas station attendant, a lumberyard laborer, and a cab company clerk. Then he joined classes at the Ben Bard Playhouse in Glendale and decided to pursue an acting career.

Rex didn't do as much television as some of the other Warners stars. He showed up from time to time on other WB series (but don't get him confused with Rhodes Reason who also guest starred in many WB episodes) and appeared in an anthology series on NBC in 1957 called *The Web*.

GARY VINSON

Gary Vinson, one of five children and son of talent scout Joe Vinson, was born on October 22, 1936, in El Segundo, California. At the age of 18, Gary organized and coordinated the El Segundo Little Theater. His work in the theater, with young kids on little league baseball teams, in Sunday school teaching, and in community development programs brought him the "Young Man of the Year" award from the city's Junior Chamber of Commerce.

At the same time that Vinson was doing the Little Theater, he was also earning extra money with appearances on television with minor roles such as a page boy on Milton Berle's show. He worked his way up the ladder and soon was guesting on a great many shows including the Warner Bros. series *Maverick*. By the time Warners decided to put him under contract, Gary already had some 62 television credits to his name. Vinson was signed to a contract to do *The Roaring 20's* and play the part of Chris Higbee. The part lasted for a season and a half.

Gary was also seen for several seasons as Seaman Christy on the *McHale's Navy* series. His next television series was *Pistols 'n' Petticoats* in which he played the part of a well-meaning, but really harmless (to the badguys), sheriff.

MIKE ROAD

Mike Road began his acting career as a teenager in Boston, working with a small theatre group. After that, he wanted to make it on Broadway, so it was off to New York and a string of jobs which he took to keep from starving. He was an usher, an elevator operator, a waiter, and even a sign painter while he worked off-Broadway stock companies.

Mike's debut on Broadway was short-lived. The play — *Doodle Dandy of the U.S.A.* — ran only ten days. *The Moonvine* was next, and it was a shortie too, but then came a leading role in *Dear Ruth* which lasted for six months. There were more lean times to follow before he finished the plays *Separate Rooms*, *The Square Needle*, and *Twin Beds*, but he again kept food on the table by taking other kinds of work.

A big break came for Road in Hollywood when he was cast as Marshal Tom Sellers in the NBC series *Buckskin* in 1958. That led to a variety of guest roles including parts in several WB series. In August of 1960 the studio put him under contract, and he was soon playing the role of Lt. Switolski on *The Roaring 20's*. He was impressive enough in the series that the part of Switolski was beefed up from a supporting character to a leading man — meaning Mike was the star of several episodes.

Road had had some directing experience in film and stage work before settling down as a TV actor. In Sweden he directed the flick *True and False* with Signe Hasso. In the repertory and stock company field, he directed Vincent Price, Luther Adler, and Kim Hunter.

In 1964–65 Mike appeared on ABC-TV as the voice of Race Bannon in the Hanna-Barbera cartoon series *Johnny Quest*.

JOHN DEHNER

On screen, John Dehner is a man you can love to love ... or love to hate; he's as much at ease playing the role of villain as hero. He's one of the better character actors ever to ply the trade.

Dehner was born on November 23, 1915 in Staten Island, New York. During his younger days, his family traveled a lot, giving John the opportunity to attend schools in Norway and France. While still in high school, John developed an interest in journalism and covered auto racing for several newspapers.

Continuing his education, Dehner attended the University of California at Berkeley majoring in fine arts. From there he went to the California School of Fine Arts and later to the Grand Central School of Art in New York. He left school to go on tour with the Jitney Players, a repertory group, but he left the group in Texas to head for Tinsel Town.

Upon arriving in Hollywood, Dehner went to work for a studio but not as an actor. He used his talents as an illustrator to land a job with the Disney Studios as an animator, working on such classics of animation as *Fantasia* and *Bambi*.

A radio career was next for John as he became the all-night man at an L.A. station playing recorded mood music. Then he tried a job as news editor for another station, finally moving on to still another spot on the dial as a newscaster. (He must have been pretty good at it. His reporting on a United Nations meeting going on in San Francisco helped win his station a Peabody Award.)

So what was left for John to try in L.A.? Acting, of course, on stage, screen, radio, and television.

On TV, you'll remember John in several roles in addition to that of Jim Duke Williams on *20's*. He was Commodore Cecil Wyntoon in the CBS series *The Baileys of Balboa* (1964); he was Burgundy Smith, a con artist complete with spats and white gloves in *The Westerner* (NBC, 1960); he was Cy Bennett on *The Doris Day Show* (CBS, 1971); in the sit-com *Temperatures Rising* he held down the part of Dr. Charles Cleveland Claver (1973); and he was Barrett Fears in NBC's adventure series *Big Hawaii* (1977).

John turned up from time to time in almost all of the WB series, usually as a heavy; in fact he had a recurring role in *The Alaskans* as Soapy Smith.

When *Have Gun, Will Travel* showed up as a radio series in 1960, John again proved his versatility by starring as Paladin. But in 1982 John Dehner returned to television in the nighttime soaper, *Bare Essence*.

The Roaring 20's — Series Index

FIRST SEASON:

Burnett's Woman

A mobster — Big Lou Burnett — tricks a rival gangster, Danny Royce, into coming to the apartment of Julie Fiore where he is killed. Lt. Switolski uncovers evidence that gets Julie accused of murder. Pat writes an article that frees Julie — but gets Switolski suspended. Julie decides to tell Pat the truth, but both are captured by gangsters. Scott and Switolski arrive in time.

Champagne Lady?

Bubbles La Peer, a pretty but naive dancer, is hired to take a champagne bath at an underworld meeting; she finds herself involved in a gangland killing. She falls in love with a crooked politician who helps Scott and Higbee capture the gangsters.

The Velvet Frame

An entertainer, Sandy, helps a bootlegger frame a department store owner on an attempted rape charge in order to get use of a warehouse to store booze. Pat Garrison is on the story.

The Prairie Flower

Garrison helps young, innocent-appearing Mary Lou get a part in a

Broadway revue—then realizes she'll do anything to get ahead. On opening night, she murders the star of the show. Pat and Switolski nab her because of a fingernail polish clue.

Vendetta on Bleecker Street

Married by proxy to Steve (a prisoner serving a life sentence), young immigrant Sophia falls in love with Steve's cousin. Steve thinks the cousin has dishonored him, escapes, and plans a murder. He's prevented by his family whom Scott has persuaded to a more American viewpoint. Steve's death frees Sophia.

Layoff Charley

Scott does a feature exposing the dual life of C.W. Webster, an honest, respectable businessman who's also Layoff Charley, an elusive racetrack czar who figures the odds for a gangster syndicate.

Brother's Keeper

In trying to scoop a story about a million dollars worth of securities missing from a bank, Pat is involved in a feud between a bank president and his playboy brother, a World War pilot hero.

White Carnation

Pinky is deeply involved with a gambler who's determined to get even with an erstwhile partner who framed him into a jail sentence.

Judge Seward's Secret

On the day of the trial of a crooked cop, the presiding judge disappears. Scott Norris tracks down the judge.

Bold Edition

A gangster murders a former henchman, then kills a reporter who was a witness. Scott locates a witness, who dies of a heart attack before he can testify. The killer panics and kills some innocent people thinking one might be the mystery witness.

The Maestro

Bootlegger Rocco is mistaken in thinking that Carbone and Gunsel are plotting the death of a famed tenor. Actually, it's Carbone's bit liquor-racket boss who is the intended victim. Rocco alerts Pat and Switolski.

Dance Marathon

Scott is fired from the paper for his persistent attempts to prove police Capt. Maples is a crook.

Big Town Blues

Supposedly killed by a jealous gangster who has stolen his wife, renowned trumpet player Buddy Benedict hides successfully until Pat inadvertently gives away the fact that he's alive.

Two a Day

Pat learns that Toto, a clown, is really Dennis, Elsa's first partner in an escape act. Elsa believes she accidentally killed Dennis, but then she learns that Alonzo, her present partner, planned the "accident" so he could take over the act.

Coney Red Hots

After a losing struggle, Gus Weber and his pretty daughter have their

Coney Island Beer Garden turned into a speakeasy by racketeer Lou Brazil. Joe Mason, in love with the girl, enlists the aid of Scott.

Black Saturday

All-American gridder Johnny Martin agrees to throw a game when a gambler threatens to reveal the story of Johnny's mother's sordid past — which would ruin his chance to marry a socialite. Pat tells the story surrounding the mother, and Johnny gets beaten up when he refuses to go through with the fix.

Lucky Charm

To avenge the crippling of his brother by a crooked gambler, likeable King Cole convinces the gambler that Pinky brings him luck ... then cheats him out of a fortune.

Pie in the Sky

Young flagpole sitter Pogo Riley says he won't come down until his girl, Evie, says she'll marry him. Rival bootleggers bet $50,000 on the result.

The Vamp

A movie Vamp leaves her producer over a money dispute. The producer then fires her publicity agent who — with Garrison's help — finds a waitress and proceeds to make her into an even bigger star.

War with the Night Hawkers

The Independent Cab Association, secretly headed by Jimmy Tate, a nightclub owner, is a protection racket preying on New York's independent cab drivers. Chris and Scott risk their lives to expose the racket.

The Twelfth Hour

Gerard North, a tailor's son pretending to be a wealthy socialite, is suspected of murder after a bookie, Ernie Hillman, plants $50,000 in Gerard's hat to divert suspicion from himself. Pat helps prove Gerard is innocent.

The Red Carpet

Helen de Bonn asks Scott to help her get her starving boyfriend Anthony Dormer out of jail. He had made a drunken threat to kill the poetry writing Queen of Romania. A crooked lawyer, Counsellor, devises a plan to kill off a judge who'll be riding in a parade with the Queen and who is trying the case of a gangland mobster.

The Salvation of Killer McFadden

When violence fails to persuade Micky (The Killer) McFadden to sell his brewery to the syndicate, disbarred lawyer Joe Quaine has his girlfriend Joan pose as a chaste mission worker to get Micky to fall for her. The scheme works, and Micky agrees to sell the brewery in order to be worthy of Joan. Pat learns of the scheme and tells Micky.

The Fifth Pin

Scott Norris helps to prove that the cop-killing for which young Joe Brown is soon to be executed was really committed by a superstitious gangster, Frankie DeLain.

Scandal Sheet

An insidious scandal sheet publisher, Mark Braddock, kills a playboy, and tries to frame Pinky. Pat sets up a trap to catch the killer.

Mademoiselle from Armentieres

Scott helps vet Hinky Dinky out of a spot when bootlegger Barney brings a perfect stranger, Suzette, from France as Hinky's "Mademoiselle from Armentieres" to deflate Hinky's bragging.

Among the Missing

Also known as "Something Borrowed, Something Blue": A West Point cadet goes AWOL to speak to his girl and accidentally witnesses a murder. He's later captured by the gunman. Pat covers the story.

Right Off the Boat — Part 1

The murder of a fellow reporter leads Scott Norris to tangle with rum-runners. Things are complicated by the fact that Pinky falls in love with one of them. Roger Moore appears.

Right Off the Boat — Part 2

Pat and Scott go after Rycker and his gang of bootleggers when a friend dies from bad booze. Scott discovers an off-shore freighter is the source but is trapped on board. Pat saves Scott and nabs the gang. Pinky's lover is killed.

Million Dollar Suit

Sandhog Tony Manaci discovers graft on the under-river tunnel project and tells Pat, who exposes the graft. The *Record* is slapped with a million dollar libel suit, and Pat is fired when Tony won't back him up.

Royal Tour

Pat takes a wistful Prince Frederick for a night on the town. The Prince has a brief romantic encounter with Susie, who's on the run from a murderous gangster.

SECOND SEASON:

No Exit

Garrison isn't having much luck with his romance with Mona Fenton, whose father is running for governor. Mona takes a bullet meant for Pat. The script for this show provided two endings: (1) Mona and her father are reconciled before she dies in a hospital or (2) she recovers and goes to a sanatorium to cure her own alcoholism.

Kitty Goes West

Irish Kitty O'Moyne gets excited about coming to America. So excited, in fact, that she falls overboard. John Dehner makes his first co-starring appearance. Glynis Jones as Kitty.

Nobody's Millions

First, Duke cooks up a news story out of thin air (which costs him his job); then he proceeds to make an amnesia victim think she's heiress to a fortune. William Reynolds guests.

Standing Room Only

Broadway producer Sheldon Farrington has been losing at the racetrack so he decides to make some money by selling a percentage of his new show to some backers. But if he wants the venture to be a success, he must sign his ex-wife — Marilyn Morgan — to star in the show. Keenan Wynn as Farrington.

Another Time, Another War

Former doughboy Ace Johnson would like to buy into the bootleg beer biz. Mobster Dutch Miller sells him a hijacked truck. Eddie Bracken is Ace; Grace Lee Whitney appears.

Everybody Loves Benny

Benny Lester (a racketeer) is a target of former associates. Pat wants the story and will live in Benny's penthouse. Peter Breck is Benny.

Duke on the Bum

A man thought to be a Bowery bum is blamed for making off with records belonging to racketeer Ed Despo. Duke finds out about it, wants the story, and heads for the Bowery disguised as a bum. He ends up being captured by Despo. Robert Strauss as Despo; Ruta Lee appears.

Pinky Goes to College

Pinky saw a gangland killing—now two gunmen are after her. But Duke has a plan: he dresses her up as a boy and sends her to a men's college.

So's Your Old Man

In his personal life, Mitch Mitchell is a respectable citizen. But when it comes to business, he's a bookie. And he's finding himself involved in a gang war with a rival. Claude Akins as Mitch.

Asparagus Tipps

Duke runs into a little lady who's quite good at handicapping the nags. The "tip service" is sold to the paper, and that hacks off the local bookies who don't like Elsie's unfailing accuracy. This episode is based on the 1920's comic strip "Asparagus Tipps," created by Will Gould who also co-authored this segment.

Blondes Prefer Gentlemen

Colleen McCullough dies when she topples through a window during a fight with her guy, bootlegger Jack Bennett. Pinky, who always seems to witness these things, does it again, and she knows it was an accident. Bennett doesn't want to take a chance on Pinky, so he has her kidnapped.

You Can't Fight City Hall

Someone has made off with one of Miklos Caravias' papers. Even though it's only worth pennies, Pinky wants to prove the value of democracy in action to the immigrant newsboy, so she insists the police investigate.

Footlights

Bug Stix is a comic who blames the death of his partner on theatre owner Desi Andreades, and he finds a way to obtain revenge. He assists the man's daughter in getting a part in a Broadway show, knowing that Andreades is against any members of his family going into show business. Robert Colbert appears.

The People People Marry

Comedian Jack Carter in a rare straight role: Higbee is sitting in for the paper's love-lorn columnist.

Afterword

Perhaps the question we've been asked the most is "why a book on Warner Bros. TV?" Well, that *is* a good question considering the shows we've covered have been off the air for so long. But that's part of the reason. The early Warners series are vintage television; they set the trend for most of the dramatic shows that are on the air today; and they are a part of history. They deserve to be remembered.

The idea for the book came up several years ago during a trivia discussion about old TV shows. As we debated which shows were of the highest quality in the 50's and 60's, the Warners series just kept coming up. Someone said, "Let's do a book."

It was a good idea, but who had the time? The project was kicked around for a year or two, and then was dropped—but it was never forgotten. After two Dallas stations began reruns of *Cheyenne* and *Maverick*, our interst was rekindled.

I wrote the introduction to the book, did some minor research, and convinced myself the idea was saleable. Bob Malsbary and Robert Strange joined me in preparing a test chapter—the one on *77 Sunset Strip*. I did the general portion of the chapter as well as the biographies of Efrem Zimbalist, Jr. and Louis Quinn. Malsbary handled Kookie (his boyhood idol) and Bobby Logan; Strange wrote the portions on Roger Smith and Jacqueline Beer.

With the style of the book thus determined, we set about the task of splitting the remaining chores. I took the private eye shows (*Hawaiian Eye, Bourbon Street Beat*, and *SurfSide 6*); Malsbary took cowboys and World War II (*Maverick, Lawman, Colt .45*, and *The Gallant Men*); Strange took the remaining westerns and adventure shows (*Cheyenne, Sugarfoot, Bronco, The Alaskans*, and *The Roaring 20's*). I acted as editor for all the chapters.

Extensive research was conducted to assemble the final product. The digging began in the files of the Dallas Public Library, continued through back issues of *TV GUIDE*, and finally took an extended trip for Malsbary and me to the Los Angeles offices of Warner Bros., and a long visit to the home of William T. Orr.

We have been diligent in our efforts to provide updated information and quotes from those who were involved in the making of these shows—people like Orr, Hugh Benson, and Carl Stucke. The "period" quotes you'll find in the book are almost all from studio press releases from the era. Some quotes in the Edd Byrnes biography are from an article by Vernon Scott and are used by permission.

There are several people without whom this book would have been incomplete, and they deserve special mention. First of all, thanks to the folks at the Dallas Public Library who opened their files to us. Avid Warners fan David Miller loaned us his collection of articles and information on Warner Bros. Grace Lee Whitney very patiently sat through a long interview and then provided us with several photos. Louis B. Marino of Warner Bros. in New York helped with stills and episode summaries. Bob O'Connor, manager of the Dallas office of *TV GUIDE*, was a tremendous help. And, of course, our appreciation goes to the folks at the Warners West Coast office including Bill Orr, Carl Stucke, and Hugh Benson.

The episode guides, we think, are one of the more important parts of the book. They were also the hardest part to assemble. At first, the task seemed impossible, but as time passed, we felt we were closing in on a synopsis of every episode of every series. The summaries used here came from a variety of sources, including Bill Orr, Warner Bros. New York offices, old periodical listings, data from fans, and through the courtesy of KXTX-TV in Dallas and KTVT-TV in Fort Worth.

We've made one other attempt to jog your memory. Each chapter title is a line from that particular show's theme song. (We always felt the WB shows were unequaled in their theme songs.) The one exception is *The Gallant Men*, a show whose theme had no lyrics.

In closing, let me say that putting this book together has been difficult—tedious at times—but always fun. We present it to you in that spirit, hoping you'll find it as much fun to read. We hope you'll remember those halcyon days—when the small screen had it all: adventure, mystery, drama—and integrity and quality. If this book should encourage more TV stations around the country to pull those Warners series out of mothballs, we won't complain. —*Lynn Woolley*.

Index